VOICE TERMINAL ECHO

*Postmodernism and
English Renaissance
texts*

VOICE TERMINAL ECHO

Postmodernism and English Renaissance texts

Jonathan Goldberg

METHUEN: New York and London

First published in 1986 by
Methuen, Inc.
29 West 35th Street, New York NY 10001

Published in Great Britain by
Methuen & Co. Ltd
11 New Fetter Lane, London EC4P 4EE

© 1986 Jonathan Goldberg

Printed in Great Britain by
Richard Clay (The Chaucer Press) Ltd,
Bungay, Suffolk

Library of Congress Cataloging in Publication Data
Goldberg, Jonathan.
    Voice terminal echo.
    Bibliography: p.
    Includes index.
    1. English poetry – Early modern, 1500-1700 – History
and criticism.   1. Title.   II. Title: Postmodernism
and English Renaissance texts.
PR531.G65   1986   821'.3'09   85-18878

ISBN 0 416 39970 3
0 416 42200 4 (pbk.)

British Library Cataloguing in Publication Data
Goldberg, Jonathan
    Voice terminal echo: postmodernism and
    English Renaissance texts.
    1. English literature – Early modern, 1500-1700
    – History and criticism
    I. Title
    820.9'004   PR431

    ISBN 0 416 39970 3
    0 416 42200 4 Pbk

One evening my Father took down his Virgil from an upper shelf, and his thoughts wandered away from surrounding things; he travelled in the past again. The book was a Delphin edition of 1798, which had followed him in all his wanderings; there was a great scratch on the sheep-skin cover that a thorn had made in a forest of Alabama. And then, in the twilight, as he shut the volume at last, oblivious of my presence, he began to murmur and to chant the adorable verses by memory.

  Tityre, tu patulae recubans sub tegmine fagi,

he warbled; and I stopped my play, and listened as if to a nightingale, till he reached

            tu, Tityre, lentus in umbra
  Formosam resonare doces Amaryllida silvas.

"O Papa, what is that?" I could not prevent myself from asking.

(Edmund Gosse, *Father and Son*)

Contents

Acknowledgements

A book, even a short one, is written over a period of time, and, in the course of writing *Voice Terminal Echo*, much has changed. Undertaken at its commencement in a critical atmosphere in which the postmodern and the Renaissance would have been regarded as incompatible, its completion coincides with a moment in which the two terms are, at least in some quarters, so comfortable as to open upon the prospect of a post-poststructuralism which some, these days, might even call formalism. There are now so many guidebooks to the postmodern, so many signs of its absorption by the structures of discourse that it sought to displace. On the other hand, what is in some quarters too comfortable is, elsewhere, still regarded with horror. The horror of so-called humanistic criticism which has not failed to see itself threatened but also, more disconcertingly, the horror of socially engaged criticism which has preferred to regard poststructuralism as a new formalism rather than confront its own sentimentality.

As I write these final words, Francis Barker's *The Tremulous Private Body* (London: Methuen, 1984) has just appeared, a set of essays on subjection that describes the emergence of bourgeois consciousness in the seventeenth century or, as Barker puts it, "what was done to us in the seventeenth century" (68) as an embodied knowledge was replaced by a disembodiment that made us minds – or texts. "As the subject, in a private condition, writes, from that blind place within which it is necessarily blind in order to see, of necessity censored in order to write, it unfolds itself now within a mode of representation which is no longer of a substance with the materiality of the old body" (63). The pages that follow could be read in terms of Barker's argument, but with a crucial difference. Textuality is not a modern invention; there is certainly a different relationship to textuality in seventeenth-century authors from that in sixteenth-century writers, one that I trust emerges in the discussions that follow; there is not, however, the naive, and romantic, bodily investment that Barker imagines precedes the opening of the modern abyss.

A book like Barker's – or like Frank Lentricchia's *Criticism and Social Change* (Chicago: University of Chicago Press, 1983) – will no doubt enrage humanistic criticism; but it is on poststructuralism that these critics whet their teeth. *Voice Terminal Echo* thus enters a battleground in which it is difficult to imagine a responsive audience, and a matter of some anticipatory regret if it meets hostility from those readers it would hope to embrace. In such times, it is thus a special pleasure to be able to thank Janice Price for her support for this project, to acknowledge Sharon Cameron for saying just the right word at the right time, and to record with gratitude the fellowship awarded by the John Simon Guggenheim Memorial Foundation that allowed this book to be completed.

Much that appears here was first tested in the classroom, as much in ancient resistances to the provocations of Edward Tayler, who may hear his questions in these pages, as in the restaging of such scenes over the years at Temple University, twice at Johns Hopkins (where Stanley Fish generously allowed the rehearsal of some of the arguments made here) and once, courtesy of Judith Herz, at Concordia, in an encounter recorded in "Reading (Herbert's *Vertue*) Otherwise," *Mississippi Review* 33 (1983), edited by Tony Brinkley, who kindly thought of including me. Thanks to Walter Benn Michaels, an earlier version of "Marvell's nymph and the echo of voice" appeared in *Glyph 8*, and Michael Fried's attentive reading made it better. "Consuming texts," in various guises, was read at Dartmouth College, at the Humanities Research Centre of the Australian National University, at Melbourne and Monash; having Richard Corum, Donald Pease, Ian Maclean, John Gillies, Ian Donaldson, Marion Campbell, Howard Felperin, David Sampson, among others, in those audiences, mattered; that David Sampson is not alive to read these pages is a great loss.

Julia and Abigail Goldberg wanted to find their names in this book, and now can. Alice Daniel gave support at a critical moment; Michael Warner provided welcome respite during the final stages of rewriting. Stephen Orgel's love made it all possible. This book is for Michael Moon, at the beginning of a sustaining friendship.

1

Terminals

Ceci (donc) n'aura pas été un livre.

Jacques Derrida, La Dissémination

Dictionaries of the future may record a new item under *voice*: *voice terminal*, a computerized telephone. No longer, then, the illusion that the instrument transmits voice at a distance, carrying it unchanged over space and time; voice now passes through the circuits.[1] Receiver and sender are at their terminals, voice terminated. The end of the voice and the beginning of the terminal: a technological image of the text, of this text, too, with its image of relays and circuits – of the short-circuiting of the voice. This newly arrived *voice terminal* suggests the historicity of this circuit, why (for example) at this moment this way of "speaking" seems necessary, why (for example) this way of "speaking" might describe the texts which it treats. The project of these pages, to be brief: to show in the Renaissance text voice-as-text, and to show it through a practice of voice terminated.

*

The project begins (began) with Marvell's "The Nymph complaining for the death of her *Faun*," a text whose critical problem has always been its voice.[2] Who speaks in the poem and how can criticism encompass a voice that seems to refuse critical coherence? The answer to these questions lies in part in attending to the nymph-as-nymph, not a creature with human coherence, but rather a demimythical/literary figure, a site through which what is *simulated* as voice passes.[3] Determined by a multitude of textual matrices – pastoral, elegiac, amorous, allegorical, Ovidian – the voice of Marvell's text is an echo, the sustained close of a number of Renaissance textual traditions. Voice, there, implicates, weaves, and terminates a history that can be read back from it, read forward into it. The poem is a compendium of strategies in the representation of loss, including the loss of the notion of the presentness of the voice. It, too, is representation, textually embedded, so overdetermined that determination of who speaks is problematic. For as much as speaking, who is in question.

The endplay of Marvell's "The Nymph complaining" opens an intertextual field into which what follows – the literary history recounted through Spenser, Shakespeare, Herbert, and Milton – takes place and precedence. For if the "wanton Troopers" glance at the historical termination of a textual practice – troopers, the OED reminds us, enter the language in 1640, used, as Elizabeth Story Donno comments, "in reference to the Scottish Covenanting Army which invaded England in 1640 in support of Presbyterianism"[4] – neither history nor textual history ends there. Milton represents another end, a terminal of transmission; his texts face the problematic of beginning, the question of what remains and the resituating of voice. With Milton begins the possibility of speaking of *his* voice; propriety enters the textual field.[5] Marvell's voice ends imaged as a statue engraving itself, a writing machine written into, dissolving voice. The Miltonic text is "marble with too much conceiving" ("On Shakespeare"),[6] a block whose solidity *prevents* closure, displacing and replacing what comes before so that *it* comes before, a germinal stone: "each term is indeed a germ, and each germ a term."[7]

To find his place in English literary history: Milton may be the first author for whom that is the question. Spenser and Shakespeare are the names around which it is raised, and Milton's first published poem appears in the second Shakespeare folio, itself a significant monument in literary history and one that makes literary history: the writer of ephemeral scripts has become the author preserved in monumental books, in multiple editions. Spenser, of course, begins his career with a book that is emphatically one, and through which claims are made. *The Shepheardes Calender* presents "the Author selfe" (as E. K. calls him) in a text replete with illustrations, glosses, commentary – a full scholarly apparatus.[8] Yet "the Author selfe" has no name, or several (Immeritô, Colin Clout); his texts register many voices and he appears through multiple figures, "shadowed" in them and in their relationships. If *The Shepheardes Calender* is the first text in which the Spenser recognized in *The Faerie Queene* appears, the problematic of appearance is linked to the curious dispersal of "the Author selfe" registered in his beginning text. The gesture towards the book is also one of disappropriation, "non-belonging – textuality as such."[9] Questions about authorial self-representation and the nature of the book become questions about the status of representation within the book, the nature of characters as voices for the poet and representations of the act of authoring. The *October* eclogue offers in particular a poetics for the articulation of these

2

questions, an opening within utterance as much platonic (the poisoned pleasures of poetry) as it is proverbial; Erasmus, for example, countenanced this voice-giving *sententia*, "ubi mel, ibi fel, ubi uber, ibi tuber," where there is honey, there is poison, where nourishment, cancer.[10]

*

(Open the sentence and find textual generation, literary history. As if the difference that determines phonemic variance were the locus of meaning, yet that 'm' should become 'f' or that 't' should come before 'u' is a matter of total indifference. The rhyme is generative, substitutive play. And it could go on. "Uber" from "ubi," *copia* in place, and "uber" is as much the breast as the copious text, "tuber" a swelling and a nourishing root.)

*

What is a character if not such letters? That, at least, is what Renaissance character writers affirm and what Shakespeare's use of the word confirms. What then of his characters, where is the author situated in relation to them? In the early *The Two Gentlemen of Verona* that question is represented by a play in which characters are little more than textual determinations, finding themselves by citing old saws, finding each other by exchanging letters, registering loss by tearing words, deforming them as they speak, wooing by figures, literal devices. These characters, then, are little more than marks on a page assuming their life; they act out a version of text, stand for the production of an author engaged in his own disappearing act. For although Shakespearian characters embody texts –and have voice only in such appropriations (they are appropriated), the text that Shakespeare writes exists only in the simulacrum of performance. The textuality of the script is played out against the books that characters become. The vaunted interiority of Shakespeare's characters is palpably in his early plays what it is when Hamlet looks within "the book and volume" of his brain, responding to the ghost's command that he be remembered with the promise to wipe his "tables" clean, a *tabula rasa*, razing "all trivial fond records,/All saws of books, all forms, all pressures past/That youth and observation copied there."[11] Characters, then, exist within texts; their interiors are texts. In this vertiginous hall of mirrors played out before our eyes, the end of speculation would produce the author, but only in the place of what Lacan would call the Other. And, as he writes, there is no Other of the Other, that is, no place where the play would have its cease.[12] In *The Two Gentlemen of Verona* that place of the author-as-Other is occupied by Ovidian metamorphoses that spawn this text, its tragic partner, *Titus*

3

Andronicus, and its afterlife, *Cymbeline*.

Milton's appropriation of Shakespeare's "When I consider everything that grows" in "When I consider how my light is spent" represents a response to the textual/scriptive energy of the Shakespearian character, just as the teeming marble of the poem "On Shakespeare" recasts the ghostly command to wipe the slate and at once to submit it to the new pressures of a stylus. If his concerns about authorship are played against the disappropriations represented variously by Spenser and Shakespeare, the possibility of writing the poem "doctrinal and exemplary to a Nation"[13] could be resolved only by facing an even more authoritative book, the Bible. Herbert, too, faces that master text, and he, too, writes the book, one testifying everywhere that "A HEART alone/Is such a stone,/As nothing but/Thy pow'r doth cut" (*The Altar*).[14] Yet, the text of *The Temple*, however much occupied by other voices, incised by the cutting edge of scripture, practices, too, acts akin to Ovidian and pastoral metamorphosis – collating, collocating, intercalating – thereby opening the prior text to its indeterminacies. As Edward Said suggests at one point, the Christian community has never stopped writing the text of Christ's death:

> Publication of a text, or at least the appearance of the text as an object to be diffused, is a ceremonious repetition of the parricidal deed by virtue of which copies proceed to supplant . . . an inaccessible source. . . . If Jesus is the father of the Christian community, every instance of writing signifies his death, or at least the transfer of his spoken words to a written document and the community's ambivalent relation to it.[15]

Herbert's *The Bag*, in which Christ's death wound becomes a mailbox for subsequent letters, figures the textual space of *The Temple* as the book of replacement and, thereby, Herbert's submission to and raising of other voices within the echo chamber of the dead letter box, "a box where sweets compacted lie" (*Vertue*). The changes his texts toll on a word like "sweet" provide one index to the echo of Herbert's voice.

This, then, is the argument in the pages that follow.

What remains, what more is there to say? Simply that the argument rehearsed above is an argument that could be made on the basis of what follows, but not the only argument that might be constructed. For what follows is not structured as an argument and resists such structures, eschewing (so far as possible) the critical impulse to totalize and the historical drive towards teleological closure. The voice on these pages is not singly determined to a procedure of logical demonstration. Multiple and fractured, it responds to texts and recounts them, pursuing and permitting disseminative practice. In some respects, an index to this volume might provide a better introduction than what stands above, for the pages that follow could be regathered through the tropes and semes scattered on them, the passages from the *Metamorphoses* or *Eclogues* that recur with some frequency. In a certain way, these pages could also be read as an account of the fortunes of Ovid in the English Renaissance, or as some further versions of pastoral, particularly in its elegiac voice. In another light, they are a set of readings of texts that are not fully assimilable to such generic or literary-historical concerns, but are, rather, demonstrations of techniques of reading consequent upon the work of writers like Maurice Blanchot or Jacques Derrida, and from that perspective the argument implicit in these pages concerns matters of critical practice. In the opening pages of a brilliant essay on an image in *Paradise Lost*, Geoffrey Hartman remarks that "the theory of criticism does not seem sufficiently advanced to solve problems even of this elementary kind"[16] – the problem of the decorum of the image; the pages that follow are pre-critical in the way that Hartman's essay is (though they cannot hope to achieve his acid-rock wit). Images are allowed to baffle critical procedures and the panoply of formalistic techniques used to restrain the divagations of texts.

A certain kind of historicism and a practice of analysis is nonetheless explored in these pages. Hartman can once again point to it, when he remarks that there is a history to "the joyful wandering of the written word" most easily remarked in "the literary evolution of the vulgar or vernacular tongues" since "dissemination . . . clearly belongs in a differentiated series with imitation, translation, contamination, secularization and (sacred) parody."[17] Some of those pathways have been marked recently, in Terence Cave's *The Cornucopian Text* or Thomas Greene's *The Light in Troy*, to take two examples. Cave considers *copia*, the technique of writing that replaces antecedent texts through a simultaneous fragmentation and multiplication, opening up antecedents (mining them and undermining them) and replenishing a full store. Perpetual deferment becomes the rule in the perpetuation of texts, both in the attempt to recapture past texts and to write new ones. Writing runs ever towards an end it never reaches and back to a source it never recovers (and which, if it did, would make all writing a text like the one that Borges' Pierre Menard inscribes), and the writer does not so fully control language as to bend it towards either of these aims. "The exiled *sensus* is seen to shift with the surface, pointing endlessly towards some absent *proprietas*, and thus inviting the game of language to continue."[18] However much authors attempt to represent their voices in texts, what they offer instead is "a kind of perpetual *prosopopeia*: a figure of speech presenting a speaking figure."[19] The crisis in sixteenth-century France that Cave explores is precisely one of those moments towards which Hartman points. It forms a chapter in Greene's wide-ranging study of imitation and discovery in Renaissance poetry from Petrarch to Ben Jonson.

Greene's work offers an elegiacs (as if his were the voice that Petrarch gave, "an eternally weeping lover," in John Freccero's words)[20] on the pathos of recovery, the historical solitude of the Renaissance writer or the modern critic. Imitation and discovery are infolded in invention, Cave's starting point as well, finding what more can be said in a place previously marked. That place is both lost and imagined as once having been complete; its pressures on the present are overwhelming, yet the present itself invents the past as well as the possibility of a future, finds itself drifting, cut off, fabricating. Assurance lies elsewhere, and the present of the text can only be (as Derrida claims) a future perfect (*futur antérieur*),[21] or, as Greene says, the Renaissance text grapples with the problem of anachronism. "In Heideggerian terms, the text can fulfill itself only as a projection into the future, an *Entwurf*, by acknowledging its *Geworfenheit*, its finite and contingent temporality, its existence in a specific cultural situation with its own particular and cultural vulnerabilities."[22] In the English Renaissance texts studied on the pages that follow, the possibility of writing is haunted as much by what has come before (classical and Biblical texts) as it is by a futurity that may never arrive. Herbert aspires to write the book, and dies ordering its destruction; Spenser leaves *The Faerie Queene* a fragment; Milton waits for history to allow him to write *Paradise Lost*, gambling on a future. The texts read here often glance at these ends, on the future that would retrospectively justify study of *The Shepheardes Calender* or Milton's poem "On Shakespeare." The accidents of history, which these pages engage, are written into the Renaissance texts and the account of them offered below.

Written, granted, in a style that does not assume that history as an inevitability, no more than the authors that Cave and Greene describe could write with security or be convinced that their inventions had earned them a place in literary history. Thus, the version(s) of the poet's life offered in the ensuing pages does not subscribe to the model that Lawrence Lipking offers in *The Life of the Poet*, with its marking of stages, and its notion that poets mature and develop, living off themselves and their antecedents by informed critical readings that point them where to go.[23] Lipking's systematized common sense begs more questions than it answers; its teleology and its rationalism suppress "the joyful wandering of the written word" as well as the terror, what Maurice Blanchot describes as the dread of an essential solitude: "a writer never reads his work."[24] That is the condition necessary if he is to write.

6

Although Blanchot's pronouncement can seem as totalizing as Lipking's (*the* life, *the* poet), they lack the metaphysical supports of Lipking's common sense, or, at the very least, bear them uncomfortably. Ontological insecurity haunts Blanchot's pages and marks out the space of writing. What is "essential" for him hardly fits within an idealistic definition of essence.

The path that opens following Blanchot or Derrida (inscribing their practices within the intertextual Renaissance field) eschews the construction of a master narrative of transmission or development, the neat parcelling out and marking of stages in a poet's production, whether individual texts or the entire work is examined. The way lies through the medium of iterability, allowing the drift of language, refusing inevitability. The possibility of criticism rests on the most insecure of bases, the endless decipherability of texts–and their endless withholding of ultimate answers. Texts are as unreadable as they are readable. To write permitting bafflement, acknowledging the excesses and outrages of texts (courting them, even, if only to refuse the containment of formalistic procedure) means a practice of a certain *impertinence*. Literary tact is not pursued in the pages that follow. But literary tact is a recent invention; E. K.'s glosses are no less guilty of their excesses. Literary history as it has been written (for the most part) in this century has followed the model of T. S. Eliot's "Tradition and the Individual Talent" (Lipking's model as well). A modernist version of history has been the consequence, a string of autonomous texts recounting a single tradition, what Eliot referred to as "the European mind." Seen from the perspective of Derrida, that history is one further inscription within the book of western idealism. And what follows, then, could be regarded as a re-engagement with the materiality of texts in all their historical contingency.[25]

In such a reading, every page trembles, vulnerable to manifold incursions–of prior texts, of future accidents, of reading and writing. To write now, then, open to the historicity of Renaissance texts and to the historicity of criticism invites (demands) a style assaultive in its refusals of the tactics of making sense, yet this is not (as is sometimes claimed) simply a practice of reversal or a pursuit of a *via negativa*, transcendent in its own fashion. Reinscribing loss, facing annihilation, texts lose their monumental status, and regain it–as memorial stones, implacable in their refusals as much as in their recording. The value of texts lies in their contingency, not in some security or consolation they may offer. If an elegiac strain is often heard, it testifies to the struggle of writing, its impossible desires and designs. Death haunts the "joyful wandering of the written word." Or, as Hartman also writes, "If there is a primal

7

scene of writing it is having one's name inscribed on a monument or tomb."[26]

Derrida's style (the plural would be better) is a central concern in *Saving the Text*, and its features have been succinctly summed up by Barbara Johnson in the introduction to her translation of *Dissemination*: "unspeakable," allusive, disconnected, multiple, lyrical, fragmentary, dense, insubordinate – a challenge, in short, to logical discriminations.[27] He offers a model for critical practice as re-marking, imitation as mime (simulation) not mimesis, criticism questioning its representational status and the status of representation in the texts it cites. Permeable to the invasions of what it invades (slicing texts), it is writing in quotation marks and marked by quotation. Mirror writing, reversible, a medium of exchange: texts made terminals, history the exchange of letters from —— to ——. These procedures seem apt for an inquiry into Renaissance texts, throwing voice in question, allowing the disturbing claims of echo to be heard. This, then, is what remains, in the pages that follow; these are the terms, voice and (or, as) echo.

No one can write about voice without taking into account Derrida's deconstruction of the metaphysical claims of phonocentrism (his argument is outlined in "The *phone*," in "The dead letter," below). Voice has a technical grammatical meaning as well, defined by Emile Benveniste as "the fundamental diathesis of the subject in the verb; it denotes a certain attitude of the subject with relation to the process . . . by which the process receives its fundamental determination."[28] Active and passive are the usual marks of voice, but Benveniste argues that Indo-European languages originally were divided into active and middle voices; taking his examples from languages that mark the middle voice (the aorist), Benveniste suggests that the fundamental distinction involves actions that do not require a subject ('he throws the ball') and actions that make a subject ('he is born,' 'he speaks'). In the active voice, the subject governs a process in which s/he is not located – thus, in the example above, the ball moves independent of the subject that throws it and its movement is not self-determined; in the middle voice, the subject partakes in the action, which also locates the subject – being born cannot take place without someone being born, speaking does not occur without a speaker.

> The principle of a properly linguistic distinction, turning on the relationship between subject and process, is brought out quite clearly by this comparison. In the active, the verbs denote a process that is accomplished outside the subject. In the middle, which is the diathesis to be defined by the opposition, the verb indicates a process centering in the subject, the subject being inside the process.[29]

What would seem to have happened historically, as the passive replaces the middle voice, is that the subject rather than being constituted in language is *subjected*. In the active/passive dichotomy, the subject is not in the verbal action; the modern dichotomy, in short, alienates the subject from its constitutive being. That "being," however, it should be said, was – and remains – only in language.

That point, in fact, Benveniste argues in several essays on the subject in language, a question clearly related to voice since voice marks the position of the subject. In a definition that is central to Roland Barthes, Benveniste defines the subject as entirely a linguistic phenomenon: "what does *I* refer to? To something very peculiar which is exclusively linguistic: *I* refers to the act of individual discourse in which it is pronounced, and by this it designates the speaker. . . . The reality to which it refers is the reality of the discourse. . . . And so it is literally true that the basis of subjectivity is in the exercise of language." Or, more summarily, "'Ego' is he who *says* 'ego'."[30] *I* does not exist save in language, and as *I* is voiced (active or passive) language exceeds any attempts of the subject to own language. Language places and displaces the subject. And what is grammatically true is also, according to Lacan (who in this instance, at least, repeats Freud), psychologically true. Lacan investigates a "speaking subject" and administers a talking cure.[31] The discursive truth he seeks (never to find) is that of the unconscious (structured, as Lacan argues, like language), the truth that would guarantee utterance and secure it. What he can find is the subject alienated in speech from the language that speaks the subject; he can find, that is, the psychological equivalent of the grammatical (dis)location of the subject.

Lacan may at times have entertained a notion of full speech,[32] an end to interminable analysis that would mark a recovery, and it is possible, too, that Benveniste's reconstruction of an original active/middle distinction may be aimed at a fuller being in language than the present dichotomy affords a subject. Derrida holds out no hope for such a beyond or origin. Lacanian alienation is his *différance*, the non-identity with itself upon which identity is founded. *Différance* is his middle voice, not conceivable in the oppositions of presence and absence or active and passive, and thus not reducible to the ontological terms of western metaphysics.

> There is no subject who is agent, author, and master of *différance*, who eventually and empirically would be overtaken by *différance*. Subjectivity – like objectivity – is an effect of *différance*, an effect inscribed in a system of *différance*. That is why the *a* of *différance* also recalls that spacing is temporization, the detour and postponement by means of which intuition,

perception, consummation – in a word, the relationship to the present, the reference to a present reality, to a *being* – are always *deferred*. Deferred by virtue of the very principle of difference which holds that an element functions and signifies, takes on or conveys meaning, only by referring to another past or future element in an economy of traces.[33]

To the literary critic, the simplest way to grasp Derrida's argument is to extend the "being" of literature into the world (to imagine with Borges a universal textuality), and thus to agree with Derrida's problematization of the *is* in the question, what is literature.[34] In the pages that follow, *echo* "answers" that question. So, too, does a jotting of Mallarmé's:

> écho.
> ego. je.

In "The Voice of the Shuttle: Language from the Point of View of Literature," Geoffrey Hartman claims for his title a phrase from a lost play by Sophocles describing the tapestry woven by Philomela after her rape and the ravishment of her tongue.[35] Although this chain from lost tongue to lost text to borrowed title might make a disseminative allegory, Hartman's concern is the substitutive structure of the trope; voice for picture, shuttle for tapestry. The substitution reverses causes and effects – it names the effect of the tapestry, its voice, rather than the image on the tapestry that "speaks"; it designates the tapestry as the shuttle that made it; indeed in so naming the tapestry the substitution names a part for the whole, the shuttle for the loom. Hartman charts the image, visualizing the substitutive chain and the space between terms that it opens:

(effect)		(cause)
voice		*shuttle*
(cause)		(synechdoche)
pictures		loom
(cause)		(effect)
tapestry	tapestry	

Between "voice" and "shuttle" the diagram marks the "tacit middle term" (as Hartman calls it elsewhere),[36] an indeterminate middle between overspecified poles. Yet this middle is as much overdetermined as indeterminate: both sides of the phrase terminate in the tapestry, but, as cause and effect, the tapestry cannot bring to a halt the suggestiveness of the (circum)locution. In this exemplary (or as Hartman would have it, archetypal) trope lurks the possibility that all metaphor is far-fetched, catachresis not the abuse of metaphor but the founding instance of the "truth" and "being" of language.[37] For the point in the Sophoclean trope is not that one might substitute the denotative *tapestry* for the allusive "voice of the shuttle." And in the trope itself the false economy of such a substitution is itself marked. It takes little effort to realize that the suppressed tapestry is itself a metaphor for the woven text that never can be unbraided entirely.

The disseminative allegory that Hartman's title implies (implicates, folds) could thus be said to be the temporalization of the trope. It, too, is a trope, named by John Hollander (after Harold Bloom, after Quintilian) metalepsis, the trope of transumption.[38] Metalepsis designates the diachronic movement of allusiveness, the echo effect of texts. It is a trope of ellipsis, seeking as well the "tacit middle term." Hollander's example of metalepsis from Quintilian is as telling as the Sophoclean trope: "The commonest example is the following: *cano* is a synonym for *canto* and *canto* for *dico*, therefore *cano* is a synonym for *dico*, the intermediate step being provided by *canto*."[39] As Hollander comments, Quintilian's synonyms are also a history. When Virgil announces he sings (*cano*), he in fact speaks; what lies behind his utterance is the fact that Homer delivered his poem by chanting it (*canto*). And, as Hollander adds, Virgil's *cano* also suppresses *scribo*, and thereby glances at a futurity; now when someone *writes*, in all likelihood s/he types or processes words. The example of metalepsis is itself metaleptic, engaging and suppressing at once the production of texts involved in the production of texts, making synchronous in the text a suppressed diachrony. That diachrony is itself unmarked (as ellipsis) and remarked (within echo). Unmarked and remarked, it is not exactly *there*, nor exactly *present*. To attend critically to echo–to the *figure* of echo–one marks a *tacit* and reverbatory middle, a between. Or, as French has it, an *entre* that is also an *antre*.[40] Echo inhabits a cave.

Echo's story is entwined with Philomel's, for in her metamorphosis the chatterbox is transformed into the *image of voice*. As told by Ovid, her story cannot be separated from the tale of Narcissus, and with it, as Hollander comments, sound and light, fullness and emptiness, absorption and reflection are mutually entailed. But, as he further demonstrates, the etiology of Echo catches hold of the realm of Pan; Longus reports her dismemberment at the hands of shepherds, and Ovid's story of the transformation of Syrinx into a vocal reed makes the instrument of writing a function of Echo. Bacon conflated Echo and Syrinx to offer an image of true *"discourse* . . . which echoes most faithfully the voices of the world itself, and is written as it were at the world's own dictation, being nothing else than the image and reflection thereof, to which it adds nothing of its own, but only iterates and gives it back."[41] Mere iterability, Echo is profoundly an image of the origin of iterability. Hers is the story of the original echo, its origin, that is, as a figure and image of voice–its origin as a trope (as the trope of troping); echo, in short, as text and textual history.

"A girl dies, song is born. . . . Voice is intrinsically elegiac." So Hartman summarizes the story of Philomela–and so, too, could the story of Echo be told, along with what Hartman adds to complicate the tale: "the myth deals with loss of voice, not only with loss."[42] Philomela must lose her tongue to give the shuttle voice; Echo must become the hollow of reverberation. These tales–to extend an insight of Hartman's–offer an etiology of fiction (where do poets' words come from?), an etiology of the fiction that words in texts speak, *have* voice. "We know," Hartman remarks, "that the nostalgia for an 'inviolable voice' is based quite consciously on the fact that such a voice is a fiction. It is always associated with prior loss or violation, as the Philomel myth perfectly expresses."[43] This fiction of one's own voice defines the poet's character; "it has become customary to use 'voice' as a metonymy for 'character,'" Hartman notes, to identify, that is, the essential nature of a poet in a particular mode of casting his voice. Hartman suggests instead that a study of voice might reveal a moment, between the pre-oedipal and oedipal, in the formation of character, that it might locate as well the place of a poet in literary history.[44]

The myth of Echo and Narcissus might represent that moment in the formation of the character of the poet and the place of that moment in literary history. In Narcissus, the solicitude of the mirror, in Echo, the disturbance of the mirror of reflection: the disturbance, to return to Hollander's argument, marks the *origin* of the image. Its after-effect is an original effect, and thus may relate to a Freudian paradigm of recovery and representation, and to the Lacanian rewriting of the Freudian pre-oedipal and oedipal stages as the Imaginary and the Symbolic. Derrida's concerns speak to these issues, too, in investigating the "complicity between . . . voice and ideality,"[45] for he argues that the representation one makes to oneself of thinking as the hearing of a voice within suppresses the spacing in that representation. Consciousness represses a temporalization and distantiation that breaks the idealizing proximity of voice and self. This idealization is, in Hartman's terms, the poet's fiction, and the critical fiction, too, that texts offer voice unmediated by the textual relay that short-circuits and recirculates voice. In the texts considered in the pages that follow, the registering of the poet's voice in other voices–particularly in the voices of women, descendants of Echo and Philomela and Syrinx–disturbs the mirror of Narcissus and the fiction of the transparent text.

For, as Derrida remarks, commenting on a text by Valéry, Narcissus speaks. Looking at himself, Narcissus speaks to his reflection; the mirror is shattered, the return to himself occurs in the resonance of voice – the resonance of Echo. "The sonorous source attempts to rejoin itself only by differentiating itself, dividing, differing, deferring without end."[46] The source is "like an echo that would somehow precede the origin it seems to answer. . . . This is why the '*echo*' is an '*incision*' . . . . The 'effect' becomes the cause."[47] The "incision" cuts into the idealizing fiction of reflection. As in the Ovidian myths, it makes the original voice the echo effect produced by a text or a textual instrument – the reed that Syrinx becomes, the tapestry that Philomela weaves, the cave of Echo (a tomb, stones ready for an inscription). The "incision" mediates immediacy, cutting into the present. It cuts into the space of representation, provides the cut of the "tacit middle term": the middle term represented by the blank space on Hartman's chart, a space in which cause and effect, part and whole, pursue each other endlessly, the graph of a graft, the path of iterability. This incisive place locates criticism as much as it locates voice. As Aristotle suggests, sound becomes voice when it becomes phonemic, when a stream of sound is cut into. Uttering *letters*, voice emerges as the instrument of imitation, miming logos, founding mimesis in a mimic voice.[48] Voice in Plato, Derrida argues (on the basis of *Philebus* 38e-39e), is the after-effect of an internal writing and painting. Voice passes through a textualization, its truth is cut into by representation.

In all these formulations, cause and effect remain undecidable, text and voice in a productive (hermeneutic) circle, inner space and externality – as Bacon suggests – indistinguishable from the troping of discourse. "Being" rests on representation, as Ovid's *Metamorphoses* intimates, incapable of naming a flower or tree without telling its tale – a tale, more often than not, about a devastating violation. When Virgil opens his *Eclogues*, he situates pastoral in a dialectically compensatory position. The displaced and soon to be exiled Meliboeus sounds the echoing effect of pastoral verse: "tu, Tityre, lentus in umbra/Formosam resonare doces Amaryllida silvas" (*Eclogue 1*, lines 4-5).[49] Tityrus, secure in the shade, can teach the woods to echo the name of his beloved Amaryllis. The woods return a name; they do not deliver the girl. And their name – *silva*, as the pages that follow insist – is a resonant one.[50] The forest, as Ben Jonson's title suggests, gathers poems; flowers, the flowers of rhetoric. Voice and echo: "echo is voice's self"[51] "*when the text is interrupted, folds back upon itself, lets the voices come back like an endless recording –*";[52] "*That device was me, it is that device which just wrote this sentence.*"[53]

2

Marvell's nymph and the echo of voice

What is to be made of loss? Perhaps this is every poet's question; certainly it is Andrew Marvell's. Whether considering politics, amatory experience, or the way that the mind works, Marvell joins creative energy to annihilative loss. His poems are replete with emblematic moments of creative annihilation: Cromwell and the severed head; Appleton House and the ruined abbey; the mower and his scythe. If every creative act in Marvell entails "annihilating all that's made," we are probably safe in assuming that these emblematic moments are also deeply self-referential images for poetic activity, that it is not only the lover in "To his Coy Mistress" who hears his "ecchoing Song" in a vaulted burial chamber,[1] not to his ears alone that soundings come as from across an abyss. In no text can the relationship of poetry to such an emblematic moment be more clearly demonstrated than in "The Nymph complaining for the death of her *Faun*." It is a poem whose plot entirely comprises that moment of creative annihilation and, as will be suggested in the pages that follow, it is a text that offers Marvell's most elaborated version of the meaning of that moment for his poetry and for himself as poet. The poem has long baffled criticism; in the interpretation offered here, an explanation for the difficulty of the poem may be found. The poem defies referentiality. It is only, and entirely, self-referential, "about" itself, about how the text comes to be, how it relates to antecedent texts, what it represents in the world.[2]

Here I need to acknowledge my debt to the brilliant introductory pages in Geoffrey Hartman's essay on "The Nymph complaining."[3] Like him, I wish to respect the terms of the poem, to regard the nymph as a nymph, "a mythic being in a privileged relation to the wood-world of the poem, the world of fawns and nature" (175), and yet to see "a conspiracy between nymph and poet" (176). And his understanding of the poem as "an apotheosis of the diminutive powers of poetry" (179) informs my own. I want to extend the implication of his provocative remarks, to answer his question, why allegorize, in the terms he suggests, by showing that the text is about its own deeply problematized voice, a voice called the nymph's only in the title of the poem. It is not precisely a human voice that we hear in the poem, nor is it a human object lamented in this elegiac occasion for speech. These transformations define the annihilative ground for the voice in the poem. That voice traverses, I will suggest, four modes of organizing speech: antithesis (lines 1-24), repetition (lines 25-34), allegory (lines 55-92), and epigraph (lines 93-122). Disjunctively, four modes that epitomize the major Renaissance genres available for handling loss – sonnet, lyric stanza, Spenserian epic, and epigram – are reviewed and reduced, and the possibility of reassembling a "vision of lost and original unity" (191), which Hartman sees as Marvell's aim, is finally relinquished.

Limitation upon limitation; a reduced speaker, on the margins of human speech, addresses the question of loss in a language marked by the constriction of all the modes of discourse available. Yet, all is not lost. In the excessive wake of these shrunken possibilities, Marvell allows us to hear the echo of voice that is his own.

Antithesis: "There is not such another"

Who is speaking here, in the opening twenty-four lines of the poem? A voice, inconsolable, brought up short from an idyllic union, made to comprehend an event excluded from all prior modes of knowledge, all previous experience; a voice that names a bond with a stricken fawn and recoils from his irremediable wound. Yet, is this the entire content of this voice? Is this all it says? And how does it speak about this event? The voice here can see only one way to say what it has lost, can only frame discourse in the stark antitheses of shattered continuity, by noting an entrance hitherto unknown and unprepared for.

> The wanton Troopers riding by
> Have shot my Faun and it will dye.
>
> (1-2)

Yet, we know, reading on, that there has been a preparation, that the fawn's death is not the first loss that it initially appears to be.

Something is not being said.

Not only is the past suppressed as this voice starts speaking, not only is the history of the figures involved implicitly denied; this voice speaks

15

as if it were discovering loss for the first time, but it speaks in terms that have been provided for it, that come before it. There is not only a story before this story, the story of Sylvio which the text reserves to tell after, there is a language before this entrance into language, the language of (Petrarchan) antithesis. Or, more starkly, there is before this voice speaks, language (in its binary structure) *as* antithesis. The voice here summons up antitheses, trying to control the situation of loss: wanton/innocent; good/ill; forget/register; justice/guilt; life/death. But the situation of loss is already, beforehand, written in antitheses: losing and having are an indivisible pair. The voice speaking here is caught in a priority that undoes the myth of priority that it presents. The voice says, here is first loss; but it says too, here is second loss, and not only by suppressing the story of Sylvio. It says it by entering language. The secondarity of speech signifies that it is the falsity of the notion of first speech that is being seen through–revealed and enabling utterance–the falsity, then, that the poet knows when he speaks. "It appears, strange as it may seem, that 'signifier of the signifier' no longer defines accidental doubling and fallen secondarity."[4] Rather, as Derrida's sentence suggests, it defines an origin robbed of priority, robbed of its single status: original secondarity.

Who speaks here? She is called a nymph, a creature both natural and divine, and she embodies the notion of divine presence in nature. Of what loss does she speak? Of a fawn, the embodiment of animality on the verge of humanity (fawn/faun). They are two marginal figures, two figures of marginality, representing encroachments and extensions, and yet exclusions from some central norm, the category of the merely natural, or the entirely human. Into this categorical void, the "wanton Troopers" come. Excluded from and antithetical to the pastoral idyll of nymph and fawn, they have no place–no place, that is, except the one that the categories of more and less than human have made for them. They are the human, a necessary middle. The schema of antithesis that would deny them a place creates their place.

Nymph and fawn define one pair of antitheses; each of them is related (through further antitheses) to the troopers. The fawn's relationship to the troopers is simultaneously glancing and absolute, casual (they are simply "passing by") and causal ("and it will dye" (line 2)). Totality of union has been replaced with its opposite, total loss and abandonment; the idyllic union of fawn and nymph replaced by the shattering union of fawn and troopers. And for this disruption of pastoral pathos – a situation in which thoughts produce acts, in which union is intimate and total, in which categories are crossed and joined (a relationship signalled in the affective "thee" (line 4), the proprietary "my" (line 2), and in the absolute knowledge that stands behind "thou neer didst alive/Them any

16

harm" (lines 4-5)) – for this disruption, explanation founders. All that remains is a voice caught in total opposition, irremediable, inexplicable antithesis. Antithesis, then, *as* explanation.

Antithetical oppositions define the multiple relations of fawn, nymph, and troopers. If not a causal principle of explanation, it nonetheless carries its own inevitability, one traced in an opening series of negations: "un-," "cannot," "neer," "nor," "never," "nor . . . nor":

Ungentle men! They cannot thrive
To kill thee. Thou neer didst alive
Them any harm: alas nor cou'd
Thy death yet do them any good.
I'me sure I never wisht them ill;
Nor do I for all this; nor will.

(3-8)

The lack of explanation, the generation of exclusionary negations, carries the force of necessity, the necessity of antithesis. Thus exclusionary negation, which barred the troopers from the pastoral idyll, defines their place: it is a discursive site. It is where the voice speaks in this opening section of the poem. The entrance into speech establishes and naturalizes antitheses; antitheses multiply within antitheses (fawn and nymph vs. fawn and troopers; fawn vs. troopers; nymph vs. troopers). What emerges from these multiple antitheses, as boundaries blur and centers shift, are identifications. Echo enters.

If the troopers are a necessary middle that embodies the antithetical identification of exclusion and inclusion, they go beyond this center to occupy an even more startling place, a more unsettling center. Excessive, "wanton," they are beyond the category of the human, and in much the same way as the nymph and fawn are. The troopers have a central place in the idyll as "ungentle men," as men, that is, who are not men but animalistic. The prefix "un-" that triggers the sequence of negations negates the category that should include the troopers, the human race (*gens*), and creates as central a category of excess. The center is excessive by being a double center, affirming and denying the category of the human. Moreover, as transgressors of the boundary of the pastoral idyll, the troopers trespass those exclusionary limits in precisely the antithetical form of the one upon whom they have encroached, the fawn. Antithesis approaches identification. The idyll had involved, in the figures of fawn and nymph, the exclusion of the human; their marginality, at once excessive and privative, put antithesis at the center. As "ungentle," the troopers occupy the fawn's position. That double center of fawn and troopers implies yet another antithesis to complete the pattern – and to

17

undo the idyll. For if the idyll represented the antithetical union of fawn and nymph, the replacement of the fawn by the troopers might imply as well the antithetical opposition of fawn and nymph, the nymph now joined to the troopers.

Within the idyll, one sign of this is the alternate naming of the fawn in terms both of identification and opposition, inclusion and exclusion, excess and privation. The fawn is named "thee" (a human designation) and "it" (as an animal). Telling the story of the idyll, the voice speaks within the wound inflicted by the opposing, antithetical, "ungentle" troopers; the account is generated from this principle of nomination, the wound gives the voice words. The fawn, in short, cannot be named without the troopers. The wound is the center, the place of meeting, the place of echo and voice. The empty space between categories is the exclusion necessary for union with the fawn. Pastoral pathos is founded, one might argue, on the wound of privation. This line of thought suggests the unthinkable, a complicity between the nymph and troopers, and not only in the alternate naming of the fawn. It is there in "I'me sure I never wisht them ill" (line 7); the troopers have been in mind before their violation of the idyll. The totalization of the idyll cannot exclude what it claims to exclude. Hence, in a final exclusionary gesture, the nymph prays *for* the troopers:

> But, if my simple Pray'rs may yet
> Prevail with Heaven to forget
> Thy murder, I will Joyn my Tears
> Rather then fail.
>
> (9-12)

The prayer to forget is the hope of re-membering the fawn, of reconstituting the fawn through forgiveness, through the admission of destruction in the pastoral union. The voice in prayer re-enacts the casually murderous entrance of the troopers into the poem – pays the price of entering into language.

Into what language? As already suggested, it is an old story renewed here, the story of the lover who laments an absent or a denying or a denied beloved, in one way or another a beloved who is removed – improbably chaste, impossibily married, or thoroughly wanton. Or dead. Eros drives the lover to want what cannot be had. The lover cannot comprehend what he wants; if he does, he sees that he wants to want, sees, that is, that Eros and the beloved are complicitous in his frustrating desire. Wyatt sounds this note first in the English Renaissance: "She that me lerneth to love and suffre" (no. 4, line 5), domesticating the Petrarchan tropes as traps, the prison of antitheses: I want/I love; I burn/I freeze;

I am sick/I am well; I am wounded/I am whole.[5] What is a sonnet if not a momentary monument built on denial and refusal, on antitheses that cannot be overcome, perhaps self-contained and isolated as a unit, yet continually replicating unfulfilled desire. The "pretty roomes" of the sonnet, as Donne saw, are sepulchral. The form memorializes loss. Its wit, the epigrammatic twist by which it arrives at closure, more often than not involves the recognition that antithetical negations constitute the speaker's situation, locate the lover's voice.

The story in brief: the broken heart, language in the place of the lost object.

This voice has been lodged in the annihilative creativity of antithetical identification, generated by negations. Now it turns to a final antithesis and seeks a restorative reversal in the law of "*Deodands*":

> Ev'n Beasts must be with justice slain;
> Else Men are made their *Deodands*.
>
> (16-17)

Deodands refer to animals which were sacrificed to the church or to the state for causing the death of men. The word names a law that would, if it were reversible, compensate for loss in a principle of return. It might fill the void. The learned word throws the voice into question. Can it encompass this word and with it effect the antithetical reversal of "ungentle," crossing the human/animal boundary in the opposite direction? No; all that will stand in the place of loss – in the void – is the word itself, it alone the substitute for the lost object. The falsity of the human system of justice and valuation, in the law of deodands, lies in the notion of compensation, in the very idea that something can stand in place of something else and thereby redeem what has been lost, either as a replacement or as a sacrifice. Like all lovers, this voice can only say, my heart is wounded and can find absolute closure only in accepting that "there is not such another" (line 23).

The voice plays across the languages that enter it, the legalism of *deodands*, the petrarchanism of the wounded heart. Once again, then, it is located in antithesis; and once more it gestures towards identification. A final identification: union in blood:

> Though they should wash their guilty hands
> In this warm life-blood, which doth part
> From thine, and wound me to the Heart,
> Yet could they not be clean: their Stain
> Is dy'd in such a Purple Grain.
>
> (18-22)

All the participants meet in blood as it parts, wounds, and stains. Nymph, fawn, and troopers – all are constituted, made, placed, through this encompassing loss, joined in the parting, sustained in the antitheses. No law can move them into each other's place, no literalistic substitution is possible precisely because in their irremediable relationships to each other, they define the structure of loss and of frustrated desire. In desire antitheses meet, never to be overcome. The final words of the first section of the poem isolate the participants in the situation, trap them forever in their positions: irredeemable troopers, irrecoverable fawn, inconsolable nymph. These are their positions in the text; they are literary positions, tropes. Each one an occupant of the wound, no one can compensate for it. No one, that is, can constitute the presence of being-for-oneself that would obliterate the void that constitutes identity and identification.

The fawn is the nexus of all antithetical relations, the place where the nymph's desire and the "wanton Troopers'" bullets meet. The fawn names a site of loss. But the name also bears, in its etymology, a further complication. *Fawn* derives from *foetus*, offspring. The fawn is the created word, the object made in loss. Its createdness – its secondary as embodied antithesis (human/animal) and as the locus of annihilation and creation – is its origin. "There is not such another": as a beginning situation (as the beginning of the voice of this text), the fawn is the place of antithesis and negation. A beginning that is not. The fawn is a beginning, then, of an order of words that arises in separation and ends in the heart's privation, that begins in the casual encounter with the "wanton Troopers" and ends when discourse has apparently exhausted the possibilities of standing in the place of loss: "There is not such another in/The World, to offer for their Sin" (lines 23-24). This plot of beginning and ending is folded in the antitheses that shape the voice in the opening section of the poem. What is narrated is a story of loss from the beginning.

Whose voice is this? Where is this voice? In the situation of a poet, voice inside of voice, located and dislocated in the generation of antitheses, in the offspring that precedes the voice and is itself preceded. This is the situation of voice in this text – a hall of mirrors reflecting back to what comes before the possibility of having a voice. Voice in the text standing for the poet. Standing disowned.

*

Before this poem began, the voice says, there was silence. A lie. Within the timescheme of the poem there is a before that comes after. Outside the text (is there an outside the text?), there are the texts that come before this one, the text we have called the sonnet, enshrining centuries of lovers

20

in their antithetical complaints, lovers lamenting losing as having, having their words for loss instead of the beloved. Within this text, the word for loss is the (always already, from the beginning) lost object, the fawn. The fawn is what the voice made, made into speech. The fawn is, thus, what made the voice. A word, a pun, the original word that is two, animal and human, fawn and faun. The word that does violence. The h[e]art.

Repetition: "solitary time"

Disjunction, and the voice begins again, from the beginning. Has it heard itself? Now it hears, it says; it hears an echo. Here is the story, it says, I will tell it exactly as it happened; without duplicity, I will tell the story of duplicity.

> Unconstant *Sylvio*, when yet
> I had not found him counterfeit,
> One morning (I remember well)
> Ty'd in this silver Chain and Bell,
> Gave it to me: nay and I know
> What he said then; I'me sure I do.
> (25-30)

The voice insists, it says, that these are the words; insisting, it says it again. Hear that voice, it repeats, that is the voice of duplicity, punster Sylvio, heartbreaker, bestower of the fawn, giver of language. Hear him, it says; he speaks double; I hear that, but I speak single. Say it again. Hear me, the voice insists . . . "I remember well . . . I'me sure I do." I do not speak like that. Like him. That is not my voice. I admit echo, the voice says: call it Sylvio, not me.

> Said He, look how your Huntsman here
> Hath taught a Faun to hunt his *Dear*.
> (31-32)

I say, Sylvio "Left me his Faun, but took his Heart" (line 36). I repeat, I do not echo. I repeat.

Who is Sylvio, what is he? Counterfeit, "when yet/I had not found him counterfeit" (lines 25-26), a first instance of prior duplicity, the "wanton Troopers" again, at first–"unconstant" (line 25) echoes "ungentle" (line 3). Sylvio is the original violator of the pastoral idyll; he represents first loss. And more. What's in a name? Translate Sylvio: woodborn huntsman, a name already written in Ovid, in Spenser, a declension of *silva*, tree; *Silvae*, an anthology of poems. Virgil's Silvia, the girl whose pet Ascanius kills, counterfeited, a transformation already written when Guarini turned Tasso's chaste Silvia into his Silvio.[6]

"Unconstant *Sylvio*" (line 25), original pastoral duplicity, the tree become text, cross-category in and beyond nature. "Unconstant *Sylvio*": so the voice begins again. Telling for the second time the beginning story, and immediately language is double, duplicitous, and doubled again, in Sylvio's gift of the fawn/h[e]art/deer/dear. Who is Sylvio? Who, if not the original provider of the pastoral idyll, bestower of the fawn as mediating gift, giver of the word: "his Gifts might be/Perhaps as false or more than he" (lines 49-50). He provides the gift as go-between, the broken h[e]art of Sylvio and the nymph. At first the fawn is (once again) the vehicle of relationship, where the puns meet: "look how your Huntsman here/Hath taught a Faun to hunt his *Dear*" (lines 31-32). Here, then, is the etiology of the word in the first story which we are only hearing now (as the repetition of the story heard first, the story of how the h[e]art came to be wounded), etiology as explanation now: the wound inevitable, already, at first. In the beginning was the word – as repetition, substitution, doubling.

And the voice now locates the pastoral idyll ("mine idle Life" (line 40)) not as original, but as substitution, not as priority, but as a second instance. Twice over: by telling this beginning second, and within the story it tells.

> Thenceforth I set my self to play
> My solitary time away,
> With this: and very well content,
> Could so mine idle Life have spent.
>
> (37-40)

The voice that heard the counterfeit echo in Sylvio now echoes itself. Does it hear itself, hear that it counterfeits the exchange of words and gift with Sylvio when it re-counts the pastoral idyll, and recasts it as a game? Can it hear that it does with the fawn what Sylvio taught, manipulating the word as a projection of the heart?

Hear these echoes: the fawn is "light/Of foot, and heart" (lines 41-42). "Light" and therefore "unconstant"? "It seem'd to bless/Its self in me" (lines 43-44). Merely *seemed*, a counterfeit? Bless . . . wound? Who is playing with whom? ("And did invite,/Me to its game" (lines 42-43)). The hart the hunter? Playing time away, spending life, playing for keeps, or to lose? What is the economy of this game? How many times can the heart be broken?

The voice answers, once, in this "solitary time" (line 38). "O I cannot be/Unkind t'a Beast that loveth me" (lines 45-46). The voice affirms the

22

"solitary time" and the singularity of what was once, by repeating. "Unkind" the echo of "ungentle," "unconstant." Trying to undo repetition (Sylvio's gift), to deny denial ("*Sylvio* soon had me beguil'd" (line 33)) and to locate a time without loss, the voice repeats itself, loses itself in the voice of echo it admits it hears (in another, not in itself). Beguiled itself, it offers the empty idyll as content. Attempting to escape duplicity, the voice is inscribed in duplicity. The pastoral idyll is a dream of priority shaded by secondarity. It comes second, after loss. It reinscribes loss. It cannot avoid repetition.

For the voice establishes its singularity and purity, its inviolateness, by being violated. It repeats insistently: "I remember well . . . I know/What he said . . . I'me sure I do./ Said He . . . ." Doubletalk, the language of Sylvio. Insisting on its innocence, the voice echoes the duplicitous voice it would disown; its "own" voice a declension of the words of Sylvio. *He* says, "Hath taught a Faun to hunt his *Dear*" (line 32). *I* say, "Left me his Faun, but took his Heart" (line 36).

The story of the idyll is a repetitious refrain. "So short a time" (line 52) recalls "one morning" (line 27). "I am sure" (line 51) echoes "I'me sure" (line 30). "Espie" (line 52) glances at Sylvio's "look" (line 31). Repetition echoes and suspends identification; it allows the voice to go on. Commenting on "the declaration of love (a banal, *already written* sequence, if ever there was one)," Roland Barthes characterizes repetition as "very precisely, the fact that there is no reason to stop."[7] The voice repeats its declaration, and denies it does so. Denial is inscribed in the repetition, spacing it, saving it from the collapse into tautology. But not, therefore, undoing repetition, not, thereby, cutting off the idyll from the duplicities of Sylvio. The "solitary time" is inscribed within the circle of repetitions, inscribed as repetition. The space of the disjunction can be seen in the movement from "I know" (line 29) to "I do not know" (line 47):

>   I know
> What he said then; I'me sure I do.
>
>   I do not know
> Whether it too might have done so
> As *Sylvio* did.
>
>   (29-30, 47-49)

The voice that knows Sylvio's echo does not know its own, does not know what it tells in its idyllic recounting. Attempting to make the idyll immune against the incursions of repetition (the voice of Sylvio), it affirms the difference only by repeating. Difference is thereby deferred in repetition. Or, in brief, the declaration:

23

> Thy Love was far more better then
> The love of false and cruel men.
>
> (53-54)

Whose love (loving the fawn, loving men, the fawn's loving, Sylvio's)? "Thy Love" echoes "the love."

What is this "play" of echoing voices, of acknowledged and unacknowledged repetition if not the stanzaic mode of lyric poetry? For example: the sonnet sequence, piling sonnet upon sonnet so that they become stanzas in a long poem, a hundred new positions of denial and frustration re-occupying the single stance until, perhaps, frustration can be acclimatized, until the disowned voice becomes fully naturalized in the inexorableness of repetition. Or, to take another example, it is the voice of Sidney's Astrophil in song, singing Stella's words, "No, no, no, no, my Deare, let be," singing, that is, the beloved's words so that they become his, denying himself doubly by denying denial and thus, in echo, finding a way out of frustration, making a final exit. Let be: cease and continue. Or, the refrain in Wyatt's lute song, ending itself in the echo of the beloved's refusal: "I have done." The lyric stanza, another echo chamber, founded in repetition and the continual reshuffling and repositioning of words, so that the lover takes as his own the words that disown him; the lover has voice in other words. To end each stanza by echoing again–in the refrain of repetition–is also to begin again. Refrain: repeat and be stopped. That is the idyll.

The voice here has begun again by telling second the story of what came first, and by installing in the center of this story of duplicity the idyll of "solitary time." The center, however, is not immune to what circles around it. The fawn/ h[e]art/dear/deer is at the center: repetition circles through that center, penetrates the idyll, violates its solitary state. Knowing repetition, the voice attempts to undo repetition. And repeats. So, the poet of refrain stops repeating by repeating, finally playing out all the positions of the word, all the meanings it might have. Or so it seems. Is the word exhausted, does the voice arrive at a terminal, in the refrain? Or, rather, is not the refrain inevitably endless? "When thou hast done, thou hast not done . . . ."[8]

What voice is here? The voice that hears double and repeats those doubling words, the voice that hears its double words as a solitary tale. One voice, or two? Sylvio, who gave this voice words when he gave the h[e]art, gave words instead of his heart *and* gave his heart in the h[e]art; and so giving, wounded his dear. To make this story solitary and univocal, the voice that speaks it echoes the voice of Sylvio. Seeking its own,

24

speaking itself, the voice finds echo.
What voice? One or two?

*

If Echo, then Narcissus.

Allegory: "to fill:/ . . . to fold"

Let me tell you a story.

Once there was a nymph who could not speak herself. Denied her own voice, she could only speak when another did, and then could only repeat the words she heard.

And she fell in love with someone who could not know himself.

When he spoke, she spoke. "Is anyone here?" he said; "Here," she said; he thought it was his voice he heard, but when he saw her, and saw he was deceived, he fled, until he found a form he could love, a mirror of perfection, on which he fed his eyes (he couldn't hear the words he saw the image say), until, replete and empty ("Plenty makes me poor," he cried), he died, and with him the image died as well.

And she, then, lost her form, and became a stone, a hollow.

Her name, Echo; his, Narcissus.[9]

Deep within itself, denying time, denying history, denying echo, the voice says: let me tell you a story, about the garden, my garden, without Sylvio, without the troopers. This is my story, the whole story, full, replete. Do not expect to understand. I hear my voice, but you cannot. I know my story, but you cannot.

> I have a Garden of my own,
> But so with Roses over grown,
> And Lillies, that you would it guess
> To be a little Wilderness.

(71-74)

Voice of denial. Voice of pleasure. Voice of death.

*

Disjunction. Once again, a new section of the text (lines 55-92) announces itself with a "first": "With sweetest milk, and sugar, first/I it at mine own fingers nurst" (lines 55-56). The voice begins again, back in the garden again, as if that framed moment of solitude were not circled round in sylvan duplicities. But, before, it had been enclosed in the eddying circles of repetition, in the voice of echo. Now, the story is to be told as a story, a sequence, one thing after another. But not the whole story, just the story of the idyll in the garden, filling "solitary time" to meet the requirements of "first" and last.

What voice is this? One that would preserve itself – have its *own* – in that prior time, identifying itself as itself only in the garden with the fawn. Denying the whole story, it makes a part whole; denying the repetitions in the whole story (to tell that, it had not narrated a story, but had spoken as if repeating a refrain), the voice returns to the garden to elaborate the game that raises the question again, who is playing with whom? What can one's own be? The game is hide and seek: "'Twould stay, and run again, and stay" (line 68), a familiar game – of repetition, denial and negation – immortalized by Freud ("*Fort! Da!*") since it holds out the possibility of a beyond . . . beyond the pleasure principle.[10] The voice preserves itself by entering into the game. Playing with the object it becomes the object with which it plays. To preserve itself, voice objectifies itself in its identification with the object of play. The game is one of substitution, making a replacement object serve when the real object is gone – and becoming that object, having *it* as one's own. The one who plays the game and the one who is absent meet in the substitute object. In Freud, it is an indifferent object, a spool of thread thrown and retrieved, a mere thing. And in "The Nymph complaining"? How can the voice preserve itself, its purity, and avoid the contaminating eddies of repetition in which it would cease to own itself? How? By objectifying. No fawn in this section of the poem, no h[e]art; those words do not enter the voice here; it will not enter that perilous territory, overcharged and echoing. No, the voice says "it." Over and again – twenty-six times – the voice says "it." [11] The singular "it" caught in iterability.

Banish Sylvio, banish troopers, banish the heart. And what remains? Voice itself, present to itself, and the memory of the fullness in the garden, remembered totality, consummate union, one with "it" and with itself. Such is the story. A Ficinian dream?

> What . . . does the intellect seek if not to transform all things into itself by depicting all things in the intellect according to the nature of the intellect? And what does the will strive to do if not to transform itself into all things by enjoying all things according to the nature of each? The former strives to bring it about that the universe . . . should become intellect; the latter, that the will should become the universe.[12]

To make mind present to itself, to fill the mind and the universe as mirrors of each other, what must be done? Speak of "it." Merge into the object. Speak of one's own.

Speak of "it" and of nothing else. Deny every analogy that would locate "it" anywhere but in the garden. Preserve that place from the perils of echo. Preserve it from all intrusion, even from someone who might hear this voice speaking. Own it all by disowning everything.

So, first, the voice begins in excess, with a superlative that marks the superabundance and fullness of this exclusive preserve. Begins "with sweetest milk, and sugar, first" (line 55), a story of a growing perfection that has nothing to do with processes of natural growth or ordinary time or space. The voice goes beyond "sweetest" in an extraordinary declension, to "more . . . sweet," "so sweet": "It wax'd more white and sweet than they./It had so sweet a Breath!" (lines 58-59). Outstripping all comparisons, whether they mark difference ("For it was nimbler much than Hindes;/And trod, as on the four Winds" (lines 69-70), or similarity ("It like a bank of Lillies laid" (line 82)), whether it rests or moves. It joins with this "it" to go beyond compare:

> And oft
> I blusht to see its foot more soft,
> And white, (shall I say then my hand?)
> NAY any Ladies of the Land.
>
> (59-62)

"Shall I say then": the voice hears itself speaking, apprehends the excess in its question, and goes beyond it in its capital denial, joining itself to what it sees to make it voice an object beyond compare, to make its voice that object. Comparisons fill the voice – "more," "much," "so," "as," "like" – only to disable comparison, only to say: "It is a wond'rous thing" (line 63).

It: place of meeting for voice and object, wondrous fusion, oneness. Joined in one breath. Speaking, and blushing, the voice rushes to a transcendent whiteness, moving with "it" like the wind on "little silver feet" (line 64), generating, as it speaks, a garden of blushing roses and "flaxen Lillies" (line 81), generating "it" as "Lillies without, Roses within" (line 92). Mirrors upon mirrors. Voice is the generation of breath: "It had so sweet a Breath!" (line 59). Breath and blush and a white hand release "it," join with "it" in the return of breath to breath, white on white, red to red. It returns "to print those Roses on my Lip" (line 86); to lie on "whitest sheets" (line 90). Through the garden, it runs and returns, a circuit: what the white hand generates moves on swift feet. What game is this? What story of return?

The story begins, "first," nursed by hand, and it closes with a "print" (line 86) and a white sheet, moving all the while on *feet* (lines 60, 64) as white as the hand that fed it. Between the lips, uttering, kissing, there is the story itself, of voice becoming object, returning to itself in the image

27

of voice.[13] The image: where "it" moves, that place beyond comparison, made in comparison, the garden of lilies and roses, the mirror of voice and object. That place of transcendent mediation, "you" would "guess/To be a little Wilderness" (lines 73-74). You would misread the image and not see that it lies beyond compare. You would misread the voice as image. See the text.

The voice speaks of "it" as a garden that "you" would not see as it does, and it speaks, too, of an object that can't be seen; "[I] could not, till it self would rise,/Find it, although before mine Eyes" (lines 79-80). Voice: it can't be seen. Such is the story of the voice coming into its own, what it makes as its own. "I it at mine own fingers nurst" (line 56). "I have a Garden of my own" (line 71). Its own into its own; on the breath (conspiracy?); in the mirror. The voice disappears into "it" and emerges as the *image of voice*, invisible as the print of voice–as the printed page. Voice extends to "it" and extends it, letting it come and go. Sylvio's "silver Chain" (line 28) has become the "silver feet" (line 64). The full voice (full of "it"), empties into "it" (by feeding "it," releasing "it"), letting "it" come into its own–the mirroring garden of red and white. It is filled with roses, folded in lilies. Filled and folded, "it" folds back upon itself. Folds and fills the unseen and unheard. What "you" cannot see. The incorporate garden, the garden of the mind, the image of voice; "you" cannot look in the mirror that returns the voice. Here it is: repletion (the feeding) of emptiness and loss; dissolution/incorporation. Into it, the one body, the word without echo. It is not the h[e]art.

You cannot see it. Here it is: this is a voice of multiple denials, refusing analogies for the incomparable "it," denying Echo to preserve voice. To preserve it – and to deny that what is preserved is, precisely, what is denied: echo. Voice, but only in "it," in the mirror. Sustained and filled in this fold. In denial lies its pleasure: "all its chief delight was still/ On Roses thus its self to fill" (lines 87-88). Voice is emptied into "it," and fills and empties itself in "its self." Replete and full in the satisfaction of loss and emptiness, the pleasures of denial. For in its play, the object that mirrors voice–the object that *is* voice–refuses union, keeps its distance, fades in the mirror, imperceptible to voice, imperceptible as voice. Become the image of voice, acting out the voice, it plays with itself. Its own with its own, folded.

Here it is: the story of denial. No mention of Sylvio, the troopers, the fawn. Here it is: stringing out a story.

What voice is this? Voice of Narcissus. Voice full of itself, denying Echo, setting itself up in a mirror, moving towards and away from an object that it is, an object that is the image of its voice – and as insubstantial. Echo, the image of Narcissus.

28

Voice of pleasure, narcissistic gratification, luring, leading on, teasing, tantalizing, playing – and denying. Fullness of pleasure coupled with emptiness of satisfaction. The satisfaction (empty/full) of having one's own, the return of a kiss, the mirror of red and white in the garden, that place of reflection of a mind toying with itself. The full voice, Narcissus says: "plenty makes me poor." The empty voice, Echo says: "I am present." The voice is full of "it"; call it Echo. There is only one voice in this text, the echo of voice.

What voice echoes in the dissolve into "it"? Iteration, dissolving the object, defusing fusion and oneness and one's own, filling (emptying) presence with a fold. The text echoes a voice of presence to oneself, or of nature full of voice. Ovid . . . and Chaucer are *dissolved* in this text. "Whan Zephirus eek with his swete breath/Inspired hath in every holt and heeth"; "it had so sweet a Breath" (line 59) "and trod, as on the four Winds" (line 70). Breath, air, voice conspire against inspiration. Dissolve Petrarch's L[']aura; voice, landscape, beloved object, word-made-flesh. Or flesh-made-word? Such are the voices remembered, dismembering this voice. The voice of Spenserian allegory.[14]

*

Allegory is a mode making use of endless and inadequate analogies; allegories speak in a voice that keeps comparing in order to move beyond compare, in a voice of continuous metaphor that becomes "darke conceit" in its very elucidation. In its etymology, allegory (*allos-agoreuein*) means a speaking beside the point, cryptic, private utterance, voice "present" to itself, not out in the open.[15] Allegory, the voice of the veil (recall the *Fort! Da!*). And, in allegory, the figures ("characters") are parts for wholes. Recall the story of Amoret and *her* bleeding heart, which is also the story of Amoret *as* her bleeding heart, Amoret distanced, objectified, separated from her heart. When her heart is restored–when the circuit of return is "complete"–when she gets back her own, Amoret is then "perfect hole" (*FQ* III. xii. 38. 9), whole and hole. The wound remains–the wound in perfection (completion)–and closure is denied. And in allegory, narrative is woven in an endless replay. Like "flaxen lillies" (flaxen from *plectere*, to braid). Allegory a full (and empty), plaited tale. Episode upon episode (mirror upon mirror), each time the same (iteration), yet in the very sameness (wound and w[h]ole) difference, perplexing. You would mistake a garden for a wilderness. You are strung along, caught in an endless replay. You can't quite find it. You are promised an end, left "to another place . . . to be perfected" (*FQ* IV. xii. 35. 9). That beyond proves to be a before, "deepe within the mynd" (*FQ* VI, proem 5. 8), Spenser says, "another place" where ending is beginning. Allegory

29

drives towards Eden ever lost, endlessly deferred. As Paul de Man puts it: "Allegory designates primarily a distance in relation to its own origin, and, renouncing the nostalgia and the desire to coincide, it establishes its language in the void of this temporal difference."[16] The void – full, empty, and folded. The end of allegory is a "first" without end. Such is the dream of the voice in this section of "The Nymph complaining," the idyll in the garden of repletion, eternal spring ("all the Spring time of the year" (line 75)), an Eden with trips, not falls, an Eden of the mind where desire is fulfilled, time stops, everything folds. The lure of allegory is a beyond . . . beyond the pleasure principle.

*

And so, we must ask again, what voice? Must ask what is suppressed to tell this story of full time, of replete voice, luxuriant garden. And must answer: the fold is empty. Fullness is folded around emptiness. This whole (this union, this oneness of one's own) is a hole. Death has been denied in this idyll. Death is this voice, as it is the basis for all (its) Edenic longings, responsible for the voice of pleasure, for the voice of play. Allegory is the voice of death.

The ludic transformations of eros and loss into hide and seek mean to render loss and absence unthreatening, to control loss by dissolving it into the object that can be manipulated to give pleasure, into an "it," solid, stable, and completely indifferent. A spool of thread; "it" on a chain. Such merging does not dissolve loss, however; it embodies it and enacts it as the location of pleasure. All pleasure. Voice dissolved/made into "it": lost object, a reduced and displaced substitute object. Like all objects. The object that disappears and reappears in (through) the veil. Or the mirror of representation. Or the screen of memory. Or presence. Or being. This voice feeds itself with a story, pressing lip against lip, folding within a garden that mirrors the voice, folding subject and object to indistinction, filling with roses, fading with lilies. The garden offers an image of the play of mind and universe, contained and containing. L'histoire d'O?

Merging means loss. Beyond the visionary certainties (the certainties of vision), loss is registered. Blindness supports vision: "Yet could not, till it self would rise,/Find it, although before mine Eyes" (lines 79-80). It can't be seen. Its very whiteness is a blank. Folded in lilies, that blankness is annihilative. It lies in "the flaxen Lillies shade" (line 81). It lies "where it should lye" (line 78), dissolving the incorporate solidity of the "it" in iteration, folding upon itself. There is no "it self" except as it sacrifices itself:

Among the beds of Lillyes, I
Have sought it oft, where it should lye,
Yet could not, till it self would rise,
Find it, although before mine Eyes.

(77-80)

To feed the voice that generates it, it returns generation, replays it. It pays in blood. Such is the "challenge" of "the Race" (line 66). The union, the kiss, the return of breath for breath, is a union in blood, embodying loss:

Upon the Roses it would feed,
Until its Lips ev'n seem'd to bleed:
And then to me 'twould boldly trip,
And print those Roses on my Lip.

(83-86)

Those blushing roses give this voice its voice.

Filled by loss, folded in a winding cloth, this story of "first" dissolves into last:

But all its chief delight was still
On Roses thus its self to fill:
And its pure virgin Limbs to fold
In whitest sheets of Lillies cold.

(87-90)

A winding cloth, blank sheets. A page? A sepulchre? A bed? Or the coldness of a monument, sepulchre of Echo, her virgin limbs become stone, embodied/disembodied, the object at last. Still delights, unmoving. "Had it liv'd long" (line 91), the voice continues, the metamorphosis would have been complete, the dissolve perfected. "Had it liv'd long," it would not have lived at all; folded in lilies, filled with roses, it would have lived to embody its death. "Had it liv'd long": at last the voice admits iteration, repeating itself (see line 47). Admits what has been denied. It ends – voice ends – as echo. The dream of Narcissus ends. Story-telling ends in its beginning.

As narration, allegory embodies death, a realm that the mind represents to itself as a space in which the human dilemmas of time and otherness are overcome because they are finally beside the point. Spenserian allegory, which is always seeking beginnings and never finding them, driving ever "deepe within the mynd," is laid to rest by this voice. The "it" is the memorialized other, eternalized as object, located in an Eden of the mind and as a plaything in a ritualized and endless sequence that plays to avoid loss, that would avoid loss by playing with it, and which therefore keeps itself from losing only by never having at all. This is the game of hide and seek. The voice here is finally so beside the point that it says what it would deny precisely because it has founded itself on denial. Inevitably, it is already inscribed in the voice of echo. And in speaking so beside the point of desire to avoid loss by holding on to the "solitary time" and making it the entire story, the voice inscribes pure loss, inevitable loss, as its desire. The troopers' bullets, the duplicities of Sylvio, *are* this voice; "it" is the death of the fawn. "Had it liv'd long . . . "; with these words, the voice comes to itself. Comes, that is, to the end of itself, to the end of the dream of one's own. The object, sustained in the echo of iteration, is relinquished. The possibility of the inimitable "it" is laid to rest and, with it, the possibility of the sustained and sustaining voice. Its fullness folds upon itself.

*

Time now to end; time for the poem of ending to become itself, for voice and all its echoes to be undone, filled and emptied. Time for the poem to give up its voice and to be what it is – text, the blank print. Time for the most severe reductions yet. Time to end itself as itself, in its own implacable, miniaturized monumentality.

(Read under erasure: itself, its, its own, is.)

Epigraph: "not as Thee"

The voice that has been speaking now draws to an end, in ending locating its beginnings. Throughout the poem, the voice, exhausting itself in a deadly necessity (a necessity of speech), has repeatedly occupied the position of having already been written, the place of echo. And this voice, in its breaks, in its reconstitutions in the face of annihilation, has not been a dramatic voice, the voice of a character or a person. Rather, it is the situation of voice in language, of voice in the already written text, played to the end. Hence, speech is a misnomer. This voice has no name as it speaks. Named before, in the title, its name is no entitlement; "nymph" names the "signifier of the signifier," designating a situation of voice, a marginal site for the voice of dissolution and erosion, for the voice made already in the word, made in a process of taking itself away, founded on the abyss, engraved:

> For I so truly thee bemoane,
> That I shall weep though I be Stone:
> Until my Tears, still dropping, wear
> My breast, themselves engraving there.

(115-118)

Is it another voice that enters now in awareness of this? Can any voice be the locus of awareness, of consciousness of itself? No, it is not self-consciousness that enters the text now, for there is no self in the text to be conscious of itself: the voice now *enters itself*. Doing away with the fiction and the structures that would locate the voice, wearing itself away, the voice enters what makes it and is undone by what makes it, the text, the word on the page: where the voice is engraved. So, finally, it is not a voice in any commonsensical definition we might give the term, not a voice at all but the echo of voice–or silence, or, the text. "I be Stone" (line 116) tells us who speaks, who "I" is. Utterance is now located as epigraph, as writing in an "essential" guise, as *writing upon*.[17] Upon what? Absence, loss, denial, death. Writing as the inscription of loss. Inscription as the death of the voice. The "being" of writing: to be stone.

The final lines of "The Nymph complaining" reduce what has come before to a series of terminal inscriptions. The entire poem is epitomized as a set of epigrams (excessively truncated inscriptions). Everything is (at once) replayed and endplayed. Voice in a situation of excess, echo, loss supplemented and replete, voice standing incised, in the breaks, the ends, the cuts. No end to erosion. Endlessly disjunctive.

i (lines 93-100)

The engraved text offers its erosions to the reader, allows an entrance for our voice in the text. The reader is invoked: "O help! O help! I see it faint" (line 93), invited to see it dissolve, however faintly. The object of speech (or is it the subject of speech?) begins to disappear and die: "I see it faint:/And dye" (lines 93-94). Voice begins to disappear to invoke the co-presence (or is it absence?) of the reader as co-witness, co-speaker of the poem: "I see it faint . . . /See how it weeps" (lines 93, 95). What is the reader, now taken into the text, invited to "see" if not the text itself, fe/ainting, fading? Excessively, the text offers its dissolution to the reader in floods of analogies: "as a Saint," "like a Gumme," "So weeps . . . so/The holy Frankincense," "such Amber Tears . . . ." These excesses (analogies dizzying in their combinations and range of allusions) mark the reader's entrance as a place of erosion, a cut in language, a wound that permits entrance at the price of annihilation. "See how it weeps" (line 94); see the tears, the flood, the sappy tree, the flowing frankincense. See the wound of the saint, the scarred tree, releasing/congealing balm. Frankincense, gift for a singular creature ("There is not such another" recall); amber jewel for the death of Phaeton, son of Apollo, son of the sun. Flooding, dissolving, eroding: a metamorphosis unleashed and held. "The brotherless *Heliades*/Melt in such Amber Tears as these" (lines 99-

100). "Melt" in the meeting of I/eye and fawn, in the wound, or the text.

Into what text has the reader entered? The text for which, voiceless, we supply voice, sightless, we see. The text, any text, monumentally, implacably *there* as long as unread, and, when read, then where? on the page? in the reader? in the wound? The entrance into this text at this point thematizes entrance into a text, the excessive supplementation that takes place upon annihilation. The analogies here dissolve the I/eye and the object in their place of meeting. These analogies answer the antitheses with which the poem began, those antitheses that converged in an identification in the inevitability of the wound. Now the wound is explicit – open – as the entrance into the text in which the dissolve of identification takes place. This answer does not close the question; it leaves it open. As text. The voice becomes text – replaced by the analogies as the object of speech, dissolved into the reader. In the analogies, the wounded tree (a trace of *Sylvio/silva/Silvae*) is the word, dissolving, generating, eroding, maintaining; the word, in short, engraved. What was once a lover's frustration is now the reader's. These opening lines of the final section of the poem replay/reposition the poem's first words; antithesis becomes identification, a dissolve into the generation of the wounded word. Replay and endplay, back to the beginning again, beginning in secondarity, the reader in place, re-placed.

ii *(lines 101-104)*

I in a golden Vial will
Keep these two crystal Tears; and fill
It till it do o'reflow with mine;
Then place it in *Diana's* Shrine.

(lines 101-4)

Repetition once again, doubling the two tears, supplementing them in echoes: "will/ . . . fill/ . . . till," "two . . . do," "I . . . Vial . . . mine . . . *Diana's* Shrine." Merging, overflowing boundaries, the second section of the poem is replayed. Keeping the tears in the vial resituates the idyll of "solitary time." Why is the vial destined for "*Diana's* Shrine"? To double (the vial in the shrine). And why Diana? As chaste nymph and as killer of the huntsman Actaeon (h[e]artslain), Diana is the meeting place of nymph and hunter (Sylvia and Sylvio). Her name embodies transcendent purity and necessary slaughter, the coincidence of the h[e]art and the hunt, duplicitous repetition. The shrine contains the image – the statue – or the corpse, an excessive surround of venerable emptiness; a shrine (from *scrinium*) is a chest of books or papers, a storehouse of words. Diana's shrine encloses the word of denial, saying no to love, the model of the stanzaic poet's endplay: "No, no, no, no, my Deare, let be"; here endplayed, enshrined. Voice spills out beyond the limits and into an enclosure that surrounds vacuity; the word. Enclosure is violated; the golden bowl is shattered or cracked. Overcoming, overflowing the limits of form produces the form that puts a limit around emptiness. Bowl within shrine; voice within voice. Diana, the preserve of Echo, sepulchral hollow; the embodiment of disembodiment.

iii   (lines 105-110)

To the garden once more, to begin again, to play again, taking flight, dissolving into a "Now" (line 105), the present of the text of presence. For "now," the excessive declension of *sweet* is death: "Now my sweet Faun is vanish'd" (line 105). And the garden is otherworldly, deadly: "fair *Elizium*" (line 107). Whiteness a corpse's pallor: "milk-white Lambs" (line 108) the company where all that vanishes is preserved. "Vanish'd . . ./to endure": so is the entire race rerun to its end. But "it" is at an end, too, buried in the shrine, and "thee" emerges in the submergence of voice, voice at an end: "for I/Will but bespeak thy Grave, and dye" (lines 109-110). On the margins of dissolution, merging into loss, losing "itself," becoming text and, thereby, undoing "its self" and achieving what the prospect of the garden held out: union in death, *on the page forever*, there – and not there. *Fort! Da!* "O do not run too fast" (line 109).

iv   (lines 111-122)

So, now, finally, in the last lines, the poem begins, again, with a "first":

> First my unhappy Statue shall
> Be cut in Marble; and withal,
> Let it be weeping too.
>
> (111-13)

The text orders its dissolution. Echo, reversed, gives orders to make herself stone. And the engraver is told to "spare" his efforts: "but there/Th'Engraver sure his Art may spare" (lines 113-14). This reserve is coupled to excess: "and withal." The truth of the text: an untouched, ever-weeping stone: "For I so truly thee bemoane/That I shall weep though I be Stone" (lines 115-16). This statue, created in dissolution, made by erosion, images the situation and status of the image and the text: speaking pictures, Sidney might say. The self-consuming artifact, a

35

modern voice might counter.

Engraving itself in itself–such is the autonomy of the statuesque text. These lines are replete–with loss, as they engrave themselves. Everything is taken away: nymph, fawn, even the engraver. Taken away . . . and monumentalized. If the text now also re-enters Ovid's Niobe, then Apollo and Diana, the gods who separately allowed Phaeton his self-destructive flight and Actaeon his self-consuming vision, the gods who jointly slaughtered Niobe's generation, preside over the final double gesture of monumental withdrawal. Founding annihilation in going beyond. Joining sun and moon, day and night, the gods of this text image a dream of repletion (opposites the life of each other) experienced as loss. Apollo and Diana, formgivers; they order annihilation.

The statue:

> For I so truly thee bemoane,
> That I shall weep though I be Stone:
> Until my Tears, still dropping, wear
> My breast, themselves engraving there.
>
> (115-18)

Cut, worn away, "still dropping," "engraving"; the statue as image of the text. Voice becomes voiceless, entering the text, turning to stone, stonily silent. Excessively engraving (weeping, wailing, mourning, sobbing, flooding), the image emerges, incised, eroded. The more than and the less than meet in this final excess–the excess that images the text. Not the text itself, but the image of the text in the statue. Endless inscription, endless reading: such is the prospect of engraving that wears away, and offers what remains, all that remains. All that reading, our incision in the text, gives: voice, life. The statue is the image of the discursive space in which reading and writing are constituted as the text is worn away.[18]

> There at my feet shalt thou be laid,
> Of purest Alabaster made:
> For I would have thine Image be
> White as I can, though not as Thee.
>
> (119-22)

The text opens on itself, opens in its denials the space of interpretation, lays it at our feet. We have the "Image." Disowned vocalization, at last explicit, when the voice becomes the engraved engraver, wearing away all pretenses of a self or self-presence, offering the image in its full inadequacy, "White as I can, though not as Thee." The annihilative ground of being, "annihilating all that's made." Here, at last, the "real" fawn – the fawn as offspring, made – of alabaster.

36

In such final gestures, in the silencing of voice, in the revelation of the simulacrum of the speaking stone, voice is "there" (present, now–written under erasure) as the fawn is. AS WE ARE. Voice dies into the already written, into the echo of voice, into stone, the image of echo. As everything is taken away, what remains? Inscription, epigraph, acting (itself) out, a revelation: "The letter killeth . . ." and nothing given life. As the statue, "not . . . Thee," the re-cognition of the refusal of going beyond. The text is not *really* "about" something else.

*

Limit upon limit. Absence, denial, negation, loss: such are the supports of presence, such are the sources of the vast powers of the text to engage with the reader in the production of meaning. For the engraving that wears away does not open on the enclosed garden (that voice is past), but on the ever-receding horizon of an annihilative abyss upon which the reader moves, undone and ever doing.

*

Where is Marvell's voice in this text?

> I yet my silent Judgment keep,
> Disputing not what they believe
> But sure as oft as Women weep,
> It is to be suppos'd they grieve.[19]

3

Consuming texts: Spenser and the poet's economy

Spenser's entrance onto the poetic scene occurs in a dispersal of names and voices. Consider the book.[1] On the title page of *The Shepheardes Calender* no author appears, and the only proper name is Sidney's. On the verso, a poem, addressed "To His Booke," signed Immeritô. Prefatory prose follows, directed not (as one might expect) to Sidney but to "Mayster Gabriell Harvey," and not from the author but from someone signed E. K. (and who is that?). Then, finally – one might say – the text itself. Or, rather, a palimpsest: woodcut, argument, monologue or dialogue, emblem, gloss. E. K. claims to find Spenser here, in "Colin, under whose person the Author selfe is shadowed" (418), yet Colin is heard only intermittently in the eclogues; no account is made (by E. K. or elsewhere) of Immeritô, the one without value, named anonymity, the name attached to the initial set of verses. "To His Booke" suggests we look elsewhere if we seek "the Author selfe," sending the book – "as child whose parent is unkent" (line 2) to another, to lodge "under the shadow of his wing" (line 7), a patron/reader who can give authoritative shelter and shade to poetic flight. E. K. subscribes to this pattern, too, and extends the shadow of authority: "So flew Virgile . . . . So flew Mantuane . . . . So Petrarque. So Boccace; So Marot, Sanazarus, and also divers other excellent both Italian and French Poetes, whose foting this Author every where followeth, yet so as few, but they be wel sented can trace him out" (418). In short: this new poet has no name of his own, no beginning except as he is received and as he receives, no story to tell until he has been taken under another's wing, unless the text is consumed.

These are the conditions that define the entrance of Spenser, and they make problematic that very name, casting in doubt its propriety or what it can own. Recent attention to the emergence of this poet, however alert to the corrosiveness that surrounds him – whether it takes the form of an hostile or indifferent social milieu, or the imperfections of the Colin in whom E. K. would project the author, or the defectiveness of all positions voiced in *The Shepheardes Calender* – has attempted to "save" the poet and to preserve his name from the depredations represented in (and by) the text. Thus, in an essay on the anonymity of authorship in this debut text, David L. Miller concludes with a Spenser who "abides in a Yeatsian monument of his own magnificence;" anonymity has become an artifice of eternity, as it is, too, for Michael McCanles, who resolves a dialectic between the corrosive historicity of the poem and its monumental status in the direction of "a movement toward consciousness and transcendence over past perspectives on time;" and transcendence, too, Miller finds in a subsequent essay on Spenser's vocation. Even Harry Berger, Jr., whose remarkable essays on the "paradise principle" of *The Shepheardes Calender* describe a text insidious in its undermining of all positions espoused, allows Spenser the ability to play on the margins of what he performs, a complex act in which he is enabled by the cultural discourse that he also (as Berger says) deconstructs. Spenser's "deconstructive literary act" leaves little intact – except, of course, "Spenser."[2]

However much it may strain criticism and its abiding fictions of "the Author selfe," we need a poetics of the book that pursues the traces and shadows that throw the proper name in question, a passport into a community of dispersed names and shades. Read in a manner he would not approve (which perhaps indicates in its own way the limits of ownership of discourse), Paul Alpers points us where to go, to Virgilian pastoral as a community of voices joined, as he puts it, in a "sympathetic dative"; he alludes to a line in the final eclogue: "who would not sing for Gallus," where "for" translates the dative and means both "to" as well as "in place of" – in another's voice.[3] The dispersal of voice produces a theory of genre and generics, a community of shades. The sympathy that binds also dissolves; no one owns his (own) voice launched in song.

> Extremum hunc, Arethusa, mihi concede laborem:
> pauca meo Gallo, sed quae legat ipse Lycoris,
> carmina sunt dicenda: neget quis carmina Gallo?
>
> *(Eclogue 10, 1-3)*

(A final labor, Arethusa, grant me these few words for Gallus, but let Lycoris read them; a song is to be sung: who would not sing for Gallus?)

39

Under the shadow of others, in the shadow of death, *in extremis*, the voices of the text emerge in *The Shepheardes Calender* following a well-beaten path, so heavily trod that its traces are all but indecipherable, save to those "wel sent." "The Author selfe" we seek cannot be found; the text we pursue is itself all but invisible. In the Argument to the *October* eclogue, E. K. (for the moment, let us take him as if the initials signified) points our way, referring the text he prefaces to another, "his booke called the English Poete," inviting a reading of that lost (phantom) text by reading the eclogue. Perhaps, then, in *October*, inscribed beneath the Scorpion, the sign of death, the voice of the text can emerge. That, at any rate, is the hypothesis in what follows.

There are three movements in this reading of *October* as a gloss on "the English Poete" (the book/the author). In the first section of the eclogue (lines 1-36), a pastoral poetics. Then (lines 37-78), abandoning "the base and viler clowne" (line 37), a poetics for others. Finally (lines 79-120), abandonment and flight in answer to the question "O pierlesse Poesye, where is then thy place." A path of displacements traces the voice in the shadows to its sole place, the echo of *silvae*, leaf against leaf. There alone, in frustrated passion, to the hills and woods, he pours out his empty words ("Ibi haec incondita solus/montibus et silvis studio iactabat inani" (*Eclogue 2*, 4-5)). "Respondent omnia silvae" (*Eclogue 10*, line 8); woods answer all. "Omnia vincit Amor" (*Eclogue 10*, line 69).

"They han the pleasure, I a sclender prise": a poet's poet

October begins in bankruptcy. Apparently, Cuddie has no audience to recompense him, only ungrateful lads who take their pleasure but won't pay; he labors, they profit, "I beate the bush, the byrds to them do flye" (line 17), and he is not "the fuller by a graine" (line 34), not even bird's food for him. Feeding them, he has been depleted, and he cancels the former exchange with present silence, extending his present condition to them, now refusing them as they refused him.

A community of identity informs this bankrupt beginning: "Now they in thee, and thou in sleepe art dead" (line 6). However, the story is more complicated, not simply one of cause and effect, of the opposition of lads and poet followed by their communion in inanition, emptiness and depletion. Rather, bankruptcy is always already the condition of utterance, and union without recompense is an inevitability in the community of the text.

Consider lines 7 to 10:

Piers, I have pyped erst so long with payne,

That all mine Oten reedes bene rent and wore:
And my poore Muse hath spent her spared store,
Yet little good hath got, and much lesse gayne.

His was a "spared store" (line 9) to begin with, and, properly speaking, not his at all, but his "poore Muse"'s. Only without expenditure–before he played for the lads–would he have had whatever full store he might claim, although even that was not his own (save as the Muse is his); nor is it clear that his Muse was ever anything but impoverished, or that piping was ever anything but painful ("I have pyped erst so long with payne" (line 7)). In that beginning (before the beginning in bankruptcy with which *October* opens), there is poverty–a slim reed pipe–from the first. The lads' failures hardly signify when piping, no matter how it may be received, is always depletion without recompense.

Or, as Cuddie continues,

The dapper ditties, that I wont devise,
To feede youthes fancie, and the flocking fry,
Delighten much: what I the bett for thy?
They han the pleasure, I a sclender prise.

(12-15)

And from the first–and not merely as a response to their irresponsibility and unresponsiveness to the poet's sustaining labors – the lads are implicated in the economy that predates the story that Cuddie laments. From the first, the pleasures they are fed are consuming, and the lads are led . . . beyond the pleasure principle. Their status within the poet's economy (the always already depletion of the spent/spared storehouse of language, source of invention and *copia*) can be traced in their nomination: "the flocking fry,/Delighten much" (lines 14-15). E. K.'s gloss directs us to the *verbal* economy of such pleasure. "Frye) is a bold Metaphore, forced from the spawning fishes. For the multitude of young fish be called the frye" (458). The lads are engendered–"forced from the spawning fishes" – as words in a text, words "forced" from the "spared store." Existing *as* "bold Metaphore," they are 'inside' language as much as Cuddie is–as a poet (E. K.'s argument treats his name as synonymous with "the perfecte paterne of a Poete")–as much, that is, as Cuddie's ownership of his "poore Muse" or "Oten reedes" is a reversible condition. The Muse is the storehouse, however scanty, of "his" words; the instrument is a Virgilian signature, a hollow reed. Lured by pleasure, the lads are led "whereto thou list their trayned willes entice" (line 24); pleasure lures them *into* the text. The "trayned willes" answer their forced spawning within a shared verbal economy: "O how the rurall routes to thee doe cleave" (line 26). Cleaving, they join and separate at

41

once, at first – in their pleasure, before their failure to repay.

> O how the rurall routes to thee doe cleave:
> Seemeth thou dost their soule of sence bereave.
>
> (26-27)

Delighted, they are also deprived, bereaved of sense. Pursuing the poet's path, tracing his "sent," they are senseless, made shadows in his path, "trayned," "forced," and bereaved. Their pleasures are one with the poet's pains.

Thus, *October* opens as if it were posing opposing voices (Piers vs. Cuddie), as if it were explaining the poet's condition in such oppositions, appreciative Piers on one side, the thoughtless lads on the other. Yet, insistent in the figurations in this opening is another beginning that undercuts the dialectics of the story (the spacing of opposition as a sequence). In that first condition, these oppositions are dispersed, opposing voices are scattered as traces on a path of generation. In the generative beginning of expenditure and storing, of cleaving and bereaving as engendering, these opposing voices emerge, suspended, dissolved, in deadly play, fatal pleasures. "So flew Virgile . . . ." So the lads fly. Pleasure joined to pain.

There is a theory of poetry in this situation, for it refigures the vital terms of classical and Renaissance poetics, mixing the *dulce* and *utile* anew; the word becomes fatal food when the lads are caught in the poet's toils. "To teach and delight" (25) is Sidney's Horatian summary of the aim of poetry.[4] In *October*, that dead month, Piers voices this position. Cuddie's task, he says, is to lead the lads, to "restraine/The lust of lawlesse youth . . ./Or pricke them forth with pleasaunce" (lines 21-23). "Restraine" or "pricke": pleasure co-opted for moral ends. Sidney says poets show the way by giving "so sweet a prospect into the way, as will entice any man to enter into it. Nay, he doth, as if your journey should lie through a fair vineyard, at the first give you a cluster of grapes, that full of that taste, you may long to pass further" (39-40). It is ashes in Cuddie's mouth; he pipes "with payne" (line 7) and starves. He remixes the *dulce* and *utile*; they have pleasure, he has pain. And, blindly following, they are fed his line: "Now they in thee, and thou in sleepe art dead" (line 6). Death is the prospect to which their "trayned" wills are so enticed; flocking, flying, they are engendered by words that place them in the poet's economy.

"The poet is the food for the tenderest stomachs" (34), Sidney writes; the lads consume the poet, have life as he gives it, as he receives it, impoverished. Words are their food, intoxicating grapes, honeyed melody, "a medicine of cherries" (41), as Sidney says, sweet "sugared

42

invention" (27), "fruitful knowledge" (52). The sweetness deceives and shadows; they are led "to take most wholesome things by hiding them in such other as have a pleasant taste, which, if one should begin to tell them the nature of *aloes* or *rhabarbarum* they should receive, would sooner take their physic at their ears than at their mouth" (40). The deception extends the shadow of the poet: poet and lads are consumed in the text, engendered only as words spawned, disseminated.

It is an old story of how poets come to have an identity, how readers read, how texts are created. Petrarch (recasting Seneca) tells Boccaccio that what he ate in the morning he digested in the evening: "These writings I have so thoroughly absorbed and fixed, not only in my memory but in my marrow." Erasmus rehearses a hundred plus ways to write 'your letter pleased me mightily' and the words become "honey-sweet", a "sumptuous banquet," he is "tipsy" at its arrival, digesting, he concludes, a "choice morsel"; nonetheless Erasmus recommends a judicious palate. "Some *Bookes* are to be Tasted, Others to be Swallowed, and Some few to be Chewed and Digested," Bacon will put it memorably in "Of Studies."[5] To be swallowed by a text, consummation devoutly to be feared: "Now they in thee, and thou in sleepe art dead" (line 6). "I now consume in poesie,/ Yet *Homer* being my roote I can not die," Chapman boasts.[6] The poet's life, rooted in texts, living off others, food for any palate. So texts are 'inside' one another, shadowed, fledged, and spawned. Such is the poet's void (and *copia*), slim store, as he sings to the echoing woods, joining the pastoral community. The author of the *Silvae* receives life from Virgil's death, he confesses in the *Purgatorio*, in that pained meeting between Virgil, eternally damned, and Statius, living (forever) off words that could not save his patron. Dante finds Statius in the circle of misers, apprehends that he has absorbed his master's text, and discovers that this is a misapprehension: prodigality, spreading his wings too wide, spending was this poet's fault too (*Purgatorio*, 22, lines 43-45).[7]

The classic exemplar, the story of Orpheus, comes to Piers's lips:

> All as the shepheard, that did fetch his dame
> From *Plutoes* balefull bowre withouten leave:
> His musicks might the hellish hound did tame.
>
> (28-30)

In Horace, or Puttenham, or Sidney, Orpheus moves rocks and rills to make the woods echo in song. Orpheus, founder of civilization, is the humanists' theme. There is, as Harry Berger says, a "darker side of Orpheus," for the release of Eurydice bears a painful ending, suppressed by E. K.'s gloss and by Piers as well: the loss of Eurydice. Spenser, Berger argues, sustains both sides of the story; the art that Orpheus represents is impossible without the pain. Loss is to the point, perhaps is *the* point in the poet's story; it figures the essential consummation, it makes song possible.[8] To turn back and lose propels the poet forward; song after loss marks the poet's path, an economy without compensation, living off himself, singing in the void. As Blanchot puts it: "only in the song does Orpheus have power over Eurydice, but in the song Eurydice is also already lost and Orpheus himself is the scattered Orpheus, the 'infinitely dead' Orpheus into which the power of the song transforms him from then on."[9] "Hold up thy heavye head" (line 1), Piers says, asking Cuddie from the first to be the poet-as-Orpheus, to take his exemplary end as the poet's beginning, asking, in effect, that Cuddie be the singing head, dismembered, scattered.

*

He rose from the dead–he made the dead rise, then lost her by desiring her–he rose, lost, turned to stone, stunned. Then, awakening from the sleep of death, he sang, and the rocks and woods moved to his song. He sang of the boy who loved a deer, and died and became a tree. He sang to the cypress, his death, his love. Sang of the gods who loved their boys to death, of an artist who found life but only in stone, of youths who fled from desire, of children born from trees, of Adonis, told stories of those who fled to deathly embraces, who made their loves die, who gave their loves life. He rose from the dead to sing these songs, and they threw stones at him, but the stones hung in mid-air; they threw leafy branches at him, but the branches were entranced. And so they hurled words at him, howled in the air, and the stones bled and birds bathed in blood. And they heard nothing, tearing his body limb from limb, sending his severed head down the Hebrus. And he sang, Eurydice, Eurydice, and the echoing shores resounded.

Death, not marriage, is what Orpheus wants.

'You gods of hell, I loved too much; I need not tell you, for you know. The kingdom of love is established here.' They heard and wept; they gave to lose and win him back to the kingdom that is his own, the one he sang recounting their story, when he told his own.

She said nothing when he looked back. How could she? He wanted her, not the song. At last, he looked back again. Then, all lost, all was won. Shades, they could play forever, you first, then me, you first, then me, repetitions without loss when all is lost. No voices then, no texts: consumed to be the text.

*

44

Here is the man who scorns us.[10]

After loss, Orpheus sings for love, the love of boys. He leads lads, too. Gloss: "In thys place seemeth to be some savour of disorderly love, which the learned call pæderastice: but . . . such love is much to be alowed and liked of, specially so meant, as Socrates used it; . . . And so is pæderastice much to be præferred before gynerastice . . ." (*Januarye*). Enticing the boys, leading them in country pleasures, he engenders them in an economics of consumption, repletion, identification. Theirs is the pleasure of the text "as Socrates used it."

Socrates to Phaedrus:

> My appetite is for learning. Trees and countryside have no desire to teach me anything; it's only the men in the city that do. You, however, seem to have found the remedy to draw me out. Just as men can lead hungry beasts by shaking a bait of fruit or leaves in front of them, so you brandish me words in books and could lead me on a tour of all Attica and anywhere else you pleased.
>
> (*Phaedrus*, 230)

Later, Socrates will tell Phaedrus that he speaks his words, his text, baited, drawn, fed, opening his second speech, for example, by declaring that his first one "was that of Phaedrus" (244). Love and texts are consuming passions, both can be called "a remedy to draw me out," into the fields, out of himself, bereaved of "sence," in a lover's condition. For the "remedy" that Socrates names, that sweet bait "of fruit or leaves" (honeyed words, echoing woods) is nothing other than poison. After Derrida's essay on "Plato's Pharmacy," no one needs to be reminded that the word for *remedy* that Socrates uses means both remedy and poison, or that, using it, Socrates is drawn into "the graphic relations between the living and the dead," as Derrida puts it (*Dissemination*, 65), for the lure of love is also the lure of the text, "words in books." Drug, poison, philtre, bait, potion: the consuming text, disseminated in reading; the community of poets and lovers, eating the banquet of the word. Consumed by words.

*

Cuddie answers text with text; to Orpheus he counters Argus, a tale within a tale, another account of the origins of poetry, in this case the etiology of the poet's instrument and voice:[11]

> So praysen babes the Peacoks spotted traine,
> And wondren at bright *Argus* blazing eye:
> But who rewards him ere the more for thy?
> Or feedes him once the fuller by a graine?
>
> (31-34)

Argus was all ear when Mercury told him the tale of the love of Pan for Syrinx, how she became, fleeing, a slim reed, instrument of loss, the pastoral pipe. Entranced, "trayned" like the lads in the company of the spellbinding taleteller, Argus shut his eye to become all eye, and was metamorphosed into the "Peacok's spotted traine" (line 32). The "Peacocks tayle," as E. K. puts it, answers the tale of Orpheus. It tells how the hearer caught in the tale becomes the tale itself – and is consumed. To Orpheus, looking back and losing, and thereby constituting the text in his gaze, this tale responds with Argus consumed by the story of Syrinx, Argus all eye. "Such pleasaunce makes the Grashopper so poore,/And ligge so layd, when Winter doth her straine" (lines 11-12).[12] The cicadas chirp, Socrates tells Phaedrus; they make the lulling music of pastoral and, he adds, *they are made by that music*, the reciprocal pattern of the response of Cuddie to Piers, Argus to Orpheus. Socrates has another story of metamorphosis to tell:

> Once upon a time, as the story goes, before the Muses were born, these crickets were men; and, when the Muses came and song made its appearance, some of these men were so overcome by the pleasure of it that they sang and sang, forgetful of food and drink and without noticing even the approach of death. And from them the race of crickets subsequently came into being and received from the Muses the gift of needing no nourishment, the prerogative of singing on and on without food or drink from the moment of birth until they die.
>
> (*Phaedrus*, 259)

Such pleasance is the poet's pain, such plenty makes him poor.

This is a psychic economy.[13] Freud imagines the mind as the container of a fixed amount of energy, depleted as it is discharged. The model for this metaphor of fullness, this storehouse, is the mother. Identification begins in union with the mother; identity comes from the act of separation from her and in compensation for loss. The fullness once imagined in a union that did not mark the boundary between inside and outside, self and other, is replaced with those demarcations and the desire to overcome them, not in absorption in the (now recognized) other, but in self-absorption, self absorbing the other. Yet, desire (and its categories of self and other) is constituted not only by the recognition of the mother as other, but also in a recognition of the self *as other*. It is not only art that holds the mirror up to nature: in the mirror, identity takes place. The *I* constituted in the gaze: the story of Orpheus. Freud calls it primary narcissism. One Ovidian metamorphosis answers another.

> At a time at which the first beginnings of sexual satisfaction are still linked with the taking of nourishment, the sexual instinct has a sexual object outside the infant's own body in the shape of his mother's breast. It is only later that the instinct loses that object, just at the time, perhaps, when the child is able to form a total idea of the person to whom the organ that is giving him satisfaction belongs. As a rule the sexual instinct then becomes auto-erotic . . . . There are thus good reasons why a child sucking at his mother's breast has become the prototype of every relation of love. The finding of an object is in fact a refinding of it.
>
> (*Three Essays*, 124-5)

Internalization: taking the breast in when the breast has been withdrawn, putting in mind what had been in the mouth. A founding of fullness and "a total idea of the person" in *loss* of the object: this, then, is the model for the passage of the pleasures of the mouth, place of food and word, for the consuming transformation of word as food. The constitution of the *I* and the object in loss provides the scene of writing, the generation of the text. In the mirror.

The Muse is the storehouse of the word. Sidney says that poets are mankind's "first nurse, whose milk by little and little, enabled them to feed afterwards of tougher knowledges" (18). Mother's milk, sweet; and then, tough food.[14] What is received in the milk? Identity-in-identification and attachment; and then, emptiness. Only then – in loss – does primary narcissism follow. But there is loss before, loss even in attachment, retrospectively in the newly recognized categories of *I* and other, but also, startlingly, as Freud says, in attachment itself, for the mother *delivers narcissism*, and the full breast feeds the feeder. Feeding the child, the mother feeds herself. Refinding the lost object in the self (the auto-eroticism of so-called primary narcissism) entails a rewriting of the original attachment. Primal narcissism, that *secondary* state, begins the delusion of fullness, and returns to unavoidable loss.

This economy of loss within loss, this refinding of loss in generation, is the poet's, spilling his strains, painfully generating, impoverishing. "Narcissistic or ego-libido seems to be the great reservoir from which the object-cathexes are sent out and into which they are withdrawn once more" (*Three Essays*, 120). So, the *Defence of Poetry* opens by acknowledging "that self-love is better than any gilding to make that seem gorgeous wherein ourselves be parties" (17). Poetry as narcissistic defense.[15]

There can be no return in this economics. One primal state metamorphoses into another. Narcissism is masochism since auto-eroticism is nothing more or less than making love to the wounded self, desiring the self-in-loss. (To deplete this self, to spend this store, as Piers

47

would have Cuddie do, would repeat the orphic story of loss.) Expenditure is death. Identification with the Muse is death. Fullness is emptiness. Life and death both meet in the lost object, that great reservoir, the poet's store. Freud writes "The Economic Problem in Masochism" and discovers that the death drive is part of libido, that self-love contains self-hate, that primary masochism is the return of sadism.

Driven by hate and love, the poet scatters death, his own, the boys'. Death is the word. "Let us cast with what delight to chace,/And weary thys long lingring *Phoebus* race" (lines 2-3), Piers invites Cuddie. The poetics of pleasure wearies; wearing out a path of traces, it scatters the race; disseminating, it sows privation. Rivaling the sun, a struggle between the generation of life and death takes place. Rivalry with the god of poetry and civilization puts the poet in the position of Phaeton and invites his career. And not his alone. Rivalry with Apollo recurs in Ovid, in the story of Orpheus, for example, the son of Apollo who is restored to the grave by his father. Or consider the singing contest in which Marsyas succeeds against Apollo and is rewarded . . . by being skinned alive. "Why do you tear me from myself," he cries.[16] Phaeton, Orpheus, Marsyas: figures for the poet's economy. To sing, to die: the poet has only empty words. A song for the poet, who would not sing? In the text he is undone, depleted, and thus *has words*. Pastoral poetics, that community, leads only to loss. The generation of the text is the generation of death.

The section closes dispersing words into thin air:

> Sike prayse is smoke, that sheddeth in the skye,
> Sike words bene wynd, and wasten soone in vayne.

> (35-36)

"In fayre *Elisa* rest": a song for the Other

In the next section, *October* seems to offer another theory of textual production, the humanistic proclamation of the public role of the poet, the Sidneian assertion that poetry does work in the world. The model career is Virgil's. Poetic advancement, a flight from pastoral to epic, and social advancement, from the country to the court, intertwine. The internal economy of the initial section of the eclogue appears to be replaced by an external matrix of reward. Yet, these are appearances, for these public models are implicated in the dissemination of the text and in the dispersal of the voice. Piers and Cuddie again are apparently opposing voices, one advancing the argument, the other denying. But, in the economy of the text, differences are swallowed into death. Wherever we look, there is loss.

48

For example, consider the opening lines of this section:

Abandon then the base and viler clowne,
Lyft up thy selfe out of the lowly dust:
And sing of bloody Mars, of wars, of guists,
Turne thee to those, that weld the awful crowne.

(37-40)

"Turne" in line 40 suggests metamorphosis again, a further refiguration of the Ovidian economy of devastation. Rising out of dust glances at a resurrection of the dead onto the battlefield of a new site of annihilation. Resurrection, thus, is a new life pitched in perilous terms. Piers speaks as if another audience would satisfy the empty poet, as if another response would compensate. But in this economics without return, the "turne" implicates Cuddie in loss. Piers, in effect, recommends *self-abandonment*, leaving pastoral clownishness behind. In the new configuration (the turn that offers no return to Cuddie), Eliza comes to occupy the previous place of the Muse, and the poet abandons himself for her: "in fayre *Elisa* rest" (line 45). Self-determination is therefore not what Piers offers Cuddie, but an end to self-determination, a final resting place in another. To live the poet's life means to surrender to an other, authoring swallowed in authority. The consequences of this turn (the death that determines this new life) is pursued in the Virgilian analogy. For Cuddie's response to Piers's version of the Virgilian career sustains (and devastates) that model. To turn to Eliza, as Virgil, "the Romish *Tityrus*" (line 55) did to Mecoenas, leads to death: "ah *Mecoenas* is yclad in claye" (line 61). Tityrus, it appears, never abandoned the "viler clowne" (line 37) in his aspiration. And the reason for this is suggested in the image of authority: "turne thee to those, that weld the awful crowne" (line 40). Power is represented as an ability to shape. The "awful crowne" demands submission. The "turne" puts the poet on a potter's lathe or a smith's forge. Authority usurps the poet's role. Celebration of authority, making the text rest in Eliza, erects a monument that turns the text into the statue made by authority, a monument whose permanence depends upon its separation from the poet and its inscription within the domain of power. Power encompasses and straitens poetic production, producing the poet and "his" text.

Hence, the flight that Piers proposes on "fluttryng wing" (line 43) has a dying fall. Although at first, the image is expansive, indeed imperialistic – "There may thy Muse display her fluttryng wing,/And stretch her selfe at large from East to West" (lines 43-44) – it soon contracts: "And when the stubborne stroke of stronger stounds,/Has somewhat slackt the tenor of thy string" (lines 49-50). Even as Piers imagines it, putting the best face on this flight, the rise is laborious and the cost is punishing. Rather than an arrival elsewhere, Piers implies an impoverished return, an inevitable slackening in the attempt. A return without return (without compensation) is where he leaves Cuddie, despite all the pretense of flight. "Of love and lustihead tho mayst thou sing,/And carrol lowde, and leade the Myllers rownde,/All were *Elisa* one of thilke same ring" (lines 51-53). And in this return to a world of clowns, the swoop of rise and fall is grounded in a circularity, a repressive round. It is always the "same ring" and now Eliza is there as well, inescapable. In the return that Piers imagines after the aspiring flight, the pastoral has been occupied by power; rather than penetrating the realm of the Other, Eliza has extended her domain. Returning to the place formally abandoned, the poet is displaced. More than ever, his role is mere instrumentality. There is no self-advancement in leading "the Myllers rownde" (line 52).

Piers's project is inscribed within the Virgilian career. Even as he traces the progress from pastoral to epic, he undercuts his claims by being circumscribed within a Virgilian text, limited by pastoral even as he claims to escape it. For in the *Eclogues* Virgil projects a *failed* career. First, he sang the songs of Theocritus. Then, advancing to epic, a voice restrained him. Apollo plucked his ear: "Shepherds should sing of sheep and feed their flock," and he found a more responsive chord wooing again the slim reed pipe and the echoing wood (*Eclogue 6*, lines 1-12). After all, woods fit a consul, "Silvae sint consule dignae" (*Eclogue 4*, line 3). Or "*Eliza*, Queene of shepheardes all" (*Aprill*, line 34).

In the first section of *October* there was emptiness in the depleted store; in this section, there is no place to go where Eliza is not, no place (not even his "own" place) that the pastoral poet can claim. To sing to the Other in the voice of an other means confronting loss once again. And it would mean that even if advancement were possible. For the pattern of failure is inscribed even in the successful career. To advance through Eliza (indeed to be advanced by her and beyond her), to advance in her love, touches an apogee of desire coincident with defeat. The career of such desire is already written:

> Or if thee please in bigger notes to sing,
> Advaunce the worthy whome shee loveth best,
> That first the white beare to the stake did bring.
>
> (46-48)

The poet's advancement occurs "in bigger notes" that are not his own and that seem to stand before (beside, outside of) him. To gain Eliza's love, Piers recommends that Cuddie put himself in the place of the one she loves. What *his* advancement entails is suggested by the circumlocution of nomination. The "worthy" has no proper name; he is as nameless as a staked bear (brought to the stake by her love) or as a bear staker (a performer in an entertainment scarcely more elevated than the country pastimes proposed for Cuddie). E. K. glosses the nomination: "The worthy) he meaneth (as I guesse) the most honorable and renowned the Erle of Leycester, whom by his cognisance (although the same be also proper to other) rather then by his name he bewrayeth." "Although the same be also proper to other": one's own is ruled out of court in Eliza's domain. Advancement in her love involves the reduction implicit in this multiple nomination. For the text to name "whome shee loveth best," it must circumlocate any proper name and arrive at a locution that names him as other(s). There are (save hers) no proper names in Eliza's text. Absorbed by the Other (made her love), Leicester becomes an emblem. He is textually transformed, as the lads were when they became the bold metaphor of the flocking fry. Leicester becomes an emblem, a text capable of dubious decipherment; Eliza's power is disseminative, Leicester's place staked in a chain of signifiers, bounded by iterability; he is tamed to bear no name but one another might give or have. So Cuddie might fly, to be a staked text in the domain of power, already inscribed, *as this text is* when Piers so names the worthy so advanced.

The text of *October* never escapes such determinations. Cuddie's response to Piers refigures his lines. "Indeede the Romish *Tityrus*, I heare,/Through his *Mecoenas* left his Oaten reede" (lines 55-56). Seeming to pass the Virgilian impasse of pastoral limits or the demands of Apollo, Cuddie invokes the example of Virgil's career that Piers had raised to abandon. But he invokes it only to reject it. Piers's patterning of the career had led to circumlocution and no further than to "leade the Myllers rownde" (line 52). Where he would lead, following the path of the "worthy whome she loveth best" (line 47), he is "lead." Cuddie plays a reductive roundelay, teasing out a leaden echo: "Ah *Mecoenas* is yclad in claye,/And great *Augustus* long ygoe is dead:/And all the worthies liggen wrapt in leade,/That matter made for Poets on to play" (lines 61-64). He multiplies "the worthy" into a heap of corpses. Poets' texts have "leade" as their "matter" now, and that, perhaps, has always been their leading capacity, to pursue the dead letter, to write the already written, to hanker after the monument which entombs all. Poetic play appears to occur on the outskirts of an inevitability that Cuddie's plaint does not evade (and which is at the "center" of Piers's circumlocution). Depletion and nullity are the moving principles checking advancement, limiting ascent; song inevitably finds out death and is found by death–both in the words that remain after the poet and his matter have become clay, as well as

51

in the life the poet attempts to have *living in the text*. Cuddie offers a disseminative image of "the English Poete," compressing literary history as a textual trope in which the flowers of rhetoric are planted in the grave: "And if that any buddes of Poesie,/Yet of the old stocke gan to shoote agayne:/. . .as it sprong, it wither must agayne" (lines 73-74, 77). The resurrective "turne" that opened this section of *October* returns to death.

Cuddie's bleak conclusion seems rooted in a social situation. He voices Sidney's complaint about the disesteem of poets in his society: "Tom Piper makes us better melodie" (line 78). Only a debased Orpheus, Tom Piper, garners approval. The Virgilian model is ruled out of court. The poet-as-civilizer is barred from society. Yet this is not merely a social indictment. The preferment of Tom Piper (who has not risen above his lowly generic nomination) records another version of poetic annihilation in the hands of power. And thus, Eliza, named by Piers as the central figure in this economy, must be allowed a place in what Cuddie laments. Eliza occupies the position of the Muse, ruling over the realm that Orpheus found, reclaiming loss, the kingdom of death. Where else could one "in fayre *Elisa* rest" (line 45)?

The place of rest is what remains, where the poet has voice but finds himself already written, staked in aspiration. Breath. She is his rest. What remains. Rest in peace. Silence after music. Still as the grave. As the statue, engraved. As the text: lost object, found again, inscribed.

*

It may seem extraordinary to place the queen in the economy of death. There is, however, a precedent in the *Aprill* eclogue, in Colin's lay for "*Eliza*, Queene of shepheardes" (line 34).[17] Her generation there is explicitly textual as "*Syrinx* daughter without spotte" (line 50); she is the slim reed whose story Mercury told to Argus. Her transcendence is textual, and the singer, attempting to raise her beyond comparison with Apollo or Diana, stumbles. The order of celebration reveals a troubled center, memorializing the queen: "I will not match her with *Latonaes* seed" (line 86). "Forswonck and forswatt" (line 99), the singer contemplates the position he occupies drawing the comparison he says he will not draw, but has:

> Such follie great sorow to *Niobe* did breede.
> > Now she is a stone,
> > And makes dayly mone,
> Warning all other to take heede.
>
> (87-90)

Daring to compare her to Diana and Apollo, he will be (he is) in the position of Niobe; what he generates will be devastated by the words he utters. But the word he utters and the instrument he plays are inseparable from who she is, and the position of Niobe defines the text in which the celebrator and the one he celebrates meet. The stone is the monument, now rooted in the daily "mone," and its warning seems to involve the delivery of death, the progeny of Niobe. Or, as Harry Berger, Jr. has suggested, Eliza's kingdom is Elizium. The transcendence at which the abashed singer aims makes her powers of generation devastating; by the end of the lay, the singer expresses fear (line 149), and transfers the song to the mouths of others. Like Niobe, or as queen of the eternal garden planted in the underworld, Eliza generates the lay in *Aprill* that lays her to rest, the tributes brought to her, a goddess "in place" (line 131), reigning "in heaven" (line 117). They include the presentation of flowers required of an elegy.

The gloss tells the poetic relationship of Niobe and her place in the theory and economy of the text, "Niobe the wife of Amphion," the poet-civilizer who founded Thebes. Sidney writes: "Amphion was said to move stones with his poetry to build Thebes, and Orpheus to be listened to by beasts – indeed stony and beastly people" (19). Orpheus moved stones, and the stones were hurled at him. Amphion married Niobe, producing children to rival the gods after he produced an incomparable city; and the gods slaughtered his children and turned his wife to stone, made her an endless monument, an implacable text, wearing itself out and never worn. And Amphion took his own life, all that was his own having been taken from him. The stones he raised were his undoing. The stones of Amphion – the civilization he raises, the wife he weds – memorialize poetic generation, the moving text that astounds its singer. In *Aprill*, praise is founded on elegiac strains. Colin's lay glosses poetic advancement and rests in Eliza. "Now ryse up *Elisa*, decked as thou art" (line 145)–decked in words and flowers, hymned; "Up then *Melpomene* thou mournefulst Muse of nyne . . . . Up grieslie ghostes and up my rufull ryme. . . . Up *Colin* up" (*November*, lines 53, 55, 207). "Lyft up thy selfe . . . stretch . . . Advaunce the worthy." Rise and rest. The poet's advancement: to become the text, to write Eliza and, engraving her, be engraved. The text requires this Other, the patron of the text; or, as Blanchot puts it, "the book needs the reader in order to become a statue, it needs the reader in order to assert itself as a thing without an author and also without a reader" (94). Eliza at rest, the poet reduced, the text remains.

The poet's generation, a psychic economy, a family connection: father of the disseminated seed, sower of stone, Amphion is the child of Marsyas, the singer flayed, stretched, racked. "Why do you tear me from myself?"

"O pierlesse Poesye, where is then thy place?": beyond poetics

Piers's question suggests that this is the point to pause, to ponder our position, the "place" we occupy. Reading this text, we refer to Piers and Cuddie (to go no further in our pursuit of "the English Poete"), as if they named persons, distinct voices in the text. Yet these are voices *of* the text, redistributing the claims of an economy – a poetics – that surfaces and rises, undermining the stability of identity as easily as their names are respelled on the page. Conventional accounts of *The Shepheardes Calender* read the dialogues as debates, attempting to decide which voice represents the poet, or to resolve contradictions in sustained patterns of meaning.[18] Authorial intention is felt to be 'behind' or 'underneath' these voices, if not 'in' them; or, at the very least, they sustain a relationship with an 'elsewhere' where meaning resides, a transcendent beyond or material necessities. Yet, in the reading we pursue, the text keeps finding these voices (finding our voice too), and the text does not resolve into some unity or integrity (not even some false "paradise principle"). There is nothing behind or in these voices. The terms that would fix identity or establish voices are, precisely, what the text disperses. Yet "text" names no transcendental principle, and its "being" coincides with non-being; its voice (as Blanchot writes in a discussion of narrative voice) is "a neuter voice that speaks the work from that place-less place in which the work is silent" (141). The text is silent and the voices we "hear" or name accrete language without thereby emerging speaking. The text is, at the very least, an intertext, a play of text against text transferred indiscriminately from voice to voice, formally structured so that its movement fractures the formal markers and the inside is brought outside, the outside turned in, whether we take (as we have been, naming Piers or Cuddie, or marking the parts) the "speakers" or the "sections" of the text to be those formal signposts. The differences we name – for example, between an internal, intrinsic economy and an external one – are left unresolved; neither denied nor determined, they are deferred in the reading we pursue. Left, as what remains, as what we read, or, as Derrida puts it, as "the nonpresent *remaining* of a differential mark."[19] To progress we traverse the spacing of the text that allows articulation and movement but only by its very spacing, that is, by the blankness of a bankruptcy that fills the text with refigurations. In this reading, those figures offer a theory of the text composed of the elements whose relationships "define" the text – language, author, reader (or patron); the text as we read it represents the theory of the text we read.

What is a text? The question is unanswerable if we seek a definition that would give an essence or a final determination to the question. It is easier to say what it is not (not that it *is* not). It is not a space of utterance, but of writing, but it is not a writing that exists on the page, although those are the marks we pursue. But, as the lads or Eliza show, the marks are consumed *and* consuming, neither fixing identity themselves, nor "owned" by an author – much as he might wish to have the text as his own – nor by its readers either, since texts constitute already written a reading that "entrains" the reader in the eddying circles of text-within-text. The extensions of the text mirror the pool of Narcissus, which is not merely a place of auto-reflection, since Narcissus sees himself as other. He sees an image, becomes a statue entranced and, attempting to reach out for the image is transformed into a flower; an etiology that thereby undermines the merely natural existence of nature. In the mirror that this text provides, the dispersal of the book into gloss, apparatus, allusion, points to the book without limits, the total book that is endless (and thereby fragmented). The book offers the illusion of solidity and totality, but, like the statue of Niobe, it wears itself away in its reinscriptions. Its elements do not simply add up to a totality, they add to – supplanting, supplementing, never resting. *Neither the solidity nor the slippages can be privileged in a reading that pursues the footing of the traces of the author in the text.* The text is both indeterminate and overdetermined. Its motion erects an endless monument. No end, then, to our pursuit, yet death is wherever we turn. Death is the aim of life, Freud writes in *Beyond the Pleasure Principle*, and the generation of the text is linked to that vital economy and represents it.

If we move ahead now, with Piers's question attempting to finish *October* and move beyond, we can do so knowing there is no beyond text, and that this is an empty gesture. Yet, spaced and sequential, our reading leads to the question of where we are in this text, where this text is. If we have taken as our question the one that "belongs" to Piers, it is because it is his within the verbal economy that leads Piers to question the place of something "pierlesse," a question, then, which pierces Piers:

> O pierlesse Poesye, where is then thy place?
> If nor in Princes pallace thou doe sitt:
> (And yet is Princes pallace the most fitt)
> Ne brest of baser birth doth thee embrace.
> Then make thee winges of thine aspyring wit,
> And, whence thou camst, flye backe to heaven apace.
>
> (79-84)

"Pierlesse Poesye" has, among its significances, 'poetry without Piers,' and that Piers voices this nomination affects his own. On the one hand, separating poetry from its peers (and Piers) points to a transcendence.

55

Yet where Piers sends poetry is "backe," and the flight he imagines we have seen before: "So flew Virgile .... So flew Mantuane .... So Petrarque." The figure of flight maintains the beyond *within* a textuality that re-marks its indeterminate limits. But such re-marking affects as well the voice that casts itself in the beyond. Piers speaks beyond himself by the self-repudiation of "pierlesse."

The process of piercing Piers occurs in slow motion elsewhere in *The Shepheardes Calender*, in the *Maye* eclogue. Turning to it for another glimpse of Piers, it is not the *same* Piers we find (the names in the text do not refer to such identities) but rather the process of auto-reflection and remarking that makes both voice and name a rhetorical site, embedding them in textuality.[20] In *Maye*, Piers upbraids Palinode as a pleasure-seeker whose expenditure represents a false economy; Palinode spends without reserve. It is not difficult to read this as a poetic encounter; the word *palinode*, after all, is a gesture of poetic repudiation. Yet Palinode speaks for "iouysaunce" (line 25) and rhymes "pleasure" and "leasure" (lines 65-66). And Piers's reply offers an economy of non-expenditure by invoking a golden age when there was no expense because there was nothing to spend. His having is no different from refusing, much as Palinode's spending defends the poetic pleasures his name denies. Not surprisingly, then, the debate seems to find a place of reconciliation when Piers offers a story and Palinode receives it as a gesture "of felowship" (line 172). Yet reconciliation is not what occurs; once heard, Palinode rejects the tale as "furthest fro the marke" (line 307). Nonetheless, telling it, Piers has been drawn into the economy of Palinode. He had posed responsibility against pleasure, yet, telling the tale, someone else tends his sheep (line 173). His moral tale is about a fox who deceives an orphaned lamb by giving him a mirror. Yet, what is Piers's tale if not a mirror for Palinode? And, if the art of the Fox is "coloured with simplicitie" (line 303), what is to be said of the art of this beast fable, or of pastoral more generally? Who, then, is not caught in the mirror? Piers's tale in *Maye* is a palinode that re-marks his place within a verbal economy that is always "furthest fro the marke." The Fox he repudiates in his tale, he becomes telling it. The tale he tells displaces the teller.

Where is the place of peerless poetry? Neither in "Princes pallace," Piers reiterates, nor in shepherds' breasts, neither outside, nor inside. Yet, the transcendence Piers voices names no other place but, rather, the recirculation (a return without returns) that marks as well the textual space in *Maye*. Cuddie's response to Piers collapses the palace and breast in the image of his "temples" twined with ivy; he, too, posits a beyond, not, however, in heaven, but in another textual locale, the theater:[21]

O if my temples were distaind with wine,
And girt in girlonds of wild Yvie twine,
How I could reare the Muse on stately stage,
And teache her tread aloft in bus-kin fine,
With queint *Bellona* in her equipage.

(110-14)

Cuddie's hypothesis of place translates princes' palaces to the "stately stage" and makes heavenly deities the matter of "queint" impersonation. The poetic power he imagines is one in which images come to life and embodiment. His beyond, then, is the yearning for *personation* and it is punctured as much as Piers's transcendent desires are. Gestures towards a beyond text point back to the text.

The heaven of Piers's return has no further zodiac, we might say, in Sidney's phrase, than the poet's wit (24). Piers's poetic flight attaches itself to the authority of Colin, and to an alignment of erotics with perfected singing, "love does teach him climbe so hie" (line 91). "So flew Petrarque." It is within the economics of such desire that Cuddie's lines have their place: "He, were he not with love so ill bedight,/Would mount as high, and sing as soote as Swanne" (lines 89-90). Petrarchan desire: in vita, in morte. Piers sustains Colin's flight in a mirror (line 93); Cuddie literalizes the tropes. His Colin, well-served in love (either by not loving at all or by having what he desires) is also metamorphosed into a swan, a bird incapable of flight. Grounded, Colin is replanted, another nature, Sidney might say, a seed in the soil of *October*, ripe for dissemination. The soil is Ovidian, perfected song deathly; no songs more sweet than those of the dying bird.

Cygnus wept, Ovid says, at the plight of the Heliades, for they wept at the fall of their brother Phaeton; they became all tears, trees weeping amber drops. Cygnus wept seeing their mother pluck their branches, tugging at their roots. And weeping, he became a swan, the bird of mourning, fearful of the blazing sky and the sun that sent Phaeton plummeting (*Meta.* 2: 367-80). Another battle with the sun, another poetic generation. A genealogy for Colin, "under whose person the Author selfe is shadowed"? Only swan songs for him?

If we pursue Colin's path in *The Shepheardes Calender*, what do we find?[22] A sporadic, scattered voice, intermittently present to call up a landscape to answer his deprivations: "I soone would learne these woods, to wayle my woe,/And teache the trees, their trickling teares to shedde" (*June*, lines 95-96), an orphic and Ovidian poet. Alone, in *Januarye* or *December*, Colin laments a lack in love and in song. Although "he of *Tityrus* his songs did lere" (*December*, line 4), "The God of shepheardes

Tityrus is dead" and "wrapt in lead" (*June*, lines 81, 89). It is only a dead voice that he sounds or makes resound in *June*. As a sign of the consumption of voice, others sing his songs–in *Aprill* and *August*. Only once in the *Calender* does Colin sing for another and in another's presence, in *November*; he sings to Thenot and of Dido, dead, and in the words of Marot. Joined in the "sympathetic dative" of pastoral, Colin participates in its community only in an elegy in which his love and his verse have become other. Colin figures the "Author selfe" in the shadows. Poor hapless nightingale, he can only sing Echo's song in the mirror of his verse, rephrasing orphic strains. "Hence with the Nightingale will I take part" (*August*, line 183), for "*Philomele* her song with teares doth steepe" (*November*, line 141). "One if I please, enough is me therefore" (*December*, line 120), this Narcissus says; but in the glass of poetry, the voice is scattered, dispersed into the void.

As the voice of pastoral, Colin's is not an owned voice, not singular or identifiable. Collating his appearances in the *Calender*, we do not produce a character, but, rather, the position Paul Alpers describes in Virgil's eclogues where "no one sings a song that is purely his own" (216). Virgil's *Eclogues* open with a confrontation between the dispossessed Meliboeus and the seemingly secure Tityrus. By the penultimate eclogue, two poets seek to reassemble fragments of their own poems and to recall a displaced poet's poems. And, finally, a song for Gallus, Virgil effaced so that Gallus speaks, and Gallus laments the pains of love to the echoing woods. Woods answer all: *silvae*, eclogues, collections of fragments. Wherever the poet is, he is not "in" his poems; the collectivity of poetic activity points to its otherness. These posies are culled from a rhetorical garden, a florilegium. Their nature is rooted in transformation. Thus, Gallus, at the end of Virgil's *Eclogues*, echoes Daphnis, and it is the elegy for Daphnis in the fifth eclogue that suggests the turn in Virgil's collection towards its ultimate dispossessions. Underlying pastoral is elegy. Spenser joins Virgil to Ovid and the result is a further unmooring of pastoral. He builds on shifting soil, metamorphic echoes in a death-haunted landscape. Like Orpheus, Spenser's shepherd sings for death. Love makes him fly to everlasting rest–to what remains, inscribed in the "immortall mirrhor" (*October*, line 93) of the fading beauty that he admires.

We return to love and poetic flight.

CUDDIE

Ah *Percy* it is all to weake and wanne,
So high to sore, and make so large a flight:
Her peeced pyneons bene not so in plight,
For *Colin* fittes such famous flight to scanne:

He, were he not with love so ill bedight,
Would mount as high, and sing as soote as Swanne.

PIRES
Ah fon, for love does teach him climbe so hie,
And lyftes him up out of the loathsome myre:
Such immortall mirrhor, as he doth admire,
Would rayse ones mynd above the starry skie.
And cause a caytive corage to aspire,
For lofty love doth loath a lowly eye.

(85-96)

Poetic flight: the poet as bird (peacock or swan), ready for transformation; he is all soul, or so the trope implies, drawing upon Plato's *Phaedrus*, in which the poet's divine frenzy is joined to the philosopher's and the lover's. When the soul is "perfect and fully winged, it soars on high;" losing its wings, it falls to earth (*Phaedrus*, 246). And, when on earth, "the wings on which the soul is to be borne aloft must find their nourishment here" (*Phaedrus*, 248). The food is beauty: "When a man sees beauty in this world and has a remembrance of true beauty, he begins to grow wings. While they are sprouting, he is eager to fly, but he cannot. He gazes upward as though he were a bird" (*Phaedrus*, 249). (So Cuddie reports Colin's wings, sprouting–"peeced pyneons"; and full-fledged, he would become his verse, a "fit" flight, "fittes . . . to scanne," the ultimate destination of Piers's search for "fit" place for poetry; Piers translates the place into the "mirrhor".) He gazes at the lover, echo and mirror of his aspiring mind:

> Just as wind or echo rebounds from smooth, hard surfaces and returns whence it came, so the stream of beauty flows back again into the beautiful beloved through his eyes, the natural inlet to the soul. There it comes and excites the soul, watering the outlets of the wings and quickening them to sprout; so in his turn the soul of the loved one is filled with love.
>
> He loves, but does not know whom or what; he does not understand, he cannot tell what has happened to him. Like one who has caught a disease of the eyes from another, he can give no reason for it; as in a mirror, in his lover he beholds himself and does not know it.

(*Phaedrus*, 255)

Platonic metamorphoses: the rebounding of wind or echo, song from rock: voice become verse, seen not heard – a "stream of beauty," the insemination that has its destination "whence thou camst" (*October*, line 84). A disseminative quickening glance. Quickening love, returning to perfection (completion). And "he does not know . . ., he does not understand, he cannot tell. . . . he can give no reason." Empty-headed,

59

fully vacant: dumb, blind, silent. Such is perfect knowledge. And sight: "a disease of the eyes" that returns to the self-in-the-mirror. Knowledge in ignorance. Plenty and poverty, a definition of love, and Narcissus. In Piers's "immortall mirrhor" (line 93), we meet Plato's love and its Ovidian echoes, Narcissus in the pool and the gaze of Orpheus. We find, that is, the scene of writing, according to Blanchot: "Orpheus' gaze is Orpheus' ultimate gift to the work, a gift in which he rejects the work, in which he sacrifices it by moving towards its origin in the boundless impulse of desire" (102-3). The text is constituted in the desire represented by the lover's gaze or the orphic glance.

Socrates and Phaedrus talk of love, making love. They take each other's words and hear voices by the stream telling them that love and writing are one, true writing that is, "inscribed in the soul . . . implanted within the souls of others" (*Phaedrus*, 278). Seductively, Socrates inscribes Phaedrus, "like one who has caught a disease of the eyes," joining soul to soul in fertile soil, so that they meet in a pastoral place, a text, that poisoned potion. Although the *Phaedrus* appears to reject writing for speaking and country for city, in this final scene, radical relocations and dislocations occur, for Socrates brings the outside in, writing on the beloved's soul, inscribing the myth of flight in its "proper" locale. Derrida has analyzed the scene brilliantly, and he sums it up this way: "the conclusion of the *Phaedrus* is less a condemnation of writing in the name of present speech than a preference for one sort of writing over another, for the fertile trace over the sterile trace, for a seed that engenders because it is planted inside over a seed scattered wastefully outside: at the risk of *dissemination*."[23] The risk is taken in this very conclusion, for Socrates is a "far more wonderful piper than Marsyas" (*Lysis*, 215), wonderful as Eros itself, charmer, poisoner of the eye, mender of the soul. Socrates disseminates.

The mirror of love is the scene of writing, not only in Plato, but in Spenser, whose dialogic voice(s) disseminates the text by generating it as poison and potion, nourishment and devastation, fullness and vacuity. Cuddie's "denial" of Piers's platonic flight is couched in the same terms; the text of *October* divides and disassembles the text of the *Phaedrus*. The "same" argument becomes an "other" one as Cuddie speaks in the vacancy implicit in Piers's mirror, of the diseased eye that Piers admires:

All otherwise the state of Poet stands,
For lordly love is such a Tyranne fell:
That where he rules, all power he doth expell.
The vaunted verse a vacant head demaundes,
Ne wont with crabbed care the Muses dwell.

Unwisely weaves, that takes two webbes in hand.

(97-102)

"Unwisely weaves," a textual metaphor for the "graphic relations between the living and the dead" (*Dissemination*, 65), mixing eros and writing in the pool of Narcissus. The etymology confirms the weave, for it links the honeycomb and the spider–and thus the "bewitched mouth" with which Socrates speaks has consumed the Sidneian "cluster of grapes." Soon, too, Cuddie will attempt a bacchic frenzy; but his ardor cools (like dinner) once the charm of verse and honeyed melody have been on his tongue. This unwise weaving is writing, graphically. Another theory of the text here, "the speaking picture of poesy" (Sidney, 33). *Ut pictura poesis*. Woven texts are tapestries in which voice becomes gaze.[24] Voice is text.

We can unravel the sequence of fatal transformations by a glance at the Ovidian text that *October* implicates. In Book VI, we have the story of Niobe, childless, a living grave; and, then, Marsyas, the tortured poet; and, then, Philomel, the bird that sings after violation. These tales disseminate the opening contest in the book, Arachne's challenge to Minerva (the "Bellona" of *October*?). Arachne, bold as Niobe, pure as Philomel, accomplished as Marsyas, weaves a fatal text, picturing the devastations brought by the gods' love for mankind, love as ruinous as hate. On her loom, she weaves Ovid's *Metamorphoses*. As she weaves, so is she woven, and Arachne is devastated by Minerva, transformed into the spider eternally weaving and reweaving, an artist of the already written text and its fatal allure. Arachne's tale establishes an answer to Piers's question about the place of poetry; text is inside of text, its place is graphesis, an activity relating life and death.[25]

Ut pictura poesis.[26] The fatal weaving of *October* translates the sister arts into a fearful paragone. It is also *literalized* in *The Shepheardes Calender* in one of its most prominent features, the woodcut illustrations made for the text. These provide images of the text *as* an image, the text to be read. And, as might not come as a surprise, these illustrations, although made *for* the text, do not merely reproduce the text in another medium. Rather, they supplement the written text, extending the graphesis graphically. They illustrate graphesis. Thus, to look no further, the woodcut for *October* pictures a divided and reversed (and reversible) scene. On the left, the image of the poet-as-civilizer; he is crowned (in laurel, presumably) and a Renaissance city in a classicized, antique mode, rises behind him; he advances with his sheephook into the country side of this *paysage moralisé*. This figure represents Piers's argument and its claims about the functions of pastoral poetry. On the

61

right side of the woodcut stands another shepherd, gesturing towards his advancing partner, but standing firm; his sheephook reversed, it points aloft to where the deadly scorpion, cousin of the spider, rules. A heavenly flight of birds answers the advancing shepherd. Who are these illustrated figures, what do they illustrate? Are they Piers and Cuddie? If the figure on the left is Piers, he has embodied his argument, not his person (Piers "himself" is no poet); and if the figure on the right is Cuddie, the "perfecte paterne of a Poete" has no poetic attributes to distinguish him. And if this figure embodies the side of the argument that stressed the poet's poverty, why is it stationed below both scorpion and soaring birds? Should the straggly herds on both sides form part of the picture? Is it not fair to say that the picture *redistributes* elements of the argument, resowing them and re-embodying them, at the same time as it unweaves the embodiments (Piers and Cuddie) that house the argument in the text? Join picture and text and find two webs woven at once.

But the text "itself" is similarly woven, and not merely in its dialogues. It offers itself to sight; for example, as the prize for the singing contest in *August*, Willye proffers "a mazer . . ./Wherein is enchased many a fayre sight" (lines 26-27). E. K. pauses over the generic aptness of the bowl and, especially, over "enchased." "Enchased) engraven. Such pretie descriptions every where useth Theocritus to bring in his Idyllia. For which speciall cause indede he by that name termeth his AEglogues: for Idyllion in Greke signifieth the shape or picture of any thyng, wherof his booke is ful." *The Shepheardes Calender* is such a "ful" book as well, a "mazer" indeed. This storied bowl is an exercise in a palimpsestic art, a *mise en abŷme*. The picture on the bowl repeats a detail of the pastoral text and replicates the entire text whose status as image is at once partial, fragmentary and full. E.K. reads an image in the text as if it were an image of the text; mirrors within mirrors.[27]

E. K. reads and glosses. This, too, needs to be considered, for how are the glosses to be taken, what voice (as insistent as any 'within' the text, as illustrative as any cut 'outside') does E. K. designate? Subsequent, sequent, coming before in his arguments, after in his glosses, E. K., editor and reader, offers a panoply of texts as guides to this one: he leads us to Plato, Ovid, Virgil, Theocritus, Mantuan, Petrarch, draws us to the rhetorical play of the bold figures or "pretie descriptions" of *The Shepheardes Calender*. As much as Paul de Man, E. K. believes that the text is constituted by its rhetoric.[28] But what does E. K. represent in the text, this glossator written (it appears) after the text "itself"? Michael McCanles has answered these questions by the generic claims that E. K.'s voice makes; his is a present voice that aligns the poem with antique tradition, a modern commentary on a classic text. Yet, he is also part of the text, not simply "outside" it, although often the function of what he says is to posit an outside or to maintain some boundary between the text and himself (and with him a world in which he belongs and to whose existence he testifies). More mirror tricks.

Thus, to take *October* as an example. E. K. opens with an argument that equates Cuddie with the pattern of the poet who lacks support, the mouthpiece of "the Author" and "the English Poete." Yet, when he comes to gloss Cuddie, he draws back: "I doubte whether by Cuddie be specified the authour selfe, or some other." His "doubt," he explains, comes from an act of reading based on a textual comparison supported by a notion of independent character: "For in the eyght AEglogue the same person was brought in, singing a Cantion of Colins making, as he sayth. So that some doubt, that the persons be different." But is E. K. "himself" immune to this doubt? Can the "same" "person" be speaking about Cuddie? E. K.'s doubt rests on a doubtful assumption about persons, that the recurring name signals the same self, and that such selves reside "outside" the text in a real world to which the text refers. His doubt is meant to secure knowledge about that world, and to place him in it. Yet, E. K.'s voice also insists upon the play of the text. Moreover, it does not exist outside such play. In his glosses, E. K. reconstitutes the text, and his readings, rather than simply reduplicating the arguments, redistribute them and rewrite them. The doubletake on Cuddie is repeated again and again.

To continue with the gloss on *October*, we might notice how often E. K. denies the supposed differences in the text he cites. Thus, commenting on Piers's proposition that poets ravish, E. K. reads ravishment as restraint. Agreeing with the Sidneian sophistic that "moving is of a higher degree than teaching" (39), E. K. places *dulce* beside *utile* as if they were no different. Yet his example of the power of poetry (the "might . . . in musick") is Alexander's bloody rampage. E. K.'s glosses gloss difference. In his commentary, Orpheus recovers Eurydice, and second loss – the prerequisite for song – goes unsaid. So, too, Cuddie's counter-example of Argus becomes, in E. K.'s hands, an extension, rather than a denial, of Piers's arguments for the glory of the poet. The peacock's tail symbolizes the immortal text; it is a sign placed for "eternall memory."[29] (As Socrates says, writing promotes the loss of memory, and E. K. forgets death to make eternal life.) By the end of the gloss, even the theme of the social disesteem of poetry (where E. K. began his argument and gloss) is virtually abandoned; poets, he claims, have always found honor "in the sight of princes and noble men." And so, rather than a complaint, *October* becomes, in E. K.'s final reading, a celebration of the divinity of poetry and the poet's divine fury.

The gloss, thus, takes the terms of the poetics figured in Piers and Cuddie, but rather than reading their interchange as a debate, it speaks two ways at once. Materials that defined voices in the eclogue become this voice, redistributing and resowing those seeds, replanting them by allusions to other texts and to the "world." E. K.'s is *another* voice, another text, generated precisely as the voices "in" the text have been. His knowledge constitutes no authority; it represents a reading of the text and, palpably, a rewriting of it. E. K. may be an invention for this text; he is, at any rate, made possible by it. A shade away from the anonymous voice, not quite a proper name, E. K.'s status cannot be distinguished from the text "itself," or the woodcuts. All are speaking pictures, double, triple, quadruple in their overdetermination and indetermination of this fragmentary and endless text. He, too, is planted in chains of signifiers that fail to arrive at ultimate signification. In part, he is a voice for such knowledge, how unperspicacious and bold the text is, is his constant theme; but he does not escape what he would anatomize. He is not, in short, "outside" of what he registers. Language defines his place, too. The answer to Piers's question, "O pierlesse Poesye, where is then thy place" (line 79), can only be the multiplicities designated by the text, a place of radical shifts where voice emerges as the image of voice (as text, the speaking picture). E. K. is planted (and disseminated) in discursive possibility; these are the seeds sown in *October*. Or, to speak more seasonably, this is the feast that is gathered to be consumed. On these words are we fed. "For *Bacchus* fruite is frend to *Phoebus* wise" (line 106).[30]

We return, as we must, to the poet's economy, in the final lines of the eclogue:

> Who ever casts to compasse weightye prise,
> And thinks to throwe out thondring words of threate:
> Let powre in lavish cups and thriftie bitts of meate,
> For *Bacchus* fruite is frend to *Phoebus* wise.

> (103-6)

To fill the vacancy of the poet's head, Cuddie proposes the fruit of Bacchus, a tipsy solution. A consumable text, the potion and fruit of the *Phaedrus* or Sidney's *Defence*. The rhythms here are those of consumption: to take *in* the prize (to encompass it), words must be thrown out; to do that, food must be taken in. Yet, such consumption is to be both lavish *and* thrifty. But even such economies are defeated; no expense is spared, and Cuddie has no sooner offered this version of poetic afflatus than it is deflated: "But ah my corage cooles ere it be warme" (line 115). Cuddie's venture into a final version of poetic theory (what E. K. refers to as *enthusiasmus*, the platonic notion of *divinus furor*) collapses in its very erection – Cuddie says afterwards that it cooled before. The very fullness of the voice (or mouth), the fantasy of a Jove-like power (*Bellona* born from his brain – himself the mother of a fierce muse put on stage and accompanied by a tamed goddess, quaintly costumed) falls in an Arachne-like chastening. A slender pipe and a safe song in a Virgilian shade is the final prospect, diminishing further these gigantic dreams: "Here we our slender pipes may safely charme" (line 118).

Here, where the charm is poison, where heady wine cracks skulls or sends them down the stream, where content puts the best face on impoverishment, and the shades threaten and secure. "For thy, content us in thys humble shade" (line 116). Here: pastoral place, shadehaunted grove, where Apollo and Bacchus join, as they did for Orpheus, fathered and loved by Apollo (*Meta.* 11:8), singer of the mysteries of Bacchus (lines 67-70), murdered by his celebrants. Cuddie, his temples stained with wine, is an orphic poet, his vacant, singing head crowned as are the frenzied Maenads. Spent, Cuddie blazes momentarily, in a bathetic version of the transcendent voice of Piers:

> And when with Wine the braine begins to sweate,
> The nombers flowe as fast as spring doth ryse.
> Thou kenst not *Percie* how the ryme should rage.
>
> (107-9)

Transported, Piers offers a kid to feed the hungry poet, materializing voice as food in the final lines of the eclogue:

> And when my Gates shall han their bellies layd:
> *Cuddie* shall have a Kidde to store his farme.
>
> (119-20)

Piers, bewitched, has drunk Cuddie's words and offers "store" to the spent poet. They stand here in each other's place – in the place of the Muse – two names dividing a broken text and reassembling it.

*

Cuddies Embleme.
Agitante calescimus illo &c.

"There is a god in us, warming the breast;/His impulse it is that sows sacred seeds in the mind" ("Est deus in nobis; agitante calescimus illo:/impetus hic sacrae semina mentis habet").[31]

His the inspiration, his the presence, his the generation of the voice as text.

65

A final quotation, the invocation to the last book of the *Fasti*, Ovid's incomplete book of months. Cuddie speaks–and is unspoken–in these lines witnessing the inhabitation of an Otherness, proclaiming a Piers-like transcendence as the disowning of one's own voice. Another speaks in me, another writes in the soul, planting seeds there. The Other: the text within, fatal charm, swallowed. Poems "strike, pierce" and "possess," Sidney writes (32), and all voices–including ours–are ravished by the text.

To the emblematic text called Cuddie's, E. K. adds a gloss. Aptly, he records a text that is invisible, comments on a response unheard save in the gloss: "Whom Piers answereth Epiphonematicos as admiring the excellencye of the skyll whereof in Cuddie hee hadde alreadye hadde a taste." An answer to a taste: Piers speaks out (the meaning, presumably, of *phonematikos*) and speaks silently, only given voice in E. K.'s gloss. He speaks *epiphonematikos*, as an epiphenomenon generated by the text as its echo. *Epiphonematikos*: the place of the text, the generation of voice in the grammar of sympathy.

*

The scene of writing that E. K. supplies as a final gloss on *October* is akin to the one imagined at first in Immeritô's "To His Booke." The poet named as nameless sends a text which only speaks when it is spoken to, and then speaks to unsay itself, denying its generation (unfathered) and invoking an economics, an exchange in which the poet is always already depleted by the one to whom the text, for whom the text is written. This constitutive act is also an undoing. Being made to proclaim itself as base born, the text returns to tell the author what was said of him. The scene of writing is the fantasy of reading, the horror of incorporation that the alluring, charming text proffers, a generation of the text joining writing and reading, giving voice to the text, a beguiling and devastating scene of metamorphosis.

We need another voice to close, for there is no end here.

And all the while the crickets, above us in the heat, are chirping and conversing with each other and seem to be looking down at us. If they should perceive that we too, like most people, were refraining from conversation at midday, relaxing our minds and nodding our heads under the charm of their spell, they would do well to laugh at us, taking us for a couple of slaves who had come here to rest, sleepy sheep drowsing through noonday by the fountain. But if they see us conversing and sailing past them unbeguiled by their Siren voices, perhaps in admiration they may give us what the gods have granted them to bestow on mortals.

What is this gift? . . .

Once upon a time, as the story goes, before the Muses were born, these crickets were men; and, when the Muses came and song made its appearance, some of these men were so overcome by the pleasure of it that they sang and sang, forgetful of food and drink and without noticing even the approach of death.

(*Phaedrus*, 259)

4

Shakespearian characters: the generation of Silvia

What's in a name? For Silvia, it is her destiny (already written in the *silva* tradition) and her destination (both in *The Two Gentlemen of Verona* and the texts it generates). In a word, her name is a genealogy, and in the play in which she appears, her generation is the generation of the letter – literally and figuratively.[1]

> *Speed.* She woos you by a figure.
> *Valentine.* What figure?
> *Speed.* By a letter, I should say.
>
> (2.1, 136-38)[2]

Silvia moves through a chain of signifiers to arrive (in the final scene of the play) in the place her name determines, the woods. There, only the letter speaks, and the character falls silent. She is, in that final location, impressed by the letter, barred at last from any attempt to own discourse (her scenes with Valentine play out those possibilities), placed within discourse that is not her own. She is what her name betokens.

If Silvia's ultimate silence makes palpable the proposition that the character functions in a discourse of the Other, the argument could also be made on the basis of her speech. Silvia's last word in the play is "O heaven!" (5.4, line 59), exclaimed when Proteus threatens to rape her. What she says then had been written earlier; "Is she not a heavenly saint?" (2.4, line 142), Valentine asks, and he is echoed in Proteus's song to Silvia, proclaiming that "heaven such grace did lend her" (4.2, line 42), and concluding that "she excels each mortal thing" (line 51). The heaven that is on Silvia's lips is a final dissemination of the word as it has passed from mouth to mouth. It derives from Proteus's song much as his attempted rape is a translation of the violence of the song of the pastoral swain singing her to perfection, violent since it imagines perfection as termination, an ultimate metamorphosis enforced by the tropes:

> Then to Silvia let us sing,
>   That Silvia is excelling.
> She excels each mortal thing
>   Upon the dull earth dwelling.
> To her let us garlands bring.
>
>   (4.2, 49-53)

Much as her repeated appearances on the balcony, the song suggests that Silvia's excellence is not earthly. Yet it marks her perfection by offering her "garlands" culled from "the dull earth" she transcends. In the mouth of a singer in the guise of a pastoral swain, the trope has the funereal ring that Florizel hears in *The Winter's Tale* when Perdita wishes to "strew him o'er and o'er" with "garlands" (4.4, line 129). Moreover, the flower passage suggests that perfection is a replanting within the tropes of a pastoral florilegium. There is no escaping the soil from which she springs; to be no "mortal thing/Upon the dull earth dwelling," she is hymned to heaven, crowned in garlands. The song inserts Silvia within a poetic economy, Ovidian metamorphosis as her end. Poets have always affirmed that they confer immortality, as Sidney, among others, might remind us.[3] Silvia's excellence is textual; her "being," literally, is figurative. No wonder, then, that she ends up in the forest, voiceless.

Proteus's song and its re-enactment as attempted rape do not alone provide paths to Silvia's final "O heaven!" That end had already been written elsewhere; Proteus's name directs us to what might be designated the master text that determines character in *The Two Gentlemen of Verona*, Ovid's *Metamorphoses*. Here, for example, are Philomela's last words:

>   si silvis clausa tenebor,
> inplebo silvas et conscia saxa movebo;
> audiet haec aether et si deus ullus in illo est!
>
>   (*Meta.* 6: 546-48)

(If I am kept shut up in these woods, I will fill the woods with my story and move the very rocks to pity. The air of heaven shall hear it, and, if there is any god in heaven, he shall hear it too.)[4]

Philomela is carried from her father's court to forest imprisonment ("in stabula alta trahit, silvis obscura vetustis" (*Meta.* 6: 521)). The plot's trajectory suggests Silvia's story. The movement is, like Silvia's, determined by desire–and by a trope. When Tereus first sees Philomela, her beauty–"such as we are wont to hear the naiads described, and dryads when they move about in the deep woods" ("mediis incedere silvis"

(*Meta*. 6: 453))–inflames him. The trope of desire becomes Philomela's woodland confinement, literally. From it, there is no escape. Raped, Philomela yearns for the voice that would fill the woods with her story. Finally, she achieves that desire; metamorphosed into the nightingale, she can fill the forests with her song. But to move the air of heaven, she must lose her tongue. Silvia's silence, Proteus's failed attempt at rape, and the doubling of Proteus with Valentine effectively displace the tragic Ovidian story to permit a comic resolution. The Ovidian etiology of song in rape and violation is disseminated in Silvia's textual generation.

Proteus's song asks "who is Silvia," and answers by positing a more than mortal excellence for her. Yet, translated into textual terms, in which excellence means acquiring the status of a word in a text, or of a figure in a rhetorical scheme, the difference that marks Silvia is, in fact, a shared condition. "Who is Silvia? What is she,/That all our swains commend her?" (4.2, lines 39-40). The song assumes–as a trope and a disguise–a community of pastoral shepherds. Proteus sings the song (ostensibly) on behalf of Thurio; he sings as a shepherd and for another imagined as a swain; he sings for the other he *is* in song. This situation is, as Spenser's *Shepheardes Calender* and its Virgilian antecedents show, essential to pastoral refigurations. In the song, and the community it imagines, it is difficult (perhaps impossible) to separate the device and disguise (the tropes) from the (literal) truth of the scene. "All our swains commend her" also applies, after all, to Silvia's *true* love, Valentine. Alone, in the forest, he pours out his desire in the "unfrequented woods" (5.4, line 2):

> Here can I sit alone, unseen of any.
> And to the nightingale's complaining notes
> Tune my distresses and record my woes.
>
> Repair me with thy presence, Silvia.
> Thou gentle nymph, cherish thy forlorn swain.
>
> (5.4, 4-6 and 11-12)

As "forlorn swain," Valentine is like the Virgilian shepherd Corydon imploring the hollow woods to answer his echoing void: "ibi haec incondita solus/montibus et silvis studio iactabat inani" (*Eclogue 2*, lines 4-5).[5] Valentine's "complaining notes," however, are Ovidian, articulated by the nightingale, and the "presence" of Silvia that he implores would seem to be carried on a pastoral song. Valentine's words are the nightingale's and Silvia's "presence" (literally? in his thoughts? in his words?) reverses the metamorphosis of nymph into nightingale. Here, the nightingale's song delivers the maiden. Valentine's words partake of the pastoral community of Proteus's song to Silvia. The "forlorn swain" projects himself into the bird of night and finds "presence" in the Silvia that he names; thus, he is repaired with the echoing return of the name he sends into the void. His identity seems tantamount to his identification – with the nightingale, her song, and the tropes of nymph and swain. In that context, it is worth remarking that Valentine's career also traces the path marked previously in Ovid's tale of Philomela and echoed in Silvia's story; he moves from his father's house to Silvia's father's court, and then to the woods. There, he is, however exiled, at home; the outlaws choose him as their leader in part because he has "the tongues" (4.1, line 33). He can give voice to the woods and speak the language of pastoral precisely because it is the language that speaks him. As "forlorn swain," Valentine arrives at the end of the play where a pastoral trope had placed him at the start. In the first scene of the play, Speed seeks his master, Valentine, and is told by Proteus that he has left to embark for Milan:

> *Speed.*   Twenty to one then, he is shipped already,
>   And I have played the sheep in losing him.
> *Proteus.*   Indeed, a sheep doth very often stray,
>   And if the shepherd be awhile away.
> *Speed.*   You conclude that my master is a shepherd then, and I a sheep?
>
>   (1.1, lines 72-77)

Shipped to be a shepherd, Valentine's destiny is the conclusion Speed derives from the punning play of the letter.[6]

Valentine finds himself as a swain not only because of this textualizing determination of his career in a pun. His destiny is also in his name. In seeking a source for the name of the character (it does not appear in any of the sources for the play), Joseph A. Porter has suggested the romance of *Valentine and Orson* as one possibility.[7] There, Orson is a twin brother brought up by a bear, and thus incapable of speech. The romance involves the brothers' meeting, Orson's acquisition of language, and Valentine's recognition of his twin in this pastoral alter ego. Porter argues that Valentine's name is regularly one in a pair, as in *The Two Gentlemen of Verona*, and as it is, too, when it appears in *Romeo and Juliet*. There the name occurs, in the list of guests invited to the Capulet ball, as a ghost brother for Mercutio (1.2, line 68), and thus a simulacrum for Romeo, whom Mercutio gives his generic names: "Romeo! humors! madman! passion! lover!" (2.1, line 7). Not merely the swain of pastoral romance, Valentine's name means lover. Appearing *in* a letter, a valentine, one must recall, *is* a letter, a folded slip of paper on which the name of a lover is inscribed. A valentine is also a legal instrument, a sealed letter from the Crown for the apprehension of persons offending against the law. In the forest, Valentine, the outlawed lover, embodies both of these letters that name him. He opens his revery by remarking "How use doth breed a habit in a man!" (5.4, line 1). If the "habit" is his new-found pastoral guise, it is also his *interiority*, what inhabits him. Hence, the nightingale's song leads him to the Silvia "that dost inhabit in my breast" (line 7); the letter folded upon the letter, so might the inside and outside of the character be defined. Thus, earlier in the play, when Silvia's father had pulled off Valentine's cloak, he asks: "What letter is this same? What's here? 'To Silvia'!" (3.1, line 137). Inwardly and outwardly, Valentine is folded in the letter that names him and his pastoral/amatory career; he, in turn, enfolds the text 'To Silvia.'

If Silvia and Valentine are these literal figures, characters, that is, who voice the letters in which they are written, it can come as no surprise that their first scene together is played around a letter. Silvia employs Valentine as a secretary to write on her behalf to a "secret, nameless friend" (2.1, line 96). Valentine delivers the letter to her, and she returns it to him. Valentine responds by assuming he has been rejected, but Speed penetrates the circuit of the letter and realizes that it has reached its destination: "O jest unseen, inscrutable, invisible,/As a nose on a man's face, or a weathercock on a steeple!" (2.1, lines 125-26). He sees without difficulty that the letter is a figure ("she woos you by a figure" (line 136)), and authorizes his reading of the scene by concluding, "All this I speak in print, for in print I found it" (line 155). Speed knows their textual play because he knows he is a character set in type. His "consciousness" involves the recognition that what he voices has been written already, and he ends the scene demanding real food (as if that need were not scripted, too) rather than the insubstantial fare that lovers desire.

The circuit of the letter in this scene traces the path of desire. Speed's analysis of Silvia's behavior suggests how fully she is caught within the play that she stages:

> For often have you writ to her, and she in modesty,
> Or else for want of idle time, could not again reply;
> Or fearing else some messenger that might her mind discover,
> Herself hath taught her love himself to write unto her lover.
>
> (2.1, 151-54)

He speaks in print, in fourteeners that suggest that Silvia's figure is an old story. Barred from her "own" discourse even before she arrives in the position of Philomela imprisoned in the woods, Silvia can only speak to her lover if he speaks for her. Already, she has no voice. The exchange of the letter plays upon the "sympathetic dative"[8] of pastoral discourse that obscures the propriety of voice: "I have writ your letter" (2.1, line 95), Valentine says, opening the scene with Silvia, but it is precisely what "your" means that is in question.

> *Valentine.*   Madam, they are for you.
> *Silvia.*   Ay, ay, you writ them, sir, at my request,
>   But I will none of them. They are for you –
>
> (2.1, 115-17)

Silvia's manipulation of the letter is a guise of mastery, and Valentine subscribes to it; he is Silvia's "gentle servant" (line 99). Yet, her speech is entirely confined to the troping of the letter and to the duplicities and divagations possible within the device. Whereas Valentine balks at the task he has been assigned, Silvia attempts to speak within it.

> *Valentine.*   So it stead you, I will write –
>   Please you command – a thousand times as much.
>   And yet –
> *Silvia.*   A pretty period! Well, I guess the sequel –
>   And yet I will not name it – and yet I care not –
>   And yet take this again – and yet I thank you,
>   Meaning henceforth to trouble you no more.
>
> (2.1, 104-10)

"And yet" locates both Valentine's desire to escape the circuit of Silvia's dictates and Silvia's attempt to tell her desire within the turns of the trope. He experiences a frustrating and baffling lack in the situation, she points to an excess.

Clearly, as Speed says, the letter is a figure of desire. Yet, its circuit is obscure precisely because it is a figure. Reading the letter, Silvia finds it "clerkly done" (line 99), and Valentine apologizes, "For, being ignorant to whom it goes,/I writ at random, very doubtfully" (lines 101-2). Writing at the commands of another and to another, Valentine is incapable of seeing himself as the other for whom he writes. The trope that locates him dislocates him, and bars him, as well, from Silvia's designs – from the figure in which she is located, which in turn bars her from speaking any more straightforwardly than, by refusing the letter, signifying her acceptance of it. "What means your ladyship?" (line 112), the baffled servant asks, and Silvia responds by saying yes (she likes the letter, although she would like it more if it were more passionate) and no (she will not accept the letter). "If it please you, so; if not, why, so" (line 121). The letter is "for" Valentine if he can read his name as "the secret, nameless friend" (line 96). Only if, that is, auto-affection will allow him to find within himself the valentine that enfolds the letter for Valentine that another (himself as that other), writing for Silvia has written within.

The return of the letter offers a virtual Lacanian allegory in which letters always reach their destination (sender and receiver are one); yet their arrival (return) goes unrecognized since the language of desire (language as desire) deforms (metamorphoses, enfolds) those who desire.[9]

> *Speed.* You never saw her since she was deformed.
> *Valentine.* How long hath she been deformed?
> *Speed.* Ever since you loved her.

>> (2.1, 59-61)

Desire is spoken through an Other. In the scene between Valentine and Silvia, that Other has a social dimension that supports the psychoanalytical one. Silvia is barred from discourse because of the limits that patriarchy enforces; but she is also barred because the language of love puts her in the position of mastery in which her beloved must be treated as a servant. Silvia is, at once, empowered and disabled by the tropes of tyrannical desire (hers is the illusion of power), doubly disabled since her power is a trope within a discourse that she cannot control. Valentine's figurative submission to the discourse that gives him his name is what disables him from recognizing himself within the discourse to which he submits; he fails to see that his being (literally) is wrapped entirely within the figure. "O jest unseen, inscrutable, invisible,/ As a nose on a man's face, or a weathercock on a steeple!" (lines 125-26). The situation, Speed's lines say, is so clear that it requires a simile to make manifest the entirely figurative being of something so entirely literal. Why Silvia's power is as visible as a man's nose or a weathercock. And those, of course, are not figures.

It was Speed's play on the letter (ship/sheep) that led us to this scene played around the figure of the letter–a letter "writ at random" (2.1, line 102) whose contents are never revealed. Speed and Proteus continue to spin out their pastoral troping in the first scene of the play, trying out the possibilities that *that* letter is also random–is Valentine or Speed a shepherd? which one is a sheep? Their inconclusive turns come to a halt when Proteus asks, "Gav'st thou my letter to Julia?" (1.1, line 94). The letter scene between Valentine and Silvia is hardly a unique event in *The Two Gentlemen of Verona*; there is, before it, this letter to Julia.

Speed's answer to Proteus's question folds the pastoral punning into the question of the letter: "Ay, sir. I, a lost mutton, gave your letter to her, a laced mutton, and she, a laced mutton, gave me, a lost mutton, nothing for my labor" (1.1, lines 95-97). "Laced" is generated from "lost" as a variation upon the letter, and Proteus soon reports that he has nothing from this response, which is also Speed's complaint about his reward for "bearing the letter" (line 115). "Fold it over and over" (line 105), Speed says; those who bear the letter have nothing more than "a pinfold" (line 104) for their production; they are pinned and penned at once. Saying "Ay"(line 108) and nodding his head, Speed makes his body and speech produce the impression of the letter which he bears in his deformations; he says, that is, yes and no at once, and identifies 'himself' (Ay = I) thereby as a character set in print. The only way to receive the letter is so to "mistake" it (line 104). Running through these dizzying exchanges is an economics of depletion, figured in pastoral and amatory terms, Speed's empty purse and Proteus's unsatisfied desire. Speed's account of how he bears the letter suggests how desire is carried by the letter; the chain of phonemic variation, metaphorical and metonymic displacements "*insists* on reproducing itself," as Lacan writes.[10] Yet, its reproduction only produces the speaker's voice as the bearer of the letter that deforms and reforms speech along the paths of desire. Such letters reach their destination only in these divagations. The verbal play, an impediment to understanding, is, at the same time, the arrival of the letter.

Speed's punning enacts what he has done; he has carried the letter and barred its delivery since it arrives at nothing but the endless deformation of the letter, chains of signifiers that fail to arrive at signification. The next scene of the play translates this movement, for now the letter to Julia is in Lucetta's hands, Julia's nurse "being in the way" (1.2, line 39) of its delivery, and receiving it in Julia's name (line 40) from "Sir Valentine's page" (line 38). The nurse both impedes the letter and delivers it, yet Julia cannot say she wants the letter, for that would be tantamount to the acknowledgement of desire, and maids are not supposed to desire. She returns the letter to Lucetta; the nurse bears the part of the page – exactly. Julia is defeated by her literalism:

> What fool is she, that knows I am a maid,
> And would not force the letter to my view!
> Since maids, in modesty, say 'no' to that
> Which they would have the profferer construe 'ay.'
>
> (1.2, 53-56)

Her desire is the very violence of the letter that is nothing and that produces the voice that says no and yes at once. Lucetta returns, drops the letter, agreeing it is "nothing" (line 71) and Julia insists that it may "lie" (line 76) where it has fallen. Lucetta answers that it will not lie unless misinterpreted and Julia unleashes the violence of her desire for the letter by tearing it to shreds, commanding Lucetta to "let the papers lie" (line 101). The truth of her desire coincides with the violation of the letter, a palpable tearing of the words that deform speech and that name characters as the lying texts that truly speak them.

Left alone with the mangled letter, Julia reads from it only names:

> Look, here is writ 'kind Julia.' Unkind Julia!
> As in revenge of thy ingratitude,
> I throw thy name against the bruising stones,
> Trampling contemptuously on thy disdain.
> And here is writ 'love-wounded Proteus.'
> Poor wounded name!
>
> (1.2, 110-15)

Her existence is in the letter; she *is* her name and she finds herself in the written text upon which she wishes to enact more violence. Collecting each instance of Proteus's name, which love (her love) has wounded, she would "except" her "own name" (line 121): "that some whirlwind bear/Upon a ragged, fearful-hanging rock,/And throw it thence into the raging sea!" (lines 121-23). Yet, finally, finding Proteus's name coupled with her own, she decides to "fold them one upon another" (line 129), commanding them to "kiss, embrace, contend, do what you will" (line 130). Julia has found "each letter in the letter" (line 120). The letter is allowed to enact desire (kissing and contending at once), for it is desire that makes her and Proteus share the "wounded name" (line 115). In *The Two Gentleman of Verona*, desire is textual; Julia's scene with the letter enacts the being of character as letters named in a text.

Not surprisingly, then, when Julia decides to pursue Proteus, she takes as her "habit" (2.7, line 39) "such weeds/As may beseem some well-reputed page" (lines 42-43), a costume that involves the illusory power of "a cod-piece to stick pins on" (line 56), Speed's pinfold. In the lying truth of that textual disguise (at once a *page*[11] and a sylvan *weed*) she overhears Proteus serenading Silvia and knows that the pastoral singer "plays false" (4.2, line 58). As his letter-bearer to Silvia, she first offers a letter she was not meant to send (the letter that impresses her as Proteus's love?) and then the one she was commissioned to deliver (4.4, lines 119-21). Silvia receives and tears the letter, but agrees to give the picture of herself that Proteus had desired; Julia takes it and looks at it as if she were looking in a mirror, finding that a change of wigs would answer "all the difference" in Proteus's love (4.4, line 188). A simulacrum of herself (in the page's weeds) Julia contemplates another double, the image of Silvia; "Come, shadow, come and take this shadow up,/For 'tis thy rival" (4.4, lines 195-96). Desire, literally, is for a shadow, an image, a figure. The text that deforms, that offers violence, makes the lover into an image. (Recall that Philomela finds voice in the shuttle, the loom on which she weaves her story as an image.) True lovers easily play false when the discourse of love is a play on the letter that comes to nothing; Julia's textual habit is hard to distinguish from the texts that Proteus pens. So, too, Silvia returned Valentine's letter as her way of accepting it. Julia accepts Proteus's letter by tearing it; Silvia's refusal is enacted in the same gesture. Returning her picture as a response to the letter, however, is at best a knowing gesture testifying to desire as the deforming, metamorphic multiplication of images. The being of characters is their textuality. Literally figures, they are placed within an image repertoire in which they seem as exchangeable as the letters they convey (the friendship of Valentine and Proteus is, of course, rooted in their alter ego relationship). For they *are* those letters, and similitude is their being.

Launce glosses this sliding of signifier into signifier, this literal troping:

> I'll show you the manner of it. This shoe is my father. No, this left shoe is my father. No, no, this left shoe is my mother. Nay, that cannot be so neither. Yes, it is so, it is so – it hath the worser sole. This shoe with the hole in it is my mother, and this my father. A vengeance on't! There 'tis. Now, sir, this staff is my sister, for, look you, she is as white as a lily and as small as a wand. This hat is Nan, our maid. I am the dog. No, the dog is himself, and I am the dog – O, the dog is me, and I am myself.
>
> (2.3, 13-22)

Launce's identification with the dog whom he loves is his version of the lover's enfolding. The self that emerges from his attempts to literalize himself makes the statement "I am myself" another similitude, displaying the metaphorization inherent in the copula. "I am myself" divides the self, and self-ownership is as problematic here as it was when Valentine and Silvia wrangled over the propriety of the letter; for whom is it? As the play moves to its close, the violence of Proteus's attempted appropriation of Silvia is answered by Valentine's surrender: "All that was mine in Silvia I give thee" (5.4, line 83). "I know him as myself" (2.4, line 59), Valentine had affirmed, vouching for Proteus. True love plays false when all truth is trope.

As instruments of the letter, characters are impressed by its false turns.[12] No better demonstration of the point can be seen than in Valentine's wooing lesson for the Duke. Proteus has betrayed Valentine's designs on Silvia to her father, and the Duke attempts to make Valentine betray himself by asking advice on how to win a lady he would marry. Valentine does betray himself (as *true* lover) by offering the cynical instructions of an Ovidian art of love, assuring the Duke that women never mean what they say, and "That man that hath a tongue, I say is no man,/If with his tongue he cannot win a woman" (3.1, lines 104-5). As he describes her, the Duke's fictional lady comes to be the very image of his daughter, and Valentine's strategies turn into his plot to abduct her and the letter he secretes beneath his cloak. The revelation in this scene is, thus, a demonstration of the path to/of the letter, a meeting place of lies and truth, fiction and desire. In the scene, the Duke appears to occupy the place of the Other, and what Valentine articulates for him is what he has indited; the text 'To Silvia' pursues the thoughts he sends her and his desire to "lodge where senseless they are lying" (3.1, line 143). Such "lying" is the truth of his being *à la lettre*. Yet, the Duke's patriarchal powers are similarly undermined; his fiction delivers an overwhelming desire. At the end of the play, when he relinquishes his hold on Silvia, he does so out of a textual need: "I thus subscribe," he concludes, "Sir Valentine,/Thou art a gentleman and well derived;/Take thou thy Silvia, for thou hast deserved her" (5.4, lines 146-49). The patriarch submits to the power that writes him; the path of the letter (desire) is not mastered by any character, not even the nominal lord in the play. The derivation to which the Duke subscribes is the textual genealogy of character, discerned as well when the Duke turns on Valentine to rename him "Phaeton" (3.1, line 153) – the *truth* of his revolt discovered in Ovid's *Metamorphoses* – for aspiring to his sunlike powers.

The Two Gentlemen of Verona opens with a scene in which Valentine and Proteus quote old saws and "a love-book" (1.1, line 19) which determines their positions. When Launce describes the woman he loves, he reads a "cate-log of her condition. 'Imprimis: She can fetch and carry'" (3.1, lines 271-72). Launce's letter scene is, in this first item, dogged by the love that accompanies him and by the appetite that intrudes upon the list of sweets. (But ah, Desire still cries, give me some food.) Launce replays the scene between the Duke and Valentine. Opening by refusing to "pluck" out the heart of his mysterious love, he can barely name her: "'tis a woman, but what woman I will not tell myself" (lines 265-66). In his scene of reading, the letter is an impediment, and yet it carries him as far as he can go, "your old vice still: mistake the word" (line 279).

> Speed. What news, then, in your paper?
> Launce. The black'st news that ever thou heard'st.
> Speed. Why, man, how black?
> Launce. Why, as black as ink.
>
> (3.1, 280-83)

Throughout, as we have seen, exchanges of letters carry and impede the characters: Proteus holds back a letter of Julia's from his father, claiming it comes from Valentine (1.3, lines 55ff.); the exchange in letters there points to Valentine's ultimate offer to put Proteus in his place. Lucetta or Speed (or Julia-as-page) impede and deliver letters; the Duke's unveiling of Valentine puts him in a similar position to which he finally subscribes. Launce's unseen love is as black as ink; what we see in the play is similarly indited.

When Proteus arrives at the Duke's court, Valentine begs Silvia to treat him as himself. Alone, Proteus discovers himself in Valentine's place:

Even as one heat another heat expels,
Or as one nail by strength drives out another,
So the remembrance of my former love
Is by a newer object quite forgotten.

(2.4, 189-192)

These lines describe the making of character as an act of violence and violation; interiority here involves the effacement of memory and its replacement with oblivion. Yet, as we have seen, internality is itself an inscription, a letter 'To Silvia.' "This weak impress of love is as a figure" (3.2, line 6), the Duke counsels Thurio. Proteus's interiority has been invaded with a figure too: "'Tis but her picture I have yet beheld,/And that hath dazzled my reason's light" (2.4, lines 206-7). Silvia *is* the picture he has seen. And what she replaces is equally an image: "She is fair, and so is Julia that I love" (line 196). "Read over Julia's heart" (5.4, line 46), Silvia urges Proteus; later in the scene, Julia reveals her "habit" (line 105), the "immodest raiment" (line 107) that she inhabits, the page as "a disguise of love" (line 108). That text enfolds characters and gives them voice. Bearers of the letter, characters themselves and in relation to others – in relation to the deformation they undergo that makes self-identity itself an otherness, wrapped in similitude – are *impressed* with the letter. Proteus subscribes to what the Duke tells Thurio: "my love is thawed,/Which, like a waxen image 'gainst a fire,/Bears no impression of the thing it was" (2.4, lines 197-99). The love he calls his is/was Julia herself and her image inscribed on the waxen tablet of his memory. "The thing it was," he says, is "like a waxen image." Its *being* is representation, the image of an image. It is within such existence that characters speak. "But to inscribe it [the subject], it is necessary to define it in a circle, what I call the otherness, of the sphere of language. All that is language is lent from this otherness and this is why the subject is always a fading thing that runs under the chain of signifiers."[13] "How like a dream is this I see and hear" (5.4, line 26): such is the scene in the forest when the letter comes to its destination, and characters are finally inscribed.

What is a letter? Lacan's definition: "By 'letter' I designate that material support that concrete discourse borrows from language,"[14] by which he indicates that actual speech partakes of the unconscious, that the subject does not own language but inhabits it (to be displaced), that speaking is inevitably metaphoric and metonymic, that *being*-in-language always is stamped and inscribed within a *lack*-in-being. What is a letter? In Angel Day's *The English Secretorie* (1586), the first English example of a kind of manual that has a history stretching back to antiquity, here is the opening definition: "A Letter therefore is that wherein is expreslye conveied in writing, the intent and meaning of one man, immediately to passe and be directed to another, and for the certaine respects thereof, is termed the messenger and familiar speeche of the absent"(1).[15] The definition is, apparently, anything but Lacanian: writing transcribes speech, it arrives transparently at its receiver, it conveys meaning and intention. Yet, there are some hesitations even in the definition; is the letter *entirely* conveyed, or does "letter" mean only what is conveyed? Is that why "in certaine respects" it is a messenger (because "in certaine respects" it is not–for example, literally)? Is the "one man" who writes everyman, that is, one whose meanings are entirely public? Or is "familiarity" a sign of privacy? And *who*, exactly, is absent in this exchange; when a letter transcribes intention does it indite absent meaning? These questions, in fact, engage Day's definition precisely because his manual of form letters for various occasions has continually to face the discrepancies between formula letters and particular instances. "Their diversities are sundry" (2), Day admits. And, when he turns to the writing of love letters, the commonplace definition falls into question:

> And now the last of all these devisions yet unspoken of, is *Amatorie*, whereof because the humors of all sortes, therewith being possessed are so infinite, and so great an uncertaintie, as perchaunce even in the very writing of his letter, the lover him selfe is sometimes scarce certaine of his owne conceipts, the lesse must of necessity be the precepts of the same directions.
>
> (232)

Love letters may inscribe thoughts, but the thoughts arise in their writing, and intention and meaning are both infinite and uncertain. Lover's discourse is self-alienated, the inditing of an absent self.

Speed complains to Proteus that he could "perceive nothing at all from her" when he "brought your mind" (1.1, lines 130, 132), his letter. Julia muses, "I would I knew his mind," and Lucetta responds, "Peruse this paper, madam" (1.2, lines 33-34). The paper that is the mind *is* the mind, quite literally–witness Proteus's speech on the violence of his penetration by the image, or Valentine's woodland solicitations of the letter inscribed on his heart. Such letters are like those that appear in dreams; they speak those who speak. Letters, after all, are, literally, characters:

> Counsel, Lucetta; gentle girl, assist me;
> And ev'n in kind love I do conjure thee,
> Who art the table wherein all my thoughts
> Are visibly charactered and engraved,
> To lesson me and tell me some good mean

How, with my honor, I may undertake
A journey to my loving Proteus.

(2.7, 1-7)

Lucetta *is*, in this formulation, a writing table on which Julia writes. It is her character to be a letter, to bear the letter, and to return what is inscribed as a lesson. Lucetta attempts to impede Julia's desire, reading moral lessons in the journey, but eventually she falls in with her plans to be a page. Julia's "journey to my loving Proteus" takes place in disguise, and ends, as all journeys do in *The Two Gentlemen of Verona*, in the forest, the place that tropes the textual *being* of characters, a final turn to the metamorphoses, displacements, and replacements that mark their paths. Throughout, theirs is the voice of the shuttle, they exist as words/images woven in a tapestry like Philomela's. *Silva* names the trope that is their being.

*

Although the characters of *The Two Gentlemen of Verona* frequently have been accused of being wooden, the argument here is that their "woodenness" (literally) is the most transparent indication of the genealogy of the Shakespearian character.[16] The troping of the *silva* tradition of pastoral and the allusions to Ovid, and particularly to Philomela, that generate the play are not its sole property, however. These materials come together in another Shakespearian text, the contemporary *Titus Andronicus*, a play (as some recent criticism has emphasized[17]) that repeatedly stages its literariness. Marcus, for example, discovers Lavinia "*her hands cut off, and her tongue cut out, and ravished*" (2.4, s.d.), and records her textual source:

Fair Philomel, why she but lost her tongue,
And in a tedious sampler sewed her mind:
But, lovely niece, that mean is cut from thee;
A craftier Tereus, cousin, hast thou met,
And he hath cut those pretty fingers off
That could have better sewed than Philomel.

(2.4, 38-43)

Although Lavinia appears to be "cut . . . off" from the disseminative sewing of mind into text, the lines that Marcus recites implant her textually; she is a citation. And her body is a text. Her lopped arms are "two branches" (line 18), her severed hands "aspen leaves" (line 45); retrospectively, Marcus provides a genealogy for those hands, imagining them strumming a lute accompanying the orphic song of her now severed tongue. Lavinia's history is fetched from Ovid's *Metamorphoses*.

Insistently, her broken body bears the textual imprint of a violated florilegium. Marcus takes Lavinia off to Titus, to "make thy father blind" (line 52), Titus, however, commands that she be seen, made visible as a text: "Look on her" (3.1, line 110):

> Had I but seen thy picture in this plight,
> It would have madded me: what shall I do
> Now I behold thy lively body so?
>
> (3.1, 103-5)

The answer is: make her a picture. Titus had been discovered at the opening of the scene writing in dust (lines 12-13); in the course of the scene, his hand is lopped off ("withered herbs as these/Are meet for plucking up" (lines 177-78)) and, at the end of the scene, Lavinia exits with her father's dismembered hand in her mouth (line 282). Titus had attempted to "understand her signs" (3.1, line 143). With his hand in her mouth, she has become a speaking picture, and in the next scene he reads her as a "map of woe" (3.2, line 12) and "an alphabet" (line 44), counseling her to put a knife in her mouth in place of her tongue (line 16), or his hand. Writing as violence and violation.

Titus closes this scene proposing reading to Lavinia: "I'll to thy closet and go read with thee/Sad stories chanced in the times of old" (3.2, lines 82-83). A scene of reading follows, proposed as a kind of therapy ("beguile thy sorrow" (4.1, line 35)) and in remembrance of earlier times when Lavinia read "Sweet poetry and Tully's Orator" (line 14). There is, however, no escaping in a text if that is where the characters are. Voiceless, Lavinia is what she once read, and in a frenzy, she indicates that there is "some book. . .that she desires to see" (line 31). It is, of course, "Ovid's Metamorphosis" (line 42), "culled" (line 44) from the "library" (line 34) transported on stage:

> Soft; so busily she turns the leaves!
> Help her: what would she find? Lavinia, shall I read?
> This is the tragic tale of Philomel
> And treats of Tereus' treason and his rape;
> And rape, I fear, was root of thine annoy.
>
> (4.1, 45-49)

Turning "leaves," taking "root": the silvan text in which Lavinia is found. "Note how she quotes the leaves" (line 50). How? Marcus takes a stick in his mouth and writes; Lavinia imitates, inscribing rape (line 78). The scene of reading had virtually re-enacted the rape[18] (for the character seizes the book that seizes her), and writing is its violent perpetuation. Titus wishes to make Lavinia's text an unchanging monument –

> I will go get a leaf of brass,
> And with a gad of steel will write these words,
> And lay it by: the angry northern wind
> Will blow these sands like Sibyl's leaves abroad,
> And where's our lesson then?

(4.1, 102-6)

– but the answer to his question is that the dissemination of the text cannot be halted. Lavinia's rapists are branded, "deciphered . . . marked with rape" (4.2, lines 8-9), and Titus spends much of the rest of the play madly reading, dispatching texts as missiles, and ultimately re-enacting the Ovidian text, serving up Lavinia's rapists in a stew, and then murdering his daughter as a further citational act, "a pattern, precedent, and lively warrant/For me" (5.3, lines 44-45). He is enabled to act by the warrant that arrests Lavinia. Life, in these texts, is lived *à la lettre*.

Wherever the scene, it is always textualized. "The forest walks are wide and spacious,/And many unfrequented plots there are,/Fitted by kind for rape and villainy" (2.1, lines 114-16); so Aaron describes the place where Lavinia meets Philomela's fate. The "kind" of its "unfrequented plots" names a generic locale, the sylvan source of the punning leaves and branches that the dismembered characters become, replanted thereby in that (in)hospitable soil. This empty ("unfrequented") place is a virtual echo chamber, Virgilian as much as Ovidian. In the scene in which Tamora's sons pursue Lavinia, the queen hunts deer and the woods echo (2.2, line 6)–along with an allusion to the meeting of Dido and Aeneas (2.3, line 22), one of a number of references to the *Aeneid* in the play. Lavinia's scene of reading recalls a Virgilian scene, too: "I have read that Hecuba of Troy/Ran mad for sorrow" (4.1, lines 20-21).

> See, see!
> Ay, such a place there is where we did hunt
> (O had we never, never hunted there!)
> Patterned by that the poet here describes,
> By nature made for murders and for rapes.

(4.1, 54-58)

The "place" "by nature made" is made by "the poet" whose patterns "patterned" nature. What we are to "see" is that the place where characters are has been written already, and that their being is quotation, whether they voice texts or, silently ravished, embody them. Characters in *Titus Andronicus* write who they are. The "plot" that determines their character is that "place" "made for murders and for rapes" – the place of the text. Writing invades being, violating any possibility that characters have their own being or speak in their own voices. The "integrity" of

83

a character, from this perspective, is coincident with how fully it is impressed by the pattern (Lavinia is most *like herself* when she is most like Philomela). The pattern is not a straitjacket, however; "the forest walks are wide and spacious" (2.1, line 114), the permutations of *silva* allow–demand–Ovidian metamorphoses. Character is most itself when violated by the texts that determine its instability. The characters of *Titus Andronicus* and *The Two Gentlemen of Verona* seem to inhabit other texts, and to take their being from them, Lavinia and Silvia, in particular, as notable instances of the metamorphic possibilities of Philomela.

There is one more citation that should be added to this set–the example of Imogen from *Cymbeline*; for it suggests, even more than the forest revery of Valentine, how fully the *internality* of character is a matter of citation, how much, that is, the texts that characters in-habit inhabit them. This late play suggests, too, that the Shakespearian character of the early plays remains at the end.[19]

A few lines into Act 2, scene 2 of *Cymbeline*, Imogen, weary of reading, commands her servant to "fold down the leaf where I have left" (line 4); close to the end of the scene, Iachimo picks up the book: "She hath been reading late/The tale of Tereus. Here the leaf's turned down/Where Philomel gave up" (lines 44-46). The scene that occurs on stage takes place within the folds of this leaf, a rape that is, at once, a scene of reading and writing. The closing of the book and Imogen's subsequent prayer for protection from "the tempters of the night" (line 9) is answered immediately by the opening of the trunk and Iachimo's emergence from it. Imogen is saved from literal ravishment by the insistent figuration of the scene, which, like all figuration, preserves the literal precisely by ravishing it. Iachimo's trunk is a double of the book, and at the end of the scene he returns "to th' trunk again" to "shut the spring of it" (line 47); but the trunk is also his body, from which he emerges all eye (Imogen shuts the book because her "eyes are weak" (line 3)); and the trunk is *her* body. He has "picked the lock and ta'en/The treasure of her honor" (lines 41-42), has gazed on "rubies unparagoned" (line 17). The uncanniness of this scene lies in its embodiment of a dream that is both Imogen's and Iachimo's, a dream that realizes what has been written and read. "To write and read/Be henceforth treacherous!" (4.2, lines 316-17), Imogen exclaims, looking at another "trunk" (line 353) later in the play.

"The crickets sing" (2.2, line 11), Iachimo begins, an allusion, perhaps, to the Phaedran fable of the origin of song;[20] he glosses his actions with Ovid's *Fasti* (and the earlier Shakespearian rewritings of it), "Our Tarquin thus/Did softly press the rushes" (lines 12-13). Iachimo proceeds "to note the chamber" (line 24). But the space in which he moves is one of metamorphic textualization. Seeing himself in the guise of the texts he cites, he sees Imogen as Cytherea; the taper she has left burning are her eyes beneath the shut lids (hence the scene takes place there), and the lids themselves are "windows, white and azure-laced/With blue of heaven's own tinct" (lines 22-23). The chamber thus is–by metaphorical condensation, metonymic displacement–within Imogen, as she is within it. Iachimo notes, "there the window; such/Th'adornment of her bed; the arras, figures,/Why, such and such" (lines 25-27). These empty "figures" are supplied by the troping turn of the scene; Imogen lies in an Ovidian chamber; these are the pictures Iachimo sees, "the contents o' th' story" (line 27) wherever he turns.[21]

"I will write all down" (line 24); Iachimo's inscription treats Imogen's body as a text. Like Launce, or the sonneteer or writer of the blazon, he tallies the parts of the body, lips and eyes, "some natural notes about her body" (line 28) "t'enrich mine inventory" (line 30). The book he writes is a treasure chest, another trunk of jewels, materialized in the bracelet he takes from her wrist, "slippery as the Gordian knot was hard" (line 34). Ravishment is displaced in this token that "witness[es] outwardly . . . as the conscience does within" (lines 35-36). Lying as a simulacrum of death, Imogen's body is given its witness in this part that stands for all, ravished from her to be her. She is made into "a monument" (line 32) in this figuration, given the form of textual permanence. Yet, her remains are also ravished, dispersed in similitude: "On her left breast/A mole cinque-spotted, like the crimson drops/I' th' bottom of a cowslip" (lines 37-39). No way to see what she is without seeing what she is like; an inevitable florilegium, an implicit Ovidian metamorphosis (whose blood became those crimson drops?). "Here's a voucher/Stronger than ever law could make" (lines 39-40). Iachimo subscribes (and writes) a text whose very materiality lies in figuration and whose strength is the violation of the difference between inside and outside, body and word. Like Julia, he folds the letter upon the letter.

And it folds upon himself. "Why should I write this down that's riveted,/Screwed to my memory?" (lines 43-44). Before the trunk snaps shut, before he turns to the turned down page, the spring of his mind recoils upon itself. The turn of the screw. Attempting to penetrate Imogen (to get beneath her veiled eyelids), he has been penetrated, written, as riveted as Proteus is by the picture of Silvia that hammers out his memory. No need for the supplement of a text if one's inner being is a text, if one's outer existence is in a text, if one, that is, has been supplemented by a text already that claims one's existence.

At the end of *Cymbeline*, "the letter of the oracle" (5.5, line 449) tells all: the "apt construction of thy name" (line 443) in a genealogical tree: "The lofty cedar, royal Cymbeline,/Personates thee, and thy lopped branches point/Thy two sons forth" (lines 452-54). "Hang there like fruit, my soul,/Till the tree die!" (lines 263-64): so Posthumous names his wife and their relationship. Her name, the oracle rewrites as "the piece of tender air" (line 445). Imogen's "soul" is the "air" she ventriloquizes, the text that speaks in her voice, or in the silence in which she is raped and, like Philomela, rewoven in the text. "The dream's here still. Even when I wake it is/Without me, as within me" (4.2, lines 306-7). "Tender air" names her (etymologically) as woman; Cymbeline calls himself "a mother" (5.5, line 369). All the characters have been ravished by the Otherness of the text, engendered in a *family tree* that names them as the divagations of a textual play no character can own (Cymbeline casts off his fatherhood and patriarchal power; Imogen dwindles into a wife). And, as even the scenes of reading that we have considered might well suggest, this textual dispersal makes the writer (in them, of them) a further locus of inscription. There is no Other of the Other, no securing textual play. The authority of the Shakespearian character may be named Shakespeare only as that name functions within the writing that characters the Shakespearian text.

The inscription of character

What's in a name? What is a character? "I will believe thou hast a mind that suits/With this thy fair and outward character," Viola tells the helpful captain in *Twelfth Night* (1.2, lines 50-51) as she prepares to don her disguise and he agrees to be her mute: "Be you his eunuch, and your mute I'll be" (line 62). The captain's character is written in the plot he tells Viola, and her disguise figures her inscription in it, an embodiment suited to his words, and rendering him mute. Viola ascribes interiority to the captain on the basis of his character and conceals herself in "such disguise as haply shall become/The form of my intent" (lines 54-55). What becomes her she may become; the translation of intention into figuration describes character the way Angel Day depicts the lover's letter. "Conceal me what I am" (line 53), Viola asks, folding the letter; the reading of mind in the inscribed character is not the penetration of a transparency. Characters have a material opacity; they are not veils to be penetrated but surfaces to be read and reread. These lines between Viola and the captain begin with a reading of character and close with the writing of one; implicit here is what is explicit elsewhere. In *King Lear*, for example, when Edmund reads a letter ascribed to Edgar: "You know the character to be your brother's?" (1.2, line 61), Gloucester asks. The question locates exactly the position of the Shakespearian character as a locus of inscription.

Such is the Overburian definition, "What a Character Is":

> If I must speake the Schoole-masters language I will confesse that Character comes of this infinitive moode χαράξω which signifieth to ingrave, or make a deepe Impression. And for that cause, a letter (as A. B.) is called a Character.[22]

The definition, etymologically exact, accounts for the imprinting of the Shakespearian character, Proteus's impression, for example, or Lucetta's entablature. The depth of a character is a result of an inscription, what others read on the surface or, even more tellingly, what the Other that commands the deformations of desire has inscribed there. The styling of character is penned with a stylus, engraving on the wax, so that the being of character (Viola's concealed "what I am") is its becoming. Not surprisingly, in that respect, a traveller's manual published in 1633 worries that the "best wits, and purest receptacles of sound knowledge" will return from their travels "corrupted." If mind (wit) is a receptive capacity, the manual continues, then it may "easily admit any obvious impression."[23] The best minds, in this formulation, are those most open to being charactered. "By *reading* we receive what antiquitie hath left us, by writing we deliver what posteritie craves of us"(25): so Richard Mulcaster describes the genealogy of character in his *First Part of the Elementarie which Entreateth chefelie of the Right Writing of our English Tung* (1582).[24]

When the Overburian definition proceeds to describe character, it also offers an account of "those Elements which we learne first, leaving a strong seale in our memories." The mind is made by receiving letters; characters are charactered, sealed as letters are, folded. Mulcaster's *Elementarie* warns that making a child's character apt for the learning of letters must itself be the inscription of the child, a folding of the letter upon the letter.

> For if the young eies be acquainted at home with unsemelie sights: if the tender ears be more then half trained to uncomlie hearings, if the pliable minde be unwiselie writhen to a disfigured shape, if the hole conceit be unadvisedlie stained with a contrarie dy, how can that countenance be liked on in school, whose contrarie favor is most honored at home?
>
> (23)

The deep impression of tender minds, as Mulcaster describes it, is recorded on the face, a "countenance" whose "disfigured shape" may witness the violence of a tainted inscription, "stained with a contrarie dy" in the blackest ink, "writhen," miswritten.

These accounts of the elementary charactering of character could stand as an archeology for the Shakespearian character, protean in metamorphosis, disseminated in disguise, for characters who discover themselves or record others as the locus of inscription and impression. This etiology of character never locates a self, or a space of interiority, that has not been inscribed beforehand. As a further example, take the character of "A Childe" in Earle's *Micro-cosmographie*; a child, he writes,

> Is a Man in a small Letter, yet the best Copie of *Adam* before hee tasted of *Eve*, or the Apple; and hee is happy whose small practice in the World can only write this Character. Hee is natures fresh picture newly drawn in Oyle, which time and much handling, dimmes and defaces. His Soule is yet a white paper unscribed with observations of the world, wherewith at length it becomes a blurr'd Note-booke.[25]

Earle's child has not yet ventured out into the world that the traveller's guide warned against; he has not, like Valentine or Proteus (or Iachimo), been abroad. The blankness of his "unscribed" soul, however, is belied by the initial impression that makes him, at first, a copy–quite literally, a retranscription–of the Edenic Adam. His being is already inscribed, for he "writes[s] this Character" simply by being, and he has been written/painted by nature to be a first image and reflection of first man. (As much as Silvia, he is a picture.) This diminutive being (this diminution of *being*) is written as "a small Letter." Time will not enlarge this "unscribed" letter so much as it will blur and deface it. Existence-in-time is an erasure of the first impression which is itself a *copy*; existence-in-the-world is a violation, an over-writing produced by "much handling." But that first impression, we must emphasize, was itself both "unscribed" and a "Copie" of the already written. The child that Earle describes is not born with a proper, self-owned, self, but delivered as a replica of a story inevitably retraced. That biblical inscription is one with nature's drawing in oils; the child's nature is entirely textual.

What, then, do character writers do when they write characters? Joseph Hall, in his *Characters of Virtues and Vices*, the first English character book, pauses over the question when he considers the Theophrastian text that provides his model as one "drawing out the true lineaments of every virtue and vice, so lively, that who saw the medals, might know the face: which Art they significantly termed Charactery. Their papers were so many tables; their writings, so many speaking pictures, or living images."[26] The "true lineaments" of a character are as much "lively" images as the "speaking pictures" in which they are (re)written as "living images." The "face" of the character of a virtue or vice is (as in Mulcaster's "countenance" or Earle's "picture drawne in Oyle") itself a picture, lineaments already drawn. Hall's "medal" bears with it the image of stamping, engraving, and sealing–the very material translated in Proteus's image forged on his mind, or Iachimo's treasure-chest. It is only a short step from the medal to the coin and to the situation of characters as fully exchangeable, the alter egos of Proteus and Valentine, the replacement of Julia with Silvia, or the specular and dreamlike substitutions that occur in the forest in *The Two Gentlemen of Verona* or the closing scene of *Cymbeline*. Such coining of characters is not confined to the stage or to character books. John Donne, writing to Sir Edward Herbert on the day of his ordination, assures him that this metamorphosis has not removed the old stamp of their relationship, but only added a new one:

> Your power and jurisdiction, which is entirely over mee, is somewhat
> enlarged. For, as if I should put any other stampe upon a peece of your gold,
> the gold were not the lesse yours, so (if there be not too much taken by mee,
> in that comparison) by havinge, by the orders of our churche, receyved a
> new character, I ame not departed from your title, and possession of mee.[27]

Donne's existence, as he explains it, is like the situation Julia describes for Lucetta as the tablet on which she inscribes. He is a coin stamped by the impression of others. Being, in these terms, is similitude, an origin in secondarity shared by Earle's child.

Thus, the Overburian account of character turns to the writing of characters this way: "To square out a Character by our English levell, it is a picture (reall or personall) quaintlie drawne in various collours, all of them heightned by one shadowing." The "shadowing" here is like the duplication of shadows Julia sees when she looks at Silvia's picture and sees herself, or like the relationship between the "lively" "true lineaments" of Hall's virtues and vices, and the drawing of "living images" in a book of characters. It is the shadow of resemblance and representation, the rewriting that characterizes Lavinia in *Titus Andronicus*, for example. The Overburian character is similarly a speaking picture in the very image it bears; the language of picture-making is also rhetorical (the colors of rhetoric), and the picture that results – "reall or personall" – is, as those philosophical terms suggest, whether universal or particularized nonetheless identically shadowed; similitude, representation, overcomes difference. Such impressions – of persons or their inscriptions – are *imprese*. Alongside the devices of Shakespearian characters, their habitual disguising, might be placed this remark in the Overburian definition of "What A Character Is": "Character is also taken for an Egiptian Hierogliphicke, for an impresse, or short Embleme; in little comprehending much."

The Overburian definition of character had begun with the phonetic alphabet, the "deepe Impression" of "A. B." To make such a picture speak, the definition proceeds to an originary language – to language as originally written – the "impresse" of hieroglyphic writing, "in little comprehending much," like Earle's child, "a Man in a small Letter." The letters of the alphabet here (as in Derrida) do not transcribe sound but have the material density of the hieroglyphic wedding of written word and picture, two sides of a coin.[28] A similar impulse to treat the alphabetical character as a hieroglyph can be observed when Mulcaster enthusiastically describes the "many pretie notes" (111) of the vowels; he waxes eloquent over the wonders of *E*, that the letter not only designates more than one sound but that it can also be mute: "this is to be noted of E, that it either soundeth or is silent." Mulcaster "notes" these "pretie notes," and his elementary instruction inscribes a writing that exceeds sound. Writing, even the ABCs, does not, in his account, transcribe sound; sound, rather, comes from writing. Voice is the effect of charactery. The duplicity of these notes is like those Julia hears when Proteus sings 'To Silvia' ("He plays false, father" (4.2, line 58)) or like the "note" (1.2, line 81) Lucetta would have Julia return as she attempts to deliver the letter from Proteus: "Let's see your song. [*Takes the letter*]" (1.2, line 88). The Egyptian Proteus.[29]

   Mulcaster lends characters their representational status when he defines them as images; in the history of writing that he offers, letters were found out as the arbitrary indicators of sound: "whereby the peple that used them [i.e. letters] first, agreed with those, that found them first, that such a sound in the voice should be resembled by such a signe to the eie; and that such a signe in the eie should be so returned to the ear, as the aspectable figur of such an audible *sound*" (65). Mulcaster denies any natural relationship between sounds and letters, and the circuit from sound to letter, and from letter to sound, is carried entirely by figuration. Letters are "aspectable" figures, pictures that inscribe voice on their faces. Similitude is their only truth, and it is not rooted in natural resemblance, but in arbitrary agreement. "What likenesse or what affinitie hath the form of anie letter in his own natur, to answer the force or sound in mans voice?" (65), Mulcaster asks, rhetorically. The "resemblance" of letters is not the same as "likenesse" or "affinitie," but a matter of "agreement." Hence, Mulcaster concludes his account of the adoption of letters with the sealing of an arbitrary agreement: "whereunto theie subscribed their names, and set to their seals the daie and year, when their consent past" (65). Letters ratify letters, and the circuit of the letter has only the assurance of writing to secure it. In Mulcaster's account, letters are "in the way" as much as they are in *The Two Gentlemen of Verona*. There is no passage for articulation except through characters, notes upon notes.

   When Mulcaster pauses, towards the end of his treatise, to consider the essence of language, he comes to an extraordinary conclusion. Its essence is change. This is the "secret misterie, or rather quikning spirit in everie spoken tung" (158). The life of language–its being–is generative. There is, he continues, nothing that sound can do to preserve itself, or that reason can attempt to align sound to word, or that custom can do, to keep the arbitrary agreement of language intact. Despite all these, there is within language what Mulcaster terms its prerogative. "I cannot compare this customarie *prerogative* in speche to anie thing better, then unto those, which devise new garments, and by law ar left to the libertie of devise" (ibid.). The law of language is its liberty to change devices, to shift costumes; the essence of language – change – is determined by the invasion of such exteriority. The "quikning spirit in everie spoken tung" is *writing*, the garment of style; written with the stylus is an endless refiguration of language so that what comes to be on the tongue–in the voice as its very essence and spirit – was first on the page. Prerogative, Mulcaster concludes, is a "stirring quintessence the leader to change in a thing that is naturallie changeable . . . a great princesse in proces, and a parent to corruption, but withall intending to rase another *Phenix*" (159). As the term *prerogative* itself suggests, language is an ultimate, political power; as Mulcaster describes it, it is Queen Elizabeth herself, the culture's most potent figure for the Other. The power of language is imagined as its exception from any rule except its own rule of freedom to change. Such change is, at once, generative and degenerative; "a parent to corruption" in the very violence of imposition and change, yet the intention is to raise a phoenix – to be unique, to rise from the ashes of mutability as eternal (becoming and being at once). Yet, were language so *ideally* self-identical, it would necessarily be no one's property, and since the "intention" of language has not yet reached its goal (nor will it ever, until there is no more time), its being/becoming generates a self-identity even more devastating in its exclusions, a self-identity that is also difference (the difference we have seen in the similitude of writing) and which rules out an ideal *being* of language. Language remains no one's property and thoroughly arbitrary in its exclusive powers, and these are not secured by an ideality impervious to the (de)generation of writing. All of which is caught in "rase"; transcendence is annihilation in this Derridean anticipation of the Hegelian *Aufhebung*. The *being* of language is its becoming *différance*. Mulcaster's "secret misterie" (158): the alphabet is a hieroglyph. Writing–characters, letters–is the quintessence of language.

What is a character? The Overburian definition concludes: "It is a quicke and softe touch of many strings, all shutting up in one musicall close: It is wits descant on any plaine song." A close that is still an opening; a sleight of hand producing song. Note the notes. A character:

a picture of a sound, the "image of the voice," as Sandys terms Echo.[30] A note. *Much Ado About Nothing*. The writing of the Shakespearian character.

*

> Thy gift, thy tables, are within my brain
> Full charactered with lasting memory,
> Which shall above that idle rank remain
> Beyond all date, even to eternity;
> Or, at the least, so long as brain and heart
> Have faculty by nature to subsist,
> Till each to rased oblivion yield his part
> Of thee, thy record never can be missed.
> That poor retention could not so much hold,
> Nor need I tallies thy dear love to score;
> Therefore to give them from me was I bold,
> To trust those tables that receive thee more.
>   To keep an adjunct to remember thee
>   Were to import forgetfulness in me.

(Sonnet 122)

The sonnets provide fertile ground for tracing the Shakespearian character. Sonnet 59, for example, seeks an image in an "antique book,/Since mind at first in character was done" (lines 7-8) – the mind is 'originally' a locus of inscription; sonnet 108 opens asking "What's in the brain that ink may character/Which hath not figured to thee my true spirit?" In these sonnets, as in sonnet 122 above, written characters are inscribed, "within my brain" and on external tablets. A search of prior (already written) texts, or of the memory on which they are inscribed, reveals that the beloved is already written in an image repertoire that even makes seeing the beloved an act of transcription. "Mine eye hath played the painter and hath stelled/Thy beauty's form in table of my heart," sonnet 24 begins; the placing of the beloved in an internal inscription also alludes to the image repertoire provided by *Astrophil and Stella*. Writing is painting when the beloved's *being* is representation and the lover's interiority is a scene of inscription.

Sonnet 122 records the multiplicity of textual inscriptions of character by tracing a path of complex and ambiguous exchanges. The first phrase, "thy gift, thy tables" is an introduction to these opacities. Has the beloved given a gift of a writing tablet, as Stephen Booth imagines?[31] Or has the lover provided an image of himself that is written on an internal writing table – the lover's mind? Is "thy gift" something being given by the beloved or being returned to him? And is that something a blank tablet or an inscribed one? And, if inscribed, written by whom? The appositional structure of "thy gift, thy tables" seems capable of supporting readings that move in two directions at once. This is the circuit of the character, the intertextual situation of the lover and beloved, and their circulation within the exchange structure of the gift. There are no easy answers to the questions of difference (between internal and external tablets, between lover and beloved) raised. "Thy," the very mark of propriety and ownership, slides in these exchanges. The opacity of sonnet 122 doubles the obscurity of the texts it treats, since the poem serves not merely to represent them, but also, to be the writing it describes. Sonnet 122 is not, however, transparently the text in the sonnet that the lover has been emboldened "to give" (line 11). That gift, after all, may be a return of another's text, the one that the beloved has given. What further complicates the situation, as Stephen Booth suggests, is that although the same tablet may be returned by the lover, it may (or may not) be written on, just as, at first, it may or may not have been inscribed. If, at first, "thy gift" is either as "full charactered" (line 2) as the internal tablets (and thus superfluous) or blank (as opposed to the internal tablets), at the end what is given is capable of "poor retention" (line 9), which may mean that it is marked (but fails to match the beloved), but may also mean that it is not yet scored. And, it must also be added, the return of the gift (whether it is the same or another tablet, a blank one or one written upon) may also be the rejection of the gift, its "poor retention" compared invidiously with "full" charactering. In any event, sonnet 122 describes a text that calls into question sameness and difference and that doubles the question in the relationship of the poem to the text it describes. The abundance of possible meanings in the poem is a version of its sustaining deficiency, the impoverishment of character-as-mark that it records twiceover.

Sonnet 122 appears to depend upon the familiar (i.e. platonic) contrasts between internal and external writing and to attempt to preserve interiority from the violence of the letter. These are, however, appearances. Interiority is marked from the beginning by the violent intrusion of the letter, as the first two lines of the poem suggest, however they are read. Interiority, described in the opening quatrain as that which *remains* "beyond all date, even to eternity" (line 4), is a monumental inscription of the sort that appears throughout the sonnets to record *them* as what remains: "Not marble nor the gilded monuments/Of princes shall outlive this pow'rful rime" (sonnet 55, lines 1–2). The inviolability of the mind to the external pressure of the stylus is denied simply by describing the mind as charactered, incised. The "idle rank" (line 3) as easily suggests the host of texts which this celebration (inscribed in the mind) will supplant as it does the idle thoughts that vanish without a trace. It is this throng (the antique books of sonnet 59) that the lover has perused, seeking his inner state. The preservation of the beloved's image in this "full" text both supplants and renews those already written. "I always write of you" (line 9), the lover says in sonnet 76, and thereby "keep invention in a noted weed" (line 6). "Of": the sympathetic dative of the transmission of the letter, from/to; the "noted weed": the device, the garment of style that produces the voice-in-writing. There is nothing to say that does not make "antiquity for aye his page" (sonnet 108, line 12). Whose page? Who is *I*? The interior/eternal text of sonnet 122 is a reiteration-with-a-difference of all that has been written already; the mind is a place prepared beforehand to receive the impression of the character of the beloved.

Eternity is retraced and retracted in the second quatrain of sonnet 122 ("Or, at the very least . . ."); the status of memory and texts as what *remains* replaces the eternal monument – temporality, and with it the present/presence of the text/mind (of "nature," in short), as erosion, erasure, forgetfulness. "Rased oblivion" is the apparent end (Hegelian *telos*) of what remains. That plot, rather than the account leading to full characters and "lasting memory," is substituted as a second thought ("at the very least") that would seem to run concurrently with the first thought. Taken together, the first eight lines of the poem might be said to write and unwrite themselves and yet to write all the while, tracing in their movement the reversibility of "thy gift, thy tables." Time enters in line 5, but only to thematize what has come before. The text described, that "never can be missed" and that will one day be entirely effaced, is, at the same time, the movement of this text. Temporality here, as in Earle's character pad, is a layering of inscription that is also a defacement; sonnet 122 is, in Mulcaster's terms, a quintessential text of prerogative. "Thy record" separates from what it records and seems almost to have in its present what it will not have in its retention. Memory and forgetfulness here are mutually constitutive – a generative corruption – as they are in the forge of Proteus's mind receiving the impression of Silvia's picture. It seems true that both the "record" and the erasure inscribe what "never can be missed."

Hence "that poor retention" (line 9) would appear to refer to *all* inscriptions, whether external or internal, to the tablet presented to or by the lover and to the image of the beloved (the image that he *is* and will, in time, not be, or the image in the mind of the lover). "Poor retention could not so much hold" (line 9), and what is "full charactered" is simultaneously reviewed as a set of incomplete and unnecessary "tallies," markers that score (multiply and cut) and yet do not strike deeply enough to be retained. Hence *they* are given; they are the characters of sonnet 122. The gift returned is a pad whose space of inscription is at the same time a space of erasure. Whether a pad full of tallies is rejected, or whether filling a pad with tallies is rejected, both possibilities – of the written pad and the blank pad – are apparently the same scene of inscription and erosion. In this textual economy, the pad, blank or charactered, appears to be compared to "those tables" retained and receiving "more" even as the gift is returned. Yet, what renders "those tables" impervious to "poor retention"? If they always "receive thee more" can they be "full charactered"? Booth denies this appositional structure of similitude, and suggests that "those tables" are the same as the "tables" of line 1, returned as blanks so that they can be inscribed to "receive thee more." This is a possible reading, certainly; but either way, "more" suggests an excess on the margin of giving and receiving. We have remarked it tracing the return of the letter that Valentine and Silvia enact. The circuit of writing and the circuit of desire reach a destination in sonnet 122 that does not escape recirculation; has the gift been returned to incite the beloved's return? Has he received what the lover wrote – to himself? Has he *emptied* himself to receive more? Or is he giving and yet remaining "full charactered"? These questions go round in circles.

And the concluding couplet is a model of such circularity, for it posits an identification of remembering and forgetting: "To keep an adjunct to remember thee/Were to import forgetfulness in me" (lines 13-14). The adjunct: the mark/character, the writing tablet. To retain the adjunct means that the internal tablet is not full, that there is room there for a further inscription. But inscription, so described, is also the rasing of the (internal) tablet. And hence, the refusal of the adjunct *for the sake of* the integrity of the fully inscribed internal writing pad means that it has been written on – and thereby full – written on, however, by the adjunct that it refuses. Moreover, the adjunct of remembrance produces oblivion. And the oblivion it produces would be imported forgetfulness, not the intrinsic emptiness of the *tabula rasa* which is the locus of the full charactering of the internal writing tablet, the mind. The protestation of integrity in these lines summons up the image of Earle's innocent child with his *tabula rasa* as yet unwritten. Yet, its emptiness is coincident with fullness, as "rasing" a Phoenix is both destroying and creating a new one. Refusing the supplement of the adjunct, the beloved claims to be fully supplied. No need for the letter if he has the letter already written within. If one cannot tell whether this letter (adjunct) is accepted or rejected, received or returned, one can nonetheless say with Lacan that this letter reaches its destination by collapsing sender and receiver, self and other, inside and outside in the play of the signifier, the eroding impressions of supplementary letters.

The scene described in sonnet 122 cannot fail to recall Freud's comparison of the mind to a writing tablet, or Derrida's reading of that text.[32] Seeking an image that would explain the relationships between consciousness (perception) and the unconscious, and the mechanisms (e.g. delay, deferral, repression) that permitted both the retention and effacement of events, or, rather, of the *images* of events perceived or remembered, Freud recalled a child's toy, the "mystic writing pad," composed of a transparent sheet on which one writes, and a wax layer beneath, that stores the impression. When the writing surface is lifted, the marks vanish; they are retained, however, on the wax below. These two surfaces represented, for Freud, the systems of consciousness and the unconscious; their contact and separation explained the relationship of memory and forgetting and their coincidence (what is in the memory is no longer conscious; bringing memory to consciousness is also the obliteration of memory). The "depth" of the mind, in this image, is illusory; depth is also a surface marked by repeated incisions. The more the wax is marked the less easily can the marks be retrieved or deciphered: that is, more memory, more forgetfulness. It is this simultaneity of erasure/obliteration and retention that the Shakespearian character scores; it is also what Derrida remarks: "Traces thus produce the space of their inscription only by acceding to the period of their erasure. From the beginning, in the 'present' of their first impression, they are constituted by the double force of repetition and erasure, legibility and illegibility." The double layering of the mind–of leaf upon leaf–allows for surfaces capable of "poor retention," for a surface that is always ready to receive (and thus blank) which transfers the marks to another surface which retains *and effaces* the marks scored–incised multiply–upon it.

Freud's pad is (for Derrida) a reinscription of the western tradition that goes back to Plato at least. In the *Theaetetus*, for the sake of argument, Socrates invites us to "imagine . . . that our minds contain a block of wax. . . . Let us call it the gift of the Muses' mother, Memory, and say that whenever we wish to remember something we see or hear or conceive in our own minds, we hold this wax under the perceptions or ideas and imprint them on it as we might stamp the impression of a seal-ring" (191d).[33] In "Plato's Pharmacy" or "The Double Session," Derrida's task involves a reading of the platonic scene of writing within the Freudian reinscription. For Freud's image of the mystic pad aims at a solution of critical questions about the relationship between its surfaces, a solution that does not reinscribe platonic metaphysics. As Derrida reads Freud's mystic pad, the fold of these surfaces establishes the 'present' and 'presence' of the mind within the deferral and differentiation of *différance*. The layers are both in contact and separate; to receive the impression of a mark, one must re-mark; "we are written only as we write," Derrida continues. The "we" he means he terms the subject, the I that is a function of (re)inscription. "The 'subject' of writing does not exist if we mean by that some sovereign solitude of the author. The subject of writing is a *system* of relations between strata: the Mystic Pad, the psyche, society, the world."

Derrida extends the mystic pad to the spacing that constitutes the subject in a field of folds: the echoing woods of *silvae* traced on the Shakespearian character. That space, the fold that joins and separates, Lacan marks with a bar, literalizing the algorithmic graph of the linguistic sign relating signifier and signified and, at the same time, separating them: S/s. The subject, for Lacan, "is" on the bar; what linguistics traditionally designates as the "signified" is, for Lacan (and Derrida) another signifier; hence, movement on the bar is a (re)inscription in a chain of signifiers that Lacan's subject (like Derrida's "sovereign...author") cannot master. The Other, in Lacan's system, is that "absolute Master";[34] Derrida understands that designation to imply a metaphysical securing in an absolute lack. Thus, Lacan defines the Other as "the beyond in which the recognition of desire is bound up with the desire for recognition,"[35] a desire that is always frustrated. And he describes "the subjection of the subject to the signifier" as occurring "in the circuit that goes from s(O) to O and back from O to s(O)," where O is the Other and s the subject. "It is from the Other that the subject receives even the message that he emits."[36] Lacan's metaphysical leanings are perhaps as inevitable as those Derrida admits in his deconstructive project,[37] however, and it is worth sidestepping the polemics to notice that the Lacanian chain of recirculation can be compared to Derridean reinscription. On the Shakespearian scene of writing, characters remark each other and are themselves remarked, and their relationships seem to be inscribed within a system that is not their own. The argument of this essay, put simply, is this: from its earliest instances (*Titus Andronicus, The Two Gentlemen of Verona*) to late examples (*Cymbeline*), the inscription of the Shakespearian character throws into question any identification of the *system* with a "sovereign ... author." Lacan's "absolute Master" has many names; the Other is also the Phallus, the *mother's* Phallus, the "name of the Father." Derrida, too, finally locates Freud's scene of writing as a primal scene.[38] At the end of *The Two Gentlemen of Verona*, we recall, Silvia's father himself "subscribes"; Cymbeline calls himself a "mother." What would secure these testaments to the writing of the patriarch in a discourse of an Other who would not also be reinscribed? How could the chain end at "Shakespeare"? What's in a name?

*

No Shakespearian text is more regularly cited to exemplify the supposed interiority of the Shakespearian character than *Hamlet*, while the textual history of the play (the various quarto versions, the length of the folio text) and the thematizing of theatricality within the play are, with equal regularity, taken to show the author's investment within this text. It seems, profitable, therefore, to close this essay on the Shakespearian character with a brief review of this central text. Citation, rather than argument, will, at the least, suggest that *Hamlet* has a place within the echoing of *silvae*.

Polonius speaks to Laertes, offering the traveller advice; "these few precepts in thy memory/Look thou character" (1.3, lines 58-59). Hamlet, as the play opens, is also remembering ("Must I remember?" (1.2, line 143)), and suiting his being to his show; "these indeed seem" (1.2, line 83). His impression is the image within his "mind's eye" (1.2, line 185). The father who writes within Hamlet then puts in his appearance and offers his traveller's advice. His word is "remember me":

> Remember thee?
> Ay, thou poor ghost, while memory holds a seat
> In this distracted globe. Remember thee?
> Yea, from the table of my memory
> I'll wipe away all trivial fond records,
> All saws of books, all forms, all pressures past
> That youth and observation copied there,
> And thy commandment all alone shall live
> Within the book and volume of my brain,
> Unmixed with baser matter. Yes, by heaven!
> O most pernicious woman!
> O villain, villain, smiling, damned villain!
> My tables – meet it is I set it down
> That one may smile, and smile, and be a villain.
> At least I am sure it may be so in Denmark.
> So, uncle, there you are. Now to my word:
> It is 'Adieu, adieu, remember me.'

> (1.5, 95-111)

Hamlet's memory is a theater, the "distracted globe," and a scene for the inscription of character. Remembering is at the same time erasing "all pressures past." For the memory to be supplemented, it must also be supplanted. The mind is a locus of *copia*; it is a book. There is, in

Hamlet's mind, a scene of writing, and it is the one staged with the ghost in this scene of inscription. Hamlet ends this speech by writing what has been scored on his mind; "my tablets–meet it is I set it down." Has he taken out a writing tablet? Or is he still writing on his mind? Would there be a difference? What he writes is the ghost's plot, "pernicious woman," "damned villain." The circuit of writing – from internal to (possibly) external writing – passes through the ghost's words, and to them. Hamlet's word at the end–"my word"–is a quotation. He voices his father's text.

The scene of impression is not, of course, quite this straightforward; it is a circuit. The text in the center of Hamlet's speech – "pernicious woman," "damned villain"–is a scene of desire as old as the scene in the garden. Hamlet, who is "too much in the sun" (1.2, line 67), is divided by the doubling of his "own" text and the ghost's. Hamlet's being is the fold in that single cloth and it is first manifest in his initial utterances, puns on "kin[d]" and "s[o/u]n" that make his voice articulate the spacing of writing. The scene with the ghost is a reinscription of what is already inscribed, and it is horrific precisely because it fulfills Hamlet's desire –he is commanded to be in his father's place, and yet to leave the woman alone. The ghost's words are tantamount to the recognition of the Other that is the very end of desire; the ghost speaks as the name of the father (the father's law is the law of the dead father), himself constrained by a text that he cannot entirely appropriate: "But that I am forbid/To tell the secrets of my prison house/I could a tale unfold . . ." (1.5, lines 13-15). Hamlet is not torn between his "own" desire and the paternal command, but divided within the paternal that writes his desire and in which it is written. Hamlet's divided identity–and with it his delays and deferrals, his resistance to the ghostly plot, his inability to act and his compulsions to repeat–are the result of his *identification* with his father's words. It is identification that splits Hamlet. The depth of his interiority is his foldedness within a text that enfolds him and which cannot be unfolded. "So, uncle, there you are" (1.5, line 110). Thus Hamlet ends the scene of writing, and his reiteration of his father's word as his own follows that inscription.

Hamlet's response to the ghost is to write, and through much of the play that is his activity. It is a writing that takes place within the ghostly text. "Who calls me villain?" (2.2, line 557), he asks, ascribing to himself the ghost's word for his uncle. When Hamlet stages the ghost's script of the murder in the garden, he assigns himself the same part; "This is one Lucianus, nephew to the king" (3.2, line 235), he identifies the villain. The entirely written world of the play makes it a space of endless *copia*, entirely simulacral. "Look here upon this picture, and on this" (3.4, line

99

54); Hamlet draws Gertrude's eyes to the pictures of the two brothers, but cannot make her see the nothing manifest in her closet when the ghost reappears. Hamlet demands that she see difference while he is commanded by spectral identification, the text that has him ask, "How stand I then,/That have a father killed, a mother stained" (4.4, lines 56-57), where "I" stands in the active/ passive position of having being in writing. Being divided by non-being: Hamlet's great question, entirely apt for those whose "kind" is textual. Hamlet saves his life by writing. Shipped to die, his father provides: "How was this sealed?/Why, even in that was heaven ordinant./I had my father's signet in my purse,/ . . . Folded the writ up in the form of th'other,/Subscribed it, gave 't th' impression" (5.2, lines 47-49, 51-52). Hamlet writes his (father's) name with the signet/signature that impresses him. Sealed in that text, he can say, "Let be" (5.2, line 212). Let: stop/permit. Finally, he can, entirely, voice his father's text, speak as a ghost. "I am dead" (5.2, lines 322, 327), he reiterates, the impossible sentence that inscribes voice within the iterability of writing.[39] Like the ghost, Hamlet cannot tell his story, and passes it on to be told, a text to be re-enacted. "The rest is silence" (5.2, line 347). Hamlet's remains.

Silvia's silence. Textually inscribed. Engraved as a statue. Hermione. Within the father's text. Love and be silent. Cordelia.

"I could a tale unfold . . ./But this eternal blazon must not be" (1.5, lines 15, 21). The text spoken in the name of the father.

"Had I but time–as this fell sergeant, Death,/Is strict in his arrest–O, I could tell you–/But let it be" (5.2, lines 325-27). The text spoken in the name of the son.

Character: inscribed/effaced. Signed, sealed, and delivered. The letter's destination, as what remains. Arrested/permitted–"let it be"–by death. The text spoken in the name of the ghost of the sovereign author.

5

The dead letter:
Herbert's other voices

The *phone*

Who is speaking? Roland Barthes's question in *S/Z* seems apt for the texts of *The Temple*.[1] The identity of the 'speaker' of Herbert's poems is, after all, a perennial issue; do these texts transcribe the poet and articulate his faith? Are they, on the other hand, pieces of bad faith, spoken by naive and disowned voices performing a poetic activity simply beside the point of faith? Or are they exercises in poetic investment, exemplary formal acts? Who speaks in Herbert's texts? A self or a *persona*? A lapsing voice or a regenerate one?[2]

These are elementary questions, and the history of the criticism of *The Temple* could be assembled as a set of responses to them. If it were, it would reveal that the criticism of this text has afforded repeated exercises of faith – faith in the theology that the text is said to articulate (high church for some, low church for others); faith in literary expression (high Renaissance formalism for some, plain style for others). Whether the voice is regarded as transparent or opaque, it functions as a veil; the transcendence that it shadows has many names: God; Christ; or, even, the human 'self.' These texts are, in the critics' estimation, always revelations, if not of faith, then of saving ironies. Revelation is always delivered by the voice of these texts, by the supposed tone; from the sounds heard, everything follows.

And if the voice were toneless? And if no one spoke? And if there were no self 'behind' the words? No transcendence beyond the text? No voice but quotation,[3] as in the paradigmatic utterance on the cross, "My God, my God, why hast thou forsaken me?" – the articulation of being disowned cites the psalmist, the opening verse of Psalm 22. What is the tone of a voice in quotation? Can there be a tone if the context of utterance is not merely, never entirely, the immediate situation of speech? Who speaks in quotation? Who owns the words? In the paradigmatic utterance on the cross, disowning is articulated through quotation. And in *The Temple*?[4]

> Thy words do finde me out, & parallels bring,
> And in another make me understood.
>
> (*H. Scriptures II*, 11-12)

I, found by another, understood elsewhere; I, constituted in iteration, in parallels (which never meet). Found and made by other words, in other words. Owned by a disowning appropriation.

And if there were no differences to mark that elsewhere but those same words?

> As when th' heart sayes (sighing to be approved)
> *O, could I love!* and stops: God writeth, *Loved*.
>
> (*A true Hymne*, 19-20)

The heart (internality) speaks; God writes (on the heart). Typographically, speech and writing are identically recorded. The same type of mark for one's own speech and another's writing. The same locus of speech/writing: the (engraved) heart. The origin of speech within is the space God engraves. The heart voices the desire to love God, which God has written on the heart. The answer to the desire to love is the inscription in which no answer is given; the heart cannot voice its desire since it is written within God's. The subject that emerges in the desire to speak is silenced with the answer that records the subject as an inscription in another text. Loved, the subject desires to love. And is ever unable to articulate his own love; only God loves, and his desire is written. "God doth supplie the want" (*A true Hymne*, line 18): God founds the subject in a lack. The subject's words are not his own. God's writing – the subject's words – supply the desire; they supplement it; supplanting it, they maintain it.

Voice in the Herbertian text, these examples suggest, is the representation of God writing, a (dis)owning which locates both God and the subject in a text that is always in quotation marks. Who is writing when "God writeth, *Loved*," if the voice speaking is itself in quotation, already written?[5]

Who is speaking?

> But as I rav'd and grew more fierce and wilde
>   At every word,
> Me thoughts I heard one calling, *Child!*
>   And I reply'd, *My Lord*.
>
> (*The Collar*, 33-36)

Graphic displacement of voice, a final recording of the otherness "at every word," in every word; his "own" words call forth, are called for, by another, whose otherness is rendered proprietary through italicization, which is also how the voice finally owns its response. As other. Which is also how the voice finally owns "every word." As other. Which is, finally, to make manifest the moment of utterance as a present of iteration, a present in which every word of one's own is *at the same time* another's, the re-citation of a subject who has heard as his own thought the call of another. When this voice writes 'I am another,' who is speaking? In what 'present' could such a statement take place? "I rav'd," "I heard," "I reply'd": what is the temporality of that retrospection? What does "I" signify? Or God?[6]

*

Elementary questions. "What is 'meaning,' what are its historical relationships to what is purportedly identified under the rubric 'voice' as a value of presence, presence of the object, presence of meaning to consciousness, self-presence in so called living speech and in self-consciousness?" These are the questions of *Speech and Phenomena*, the text Derrida momentarily forgets in *Positions*, and nonetheless names as the founding text that he would append as a note to *Of Grammatology*, which "refers to it and economizes its development," in an 'economy' that also globalizes "the question of the privilege of the voice and of phonetic writing" raised by Husserlian phenomenology.[7] "In the beginning was the Word": the logocentrism of the Herbertian text–and of its modern readings–can be read in other words in *Of Grammatology*, particularly in its first part, "Writing Before the Letter," the 'historical' argument that precisely by arguing for writing *before* the letter displaces the privilege of the voice, and the historical/teleological plot it inscribes. (Cf. *Prayer (I)*, "Gods breath in man returning to his birth," line 2; notice that in the *second* account of human creation in Genesis, God "breathed into his nostrils the breath of life; and man became a living soul" (2.7), that in the first account, "God created man in his own image, in the image of God" (1.27); visual before verbal, writing before speech? 'original' representation?)

> The privilege of the *phone* does not depend upon a choice that could have been avoided. It responds to a moment of *economy* (let us say of the 'life' of 'history' or of 'being as self-relationship'). The system of 'hearing (understanding)-oneself-speak' through the phonic substance – which *presents itself* as the nonexterior, nonmundane, therefore nonempirical or noncontingent signifier – has necessarily dominated the history of the world during an entire epoch, and has even produced the idea of the world, the

idea of world-origin, that arises from the difference between the worldly and the non-worldly, the outside and the inside, ideality and nonideality, universal and nonuniversal, transcendental and empirical, etc.

(*Of Grammatology*, 7-8)

"The letter killeth, but the spirit giveth life" (2 Cor:3.6).

These are elementary, founding remarks. At most, at this point, they can be remarked further in a reading that unravels the implications of their economy, and that can then go on to weave the Herbertian text within their seams.

"The privilege of the *phone*." Derrida presents this as a necessity that is not an accident of history, rather a product of a conception of history and consciousness that has dominated western thought from its inception. "Voice . . . has a relationship of essential and immediate proximity with the mind" (11) in this system of thought.[8] In the beginning was the Word, manifest in speech, in spirit, in breath, in the soul. "Christian creationism and infinitism . . . appropriate the resources of Greek conceptuality" (13), the metaphysical foundation of the world and the self in a conception of presence, fullness, life. Breath is Being, nonphysical, transcendent. Ideas in the mind of God made manifest in the world, history their unfolding; ideas in the mind of man made manifest in voice, speech their articulation: such is the homology of breath and Being. The human experience of having an idea amounts to a feeling of an internality, an inhabitation of mind that offers itself as the immediacy and intimacy of a voice; we speak our minds. The intimate experience of intellection is an assurance of our being (*cogito ergo sum*); that there is no distance between our thoughts and ourselves carries the conviction of identity. When we speak our minds, we say, if nothing else, I am, I am myself. The fullness of the self is carried on the breath, our lives articulated. But more: breath is a spiritual substance, ideas are not material, voice is the sounding of an interior silence. We are inhabited by a voice; it speaks our ideas. Recall Socrates. Remember that Jesus spoke. "It is not by chance that the thought of being, as the thought of this transcendental signified, is manifested above all in the voice" (20).

"The system of 'hearing (understanding)-oneself-speak'." Derrida formulates the system in this portmanteau conception, coining a single word for the root conception. And, immediately, a gap is opened within immediacy, and self-presence and proximity begin to appear problematic. How do we represent immediacy, if not by a spacing and an overlapping? Is there not, even within immediacy, a temporalization? Is there not, even within identification, difference? Hearing (understanding): the same word in French (*entendre*); and the same meaning? The translation into English suggests not. And when I hear myself speak does not a space open between the I hearing and the self speaking? Does not a gap appear between the internality of hearing and the externality of speaking? And does it not even invade internality? Whose voice do I hear within? "The phonic substance – which *presents itself* ": presence is, in Derrida's formulation, a presentation, indeed, a representation. It represents itself as immateriality, spirit, proximity, presence; but it comes on a substance (breath), and with the density of a materiality that occludes immediacy. There is, within voice, a spacing in its presentation and a temporalization. For voice to be understood, it must be articulated; it requires time, not immediacy. It is never already there all at once. Derrida's portmanteau conception – his articulation of the privilege of the *phone* – represents the concept as always already inscribed within a system of terms that refuse coincidence and immediacy. For this "always already," Derrida has many words; in *Of Grammatology, différance, trace, supplement*.

This is an elementary deconstruction of the privilege of the *phone*. What remains? To see that the differences raised by this privileging are already inscribed within voice. The oppositions (worldly/nonworldly, physical/spiritual, transcendental/empirical, internal/external, etc.) inhabit voice, and rob it of its privilege and priority. Differences do not come from voice – it is not a transcendent origin; differences are within voice. But the very relationship of difference is involved in this identification; difference is, thus, also deferred; hence, *différance*. Immediacy is also secondarity (*supplement*). Presence is also a lack (*trace*). Or, to say this all in a single word; what remains is writing.

For the privilege of the *phone* is rooted in the opposition of voice and writing, where writing has the status of a purely external mark, an entirely physical substance, parasitically dependent upon the voice that it represents inadequately and corruptly. To reverse this opposition and find writing within voice does not privilege writing, except strategically. That is: writing does not have the metaphysical investment of voice. Its "presence" within speech does not install some new transcendental signified. From Plato on, western metaphysics has been haunted by the metaphor of an internal writing. In the Bible, the account of creation is troubled with a supplementary recounting. Deconstruction performs the critical act of recording and remarking these suppressed materials, not, however, to claim them as the truth of western thought – but to throw that truth, and the ability to make such claims, into question. Which means, that in a certain sense, deconstruction must itself be limited by the system that it shakes, for it offers nothing in its place. Which is not to say that it is nihilistic (for that would be to offer nothing as something). The strategic reversals of deconstruction also refuse the hierarchizing privileging that would allow for the reversal to signal a reprioritization. Hence, Derrida writes such terms as "archetrace" which both reinscribe writing within western metaphysics and shake the differences upon which its stands. If writing is the other of voice, there is no Other of the other. Which means that voice is divested of its privilege and reinvested within a writing which retains its unprivileged status. And has also thrown into question the metaphysical basis for the status which it retains.

What remains, then? A certain (not unproblematic) materiality, a literalism, even. For, if the privilege of the *phone* inscribes the difference signifier/signified, only signifiers remain, when the *phone* is deconstructed. "Writing is not a sign of a sign, except if one says it of all signs" (43). A literalism, then, if signs only refer to other signs and never transcend the process of signifying, never, that is, pass from the sign to the signified because the signified is itself a signifier. A materiality, then, unsupported by metaphysics, a certain embodiment: "writing, the letter, the sensible inscription, has always been considered by western tradition as the body and matter external to the spirit, to breath, to speech, and to the logos. And the problem of soul and body is no doubt derived from the problem of writing from which it seems–conversely–to borrow its metaphors" (35). But if one deconstructs Plato's and St. Paul's metaphors, their oppositions of body (letter) and spirit, signifier and signified, writing remains as an outside that has been brought inside.

> That the signified is originally and essentially (and not only for a finite and created spirit) trace, that it is *always already in the position of the signifier*, is the apparently innocent proposition within which the metaphysics of the logos, of presence and consciousness, must reflect upon writing as its death and its resource.
>
> (73)

Original, essential, always already: Derrida writes these words having put in play the metaphysical foundations that secure them. Writing Being under erasure, all terms are similarly effaced. Marks remain – hence, writing as death and resource. "The trace is not more ideal than real, not more intelligible than sensible, not more a transparent signification than an opaque energy and *no concept of metaphysics can describe it*" (65). There is no *proper* way to say this, for there is no way to be in language, nor is there anywhere else to be. Western metaphysics is the "*metaphysics of the proper*" (26), the inscription of difference (inside/outside, self/other, etc.), the marking of boundaries that insure ownership, that allow for one's interiority, for the proximities of voice. And that *disallow* materiality, externality any function but the errant transcription of spiritual essence. "The letter killeth, but the spirit giveth

106

life": the function of the dead letter, its inscription in the book, is to point to the transcendental signified; meaning is referential. The book is secured in voice, logocentrism is phonocentrism. In the reversal signalled by the Derridean writing before the letter, this system is remarked; its metaphysical foundations founder. The dead letter remains animating voice-in-citation, voice as a (dis)possessed otherness.

*

And to return to Herbert, his voice, and its recording within other voices, other texts: to see that such conceptions as the author, the ownership of voice, or the transcendent Being of the Other that so often enters Herbert's verse must be called into question. The poems so explicitly thematize the divestment of self and of authorship – raising, thereby, for modern criticism the problem of the location of Herbert in relationship to texts that he seems willing to disown, and yet continues to produce – that it is particularly the status of the voice and writing of the Other that is in question. It is the argument here that there are only other voices in Herbert's text, and that they are always explicitly represented as written, that Herbert identifies "his" writing as the recording of those voices, that this is, then, a further divestment–and investment in writing, but precisely a writing that cannot be owned. God does not "really" speak in Herbert's texts except in the way that God has spoken: in the texts that represent his voice. God exists only in writing. In the dead letter. An otherness without transcendence. Literally.

The texts that we call Herbert's record the voice of a subject, of one saying I. But as Benveniste has argued, that is no proprietary mark. In "The Death of the Author," Barthes reiterates Benveniste's argument and applies it to the author: "Linguistically, the author is never more than the instance writing, just as *I* is nothing other than the instance saying *I*: language knows a 'subject,' not a 'person' . . . ."[9] The existence of the author is in "his" writing, and it is Barthes's argument that only the reader of the text can give life to the author, that when the author has given himself over to the text he no longer is, except in the text. Barthes's argument requires the further contextualization of Michel Foucault's "What is an Author?" for Barthes writes in opposition to the classic notion of the author that Foucault articulates, the author, that is, produced by a certain way of reading and within a particular historical situation. As Foucault says, the author is always a function of the text, and, classically, a name applied to a body of texts to signify their unity and propriety; at a certain point, when property defines the nature of the self, when copyright safeguards the text as the author's property, the author emerges as one whose existence is the transcendental guarantee for his texts.[10]

107

It is that sovereign author whose death Barthes, and Foucault (and Derrida) proclaim. And that sovereign author *has yet to be born* in Herbert (or in Spenser or Shakespeare) – except in the hands of his twentieth-century critics.

Who is speaking? Roland Barthes's question in *S/Z*, and his call to "de-originate the utterance" (21) in the classic text, where voice always appears to have an origin – appears, indeed, to secure the very notion of origin – is answered by the voice of the castrato in Balzac's text. Voice in *S/Z* gives access to that broken body, site of desire and its death: the voice of the text communicates castration. And in Herbert? The voice – dissolved in other voices – speaks in the broken body of Christ. His death is inscribed on the speaker's heart, as the text he voices.[11] Herbert's texts record the voice of conscience, an internal scene of inscription. "The voice is *heard* (understood) – that undoubtedly is what is called conscience" (*Of Grammatology*, 20); but what is heard is seen. Indeed, a primal scene. Freud speculates on the nature of a watching institution that secures narcissistic gratification despite the castration complex; it is, he writes, "what we call our *conscience*." "Patients . . . complain that all their thoughts are known and their actions watched and overlooked; they are informed of the functioning of this mental institution by voices which characteristically speak to them in the third person ('Now she is thinking that again' . . .)." This condition, Freud continues, "exists with every one of us in normal life," although we are not all paranoids; for that voice we hear is a parental one.[12]

Herbert may write I, but his I is in the position of subjection; the *object* of scrutiny. He writes I as the paranoid says he. The delusion of the voice within is transcribed, materialized in the text to be seen, the text which simulates the delusion of being seen. The parental voice brings the child into civilization by installing the watching institution of conscience – conscience means a corporate knowledge (knowing with); this moment marks the child's entrance into language which enters the child. This is the founding moment of the subject in what Lacan calls the symbolic; it is the moment coincident with the castration complex. The narcissistic gratification of the text lies in its retrospective disowning of the I and its replacement in the broken body of Christ. This is the Herbertian version of Echo and Narcissus. "The voice is *heard* (understood) – that undoubtedly is what is called conscience – closest to the self as the absolute effacement of the signifier: pure auto-affection" (*Of Grammatology*, 20). Absolute effacement of the signifier 'I' in the body of the text that is the writing of the Other.

As in *Coloss. 3:3. Our life is hid with Christ in God*, where written across the text is a sentence that writes over the text, inscribing a "double motion" (line 2), a scene of reading that is a double session, a writing under erasure, crossed over. "*My* words & thoughts" (line 1) are already written; voice is text. What remains to be asked is what it means to rewrite the already written book. As in this elementary (re)transcription – a spelling of the elements that are the death and resource of the Herbertian text:

For ye are dead, and your life is hid with Christ in God.   (Coloss. 3:3)

"*My/Life/Is/Hid/In/Him/That/Is/My/Treasure.*"   (*Coloss. 3:3*).

The book

Western culture dreams the book as the total embodiment of the word, the book (either as opacity or transparency) secured by an ultimate referent, the beginning word. As any number of critical studies might demonstrate, Herbert is the writer of the book, and the order and unity of *The Temple* is a recurring problem. For to critics who assume the book–within logocentric suppositions–*The Temple* is problematic. We do not know how to read his book, for it does not secure words within the structures we recognize (beginning, middle, and end; sequence).[13] Critics who despair of describing the elusive structure of the book settle for explications of individual poems. Literary journals are full of readings of Herbert's lyrics. These, too, cannot succeed. For there is no poem within *The Temple* that does not echo against other poems; no reading of an individual poem can account for all the echoes, nor would an attempt to construct a gloss to catch every echo produce the single poem. Echoes would multiply, refusing the coherence of critical designs. The totality of *The Temple* would remain as the critical question.

(The dream of the book. God speaks, and the prophet writes down all the words. The tablets are shattered. And God *writes* them anew. Another dream of the book: to write the first book when the second book is already written; to write the immediacy of transcription. Original writing. To (re)write the shattered tablets. To write the disruption of the (second) book, the Bible. To write an original secondarity. The book before the book that is no book. This dream of the book (*The Temple*) is the end of the book and the beginning of writing.)

The title page:

THE

TEMPLE.

Sacred Poems

and

Private Eja-
culations.

———————

By Mr. George Herbert.

———————

Psal. 29.

*In his Temple doth every
man speak his honour.*

———————

What are the relationships between these items? Are sacred poems the same as private ejaculations or different?[14] Public, institutional writing and private utterance: but are not both exteriority *and* interiority on the page? Ejaculation, a figure for utterance as the spurting forth of seed and fluid: a space of dissemination. What is the relationship between the name of the author – produced by the title – and the text below, surely a sacred poem not by Mr. Herbert? Does citation secure the author's identity . . . by disowning authorship? What does "by" mean? – by way of, through, beside? What is the relationship between the title and the citation of "his Temple" that passes "by" the author's name? Where is "THE TEMPLE"? In the space of the reiterated word on the title page? "His Temple" every man's? *Speaking* whose honor? An *interiority* where every man speaks the *exteriority* of this page? Could the title be a restatement of the quotation with its joining of sacred and private (profane?), written and spoken? Or does the title, passing through the name of the author, produce the quotation? Is the quotation, then, not only a sacred text but, when removed from its context to this context, also an ejaculation? What, on this page, is *not* in citation? What happens between the lines? A literal question about the movement of the letter and the being of the book.

   (Or is the title page a scene of masturbation? Narcissistic encounter with the ideal other, a voice become a text, a scenario? Gloss the ejaculation: "We are shooters both" (*Artillerie*, line 25); "And ev'n my verse, when by the ryme and reason/The word is, *Stay*, sayes ever, *Come*"

(*Home*, lines 75-76). A scene of scattered seed, shooting stars, and the ejaculative traces of a forestalled and productive path: how to enter the temple, how to be on the page, where the words stay, yet nonetheless come.[15])

The title page (concluded):

----

*

CAMBRIDGE:

Printed by *Thom. Buck,*
and *Roger Daniel,* printers
to the Universitie.
1633.

"*The Printers to the Reader.*" follows. The graphic convention of assigning words elsewhere – italicization – extends to the names of the printers, whose proprietariness is further dispersed in their university origin, and extended to the title of their letter to the reader. And when, in 1641, Buck and Daniel dissolved their partnership, the heading drops the character 's', but the letter remains unchanged. An elementary demonstration of the (im)propriety of authorship? And, as the author slides into the printers' address, should we recall the likelihood that this letter to the readers was composed by Nicholas Ferrar? How is the author inscribed in the book? The printers' letter suggests an answer since, in many respects, it rehearses the title page with its problems of interiority and exteriority, privacy and the publicity of print; for example, by suggesting first that the true reader (the ideal spectator) of the text is God, and then by putting the reader in his place, thus offering to make the reader "privie" to a life of Herbert as remarkable for its "private devotions" as its public service, a life lived in "the Sanctuarie and Temple of God." The space of the temple remains the critical issue and with it questions of the propriety of writing and authorship. As in what follows:

> As for those inward enforcements to this course (for outward there was none) which many of these ensuing verses bear witnesse of, they detract not from the freedome, but adde to the honour of this resolution in him. As God had enabled him, so he accounted him meet not onely to be called, but to be compelled to this service.

The printers' pages are so entirely a resowing of the seeds of the title page that the life they write is, like the one Herbert wrote – *A Priest to the Temple, Or, The Countrey Parson His Character* – entirely of a textual character.[16] A life and a text as moveable as type, that is; a resowing of characters. The "witnesse" of "ensuing verses" – as if texts were readers – might gloss the "inward enforcements" of this account, as if the interiority of character were an inscription. Witness, for example, *The Odour* (the poem in which Walton read Herbert's conversion):[17] "How sweetly doth *My Master* sound! *My Master*/ . . . when *My Master* . . . /Shall call and meet,/*My servant*, as thee not displeasing,/That call is but the breathing of the sweet" (lines 1, 21, 23-25). Intercalate that ensuing text with what ensues in the printers' letter:

> To testifie his independencie upon all others, and to quicken his diligence in this kinde, he used in his ordinarie speech, when he made mention of the blessed name of our Lord and Saviour Jesus Christ, to adde, *My Master*.

Note the echoes. Interiority is the supplementary addition to speech (written, for example, in *The Odour*) that insures the freedom of the page; as in the play of "call and meet" ("he accounted him meet not onely to be called"), or the compulsive iteration of "*My Master*" or "sweet." Living a life, even merely breathing, takes place in the reglossing of words that circulate through the printers' text – which is, of course, Herbert's text, which is, of course, the text from Psalm 29 that *is inserted* in this textual play.

> The voice of the Lord maketh the hinds to calve,
> and discovereth the forests:
> and in his temple doth every one speak of his glory.
>
> (Psalm 29.9)

The printers' gloss:

> Next God, he loved that which God himself hath magnified above all things, that is, his Word: so as he hath been heard to make solemne protestation, that he would not part with one leaf thereof for the whole world, if it were offered him in exchange.

The "whole world" is the Word; the "forests" an echo chamber of *silvae*, the "leaf" that he would not part with. "His temple" (whose?) is the book. A space entirely of writing: as in *The Temple*, with its hieroglyphics which embody words on a page because there is nothing except the text. The text of generation, calving hinds – private ejaculations; the text of echo, discovering forests – leaves against leaves, leaves that do not leave (cf. *Heaven*).[18] How to magnify the word? Repeat it, re-cite it, re-plant it, a sowing without end that never goes beyond the printed page, that refuses the world or lived experience. That says "*My Master*," a quotation that is a substitution, writing words in another's mouth. Magnify and therefore diminish – and thus write the scattered text, the shattered tablets. The disowned seed.

112

Whose Psalm 29 is disseminated through the title page and printed address? The title page quotes neither the King James version (cited above), nor those provided in the Bishops' Bible or the Sternhold and Hopkins version:

> The voyce of God maketh hindes to cast their calfe, and maketh woods to be bare: therefore every man setteth foorth his glory in his temple.
>
> (1568 Bishops' Bible)

> It makes the Hindes for feare to calve,
> and makes the covert plaine:
> Then in his Temple every man
> his glory doth proclaime.
>
> (*The Psalmes of David in Meetre* (1605))

The generativity of the word: collate the texts of Psalm 29. Is revelation making the hidden (privacy) plainly visible? Or effacing, baring the visible? Discovery: uncovering, inventing? Bearing (calving) and baring (casting) as the space of *silva*, or *The Temple*, where "every man" (typographical substitution) speaks his *honour*. (Is there a text of Psalm 29?) Speaks by setting forth – in the visibility of type? Is this the license of his "honour," the title page substitute for "his glory"? So the printers write, claiming that the witnessing verses "adde to the honour of this resolution in him." And they continue by telling another honorable resolution, his earnest desire to resign the worldliness of "an Ecclesiaticall dignitie. . . . But God permitted not the accomplishment of this desire." The father's no (the *nom de père*) as the freedom of his additional, supplemental honor.[19] The license to turn a verse, to scatter the already written seed. Staying and coming at once. The freedom of denial.

The printers end – in citation, with Herbert's motto: "*Lesse then the least of Gods mercies*"; itself a re-citation: "I am not worthy of the least of all the mercies, and of all the truth, which thou hast showed unto thy servant" (Gen. 32:10), Jacob's words before he became Israel, as he received the promise of the multiplication of his seed. Followed by *The Dedication.*: "*Lord, my first fruits present themselves to thee;/Yet not mine neither: for from thee thy came,/And must return*" (lines 1-3).

"The system of 'hearing (understanding)-oneself-speak' through the phonic substance – which *presents itself*" (*Of Grammatology*, 7). Self-presentation as re-presentation of the already written, already written in the circuit of return in which the re-presenter takes the priority of an initial secondarity.

A disowning, "lesse then the least"; a magnification of the space of the text, its generativity; a supplementation that posits a loss in the prior text (God supplies the lack), that supplants the voice with the written word; that rewrites and scatters scripture. The struggle with the angel to have a name. "*And make us strive, who shall sing best thy name*" (*The Dedication*, line 4). A strife for voice that is decided on the page: "*Turn their eyes hither, who shall make a gain*" (line 5). Turn: metamorphosis. Strophic strife. The scene of writing. The primal scene. Echo and Narcissus.

The text given to the reader's hand, and eye, to "*make a gain*," invited supplementation, ejaculation, dissemination. And a warning to "*Theirs* [their eyes], *who shall hurt themselves or me, refrain*" (*Dedication*, line 6). Refrain: restrain, the bridle of reiterated versing. The space of speculation, contemplation: where author and reader meet, dangerously, violently. A temple, etymologically, an open space. For expenditure without gain: scattered seed. The turn and the refrain circulate the fruit of the word on the page, the spacing and articulation of *The Temple*.

*

Thus, *The Church-porch* opens, rewriting *The Dedication*:

> Thou, whose sweet youth and early hopes inhance
> Thy rate and price, and mark thee for a treasure;
> Hearken unto a Verser, who may chance
> Ryme thee to good, and make a bait of pleasure.
>> A verse may finde him, who a sermon flies,
>> And turn delight into a sacrifice.
>
> (1-6)

Lines that require the glossing of "sweet" (start with *Vertue* or *The Odour*; no telling where to cease),[20] the treasure written into *Coloss. 3:3*, the poetics of Horace and Sidney and Spenser, Ovidian metamorphosis, figurative troping, *The Sacrifice*, etc. These "mark" the page, the character of youth, and offer an invitation to promiscuous glossing immediately denied (the word is stay), and rewritten in the stanza that comes next:

> Beware of lust: it doth pollute and foul
> Whom God in Baptisme washt with his own blood.
> It blots the lesson written in thy soul;
> The holy lines cannot be understood.
>> How dare those eyes upon a Bible look,
>> Much lesse towards God, whose lust is all their book?
>
> (7-12)

To ward off the disseminative dispersal of the first stanza, the second recommends an internal reading lesson, a restoral of the innocency of an unblotted and already written page. An innocence, however, that seems coincident with auto-affection, eyes turned inward upon a writing

114

that produces the Bible–even God–within the space of a scopic desire, "whose lust is all their book," a desire, that is, that never escapes the page.

The marks of the Herbertian book occupy the space of this rewriting, and are produced under the impression of a forbidden desire. The voice of the first stanza of *The Church-porch* becomes the writing of the second, an original effaced impression, effaced by the very desire solicited by the initial stanza. The way "in" (to the self, to the book) is virtually barred. As it is, graphically, in the next invitation, the next set of instructions of the way "into" the book, the SUPERLIMINARE between *The Church-porch* and *The Altar,* a text *over* a doorway, marked (in the 1633 edition) by a line dividing the stanzas, a graphic threshold. (In the 1674 edition, the line is literally a threshold, and a doorway is traced around the edges of the stanzas; a typographical recognition of the claims of *The Temple* that all the world is the space of its writing.)[21] Above the bar, the invitation–come, "approach, and taste" (line 3); below the bar, "Avoid," stay.

Entrance "into" *The Temple* takes place on such a graphic line, as elegantly diagrammatic as the patterned poems that follow, suggesting that the text is whatever might be meant by space–or, when we arrive at THE CHURCH MILITANT, time. A line comparable to the Lacanian algorithmic notation, S/s, where the bar signifies the blockage of desire, the impossibility of signifier becoming signified, and thus the graphic track along which desire moves. A productive blockage. "No signification can be sustained other than by reference to another signification," Lacan writes in "The Agency of the Letter in the Unconscious."[22] Under the aegis of the Other, the speaker voices a desire that cannot be owned, in words that are already written. As in the anonymous voice of a SUPERLIMINARE, the voice of a space, a voice to be seen. The bar blocks and marks the space of an entrance not into an interiority, but onto the graphic trace. A space which enforces its understanding (literally) on the reader, invited, barred, re-invited: a perilous entrance under the violent impress of the letter:

> Avoid Profanenesse; come not here:
> Nothing but holy, pure, and cleare,
> Or that which groneth to be so,
> May at his perill further go.
>
> (SUPERLIMINARE, 5-8)

No coming here, no profaneness, except in the wiping clear of the inner tablet, the receipt of the bloody impression; inseminative birth of a page. Being only on the page, marked, barred, the baring of an internal scene violated by, delivered as, exteriority and supplementarity–the beyond the limit (superliminarie) of the limit (the bar, the line – of verse, wherever written). The space of *The Temple*, the writing, literally, of the dispersed book. Written by whom? "No workmans tool hath touch'd the same" (*The Altar*, line 4). Unmarked (blank) marks: ejaculations that "come not here," a "broken ALTAR" reared as the space of an inscription, cut, "whose parts are as thy hand did frame" (*The Altar*, line 3). The stone text (the tablets on which all the world is written; the tablets broken by writing; the text that generates the world as a space of inscription; recall Niobe). The black marks of the page represent the cuts, the bars, the negations and denials that produce the text of the Other – that make the space of *The Temple* God writing. They are the way "into" the text, the path our eyes follow as we make our way through its temporal/spatial articulation. They offer us a supplementary scene of auto-affection that never stains the page.

("As soon as writing, which entails making a liquid flow out of a tube onto a piece of white paper, assumes the significance of copulation, or as soon as walking becomes a symbolic substitute for treading upon the body of mother earth, both writing and walking are stopped because they represent the performance of a forbidden sexual act.")[23]

"Approach . . . Avoid." "God doth supplie the want" (*A true Hymne*, line 18): *The Altar* is raised on the page; graphically displacing the cut and bar, it manifests what was written on the heart before the heart was broken, a writing on stone before the tablets were shattered; it is God writing: "O let thy blessed SACRIFICE be mine,/And sanctifie this ALTAR to be thine" (*The Altar*, lines 15-16). *The Sacrifice* (whose?) follows. A *Clasping of hands*: "O be mine still! still make me thine!/Or rather make no Thine and Mine!" (lines 19-20). Writing that prior text, the hand is held – restrained – to disseminate. Writing within the father's name, the script on the heart/stone: writing the scene of writing, the forbidden scene.

*

The path broken in these various entrances into *The Temple* – the title page, the printers' address, *The Church-porch*, SUPERLIMINARE, *The Altar* – presents a circuit for reading/writing that cannot be covered, an endless itinerary that would defeat any critical attempt to master the book, or to stop its significances in an ultimate referent. All references return us to the page as the productive stone of a repeated inscription. We can, at least, note the thematizing of this path in the lines of the text, taking, for example, this citation as a witness to the way: "Thy word is all, if we could spell" (*The Flower*, line 21). If we could decipher the word, spell it into its elemental characters, "learn/To spell his elements"

(*Church-monuments*, lines 7-8), we would come to the master word, the already written rewritten here. "If" names the condition of the impossibility of the arrival at ultimate signification, and returns us to a text that approaches that condition through its appropriation of/by the already written. This is the elementary spelling lesson of *JESU*, for example, that "Jesu is in my heart. . ./deeply carved" (lines 1-2); that the broken letters are words, that words are his name. The letter, then, by being broken, is "graved"(line 6), made into the dead letter that generates; reassembled and "whole" (line 10), the letters spell a "proper name" written elsewhere – on the page, engraved on the stone heart, disseminated in the scene of the writing of the broken proper name. Even Jesus, we recall, was caught in citation.[24]

"Jesu" is the name of the activity of writing-in-quotation, the mark of the impropriety of one's own (cf. *The Holdfast* with its dissolve of voices); his is the master name for the principle of mastery by the Other, the signifier that generates signifiers in a writing that has no end. "There is no articling with thee:/I am but finite, yet thine infinitely" (*Artillerie*, lines 31-32); "Thou didst at once thy self indite,/And hold my hand, while I did write" (*Assurance*, lines 29-30). Such is the assurance of *The Temple*, that immediately ("at once") in a present that once was, a writing took place, a writing that was also forestalled (held back). The writing of *The Temple* is situated in that dead present, in the already written, yet to be written moment: the time of the text, where whatever is, is. "But how then shall I imitate thee, and/Copie thy fair, though bloudie hand?" (*The Thanksgiving*, lines 15-16); "Since bloud is fittest, Lord, to write/. . ./My heart hath store, write there, where in/One box doth lie both ink and sinne" (*Good Friday*, lines 21, 23-24). The lifeblood of ink and sin, promiscuously spilled on a page written by another, a page of simulation and *copia* that writes the death of the proper. ("For ye are dead, and your life is hid with Christ in God." [Coloss. 3:3]) "Their storie pennes and sets us down" (*The Bunch of Grapes*, line 11). *The Temple* (re)writes *The H. Scriptures*:

> This verse marks that, and both do make a motion
>   Unto a third, that ten leaves off doth lie.
>
> (II, 5-6)

The marks, scattered leaves; the path of dissemination, the scene of auto-affection:

> Ladies, look here; this is the thankfull glasse,
> That mends the lookers eyes: this is the well
>   That washes what it shows.
>
> (I, 8-10)

117

The purified pool of Narcissus; the reader(s) as the echoes of the scene.

> Wert thou not born among the trees and leaves?
>> *Echo.*   Leaves.
>
> And are there any leaves, that still abide?
>> *Echo.*   Bide.
>
> What leaves are they? impart the matter wholly.
>> *Echo.*   Holy.
>
> Are holy leaves the Echo then of blisse?
>> *Echo.*   Yes.
>
>   (*Heaven*, 5-12)

Heaven is an echo chamber of *silvae*, the holy leaves of these pages, with their spacing and what they impart. Leaves are what remain – the traces of the original marks, cuts – in the simulation of word from word, of voice from text. The simulation of the space of writing, the regained priority of the original simulation – the priority of the image and of writing before speech, the scene of writing (at first – at once) reiterated:

> Yet Lord restore thine image, heare my call:
>   And though my hard heart scarce to thee can grone,
>   Remember that thou once didst write in stone.
>   (*The Sinner*, 12-14)

> And as of old the Law by heav'nly art
> Was writ in stone; so thou, which also art
> The letter of the word, find'st no fit heart
>   To hold thee.
>   (*Sepulchre*, 17-20)

Instead, "the letter of the word," a supplementary being, finds the page that holds it, coming and staying.

The Bag

To read an individual lyric within this context: an impossible project, for the activity of spelling the letters would lead to their endless respelling, something suggested as well by the final poem of *The Temple*, THE CHURCH MILITANT with its projection of a futurity that is a circularity, a cancellative progress. If we open *The Bag* now, it cannot be with the attempt to close it, or to produce a closed reading of the poem. Rather, to demonstrate, in a text that thematizes many of the issues of writing that have engaged the discussion thus far, some of their consequences for reading.[25] A reading, then, that situates this text as if on a threshold, staying and coming on the line beyond which, into which, there is no passing. Caught within the father's no.

And to ask, once more, who is speaking? To answer, again, that the text is written, and that writing comes before speech. That the writing of *The Bag* is a writing before and in "the letter of the word." To spell these elements in their dissemination, and, thereby, to demarcate the materiality and literalism of the letter as the space of the text. The space of echo, the mirror of Narcissus, the engraved stone. The dead letter and its other voices, the simulation of the Other.

*

Away despair! my gracious Lord doth heare.
  Though windes and waves assault my keel,
  He doth preserve it: he doth steer,
  Ev'n when the boat seems most to reel.
  Storms are the triumph of his art:
Well may he close his eyes, but not his heart.

(1-6)

The opening line is an interruption, or continuation, to be read immediately within, at the least, the context of a sequence. Thus, *Longing*, immediately before, ends with the repeated call, "heare." If *The Bag* opens with the assurance that the call has been heard, it does so, however, in a manner that breaks such smooth continuity. The call of the heart of *Longing* is now (if the poems are continuous) renamed despair. But, the assurance of being heard now means that the voice must cease, despair must "away" because someone else ("my gracious Lord") hears. Whoever is speaking in *The Bag*, it is not the voice of *Longing*, except insofar as that voice – of desire, longing – longs for a belonging that it lacks (a longing for its own) and has (in being the articulation of an Other).[26] A dissolve of voices, then, in the continuity and break of this opening line, and within the line itself. For the social scene of that line posits a speaker who is not "his" despair nor his "gracious Lord," although he, too, seems to be represented as a hearer, not a speaker.

The opening in which that voice is (dis)located is graphically displayed by the indented text, which J. Max Patrick has read as the space of the heart in which the poem finally arrives.[27] In the first stanza, the syntactic marks allow the middle, indented lines to be read as a parenthesis between two independent statements. What is the circuit from hearing to the heart? Why does it pass through the scene of the storm? The "air" of "despair" dispersed in wind? (Cf. *The Storm*). A crossing of the Red Sea? *The Tempest*? Although the final closing of the eyes/opening of the heart would seem to be written within the circuit of "hearing (understanding)" and the immediacy and interiority of feeling/experience, the indented lines – as metaphoric extension, logical break, allusive images – impose an exteriority on this inner scene. The open heart receives what the eyes refuse; indeed, if the heart is a scene of writing, then the eyes closed upon exteriority are open upon interiority.[28] Interiority encloses exteriority as it does in the indented form of the stanza. The outside is the inside.

Between speaking and hearing a space is opened; hearing precludes speaking; hearing is the receiving of an impression. "Hast thou not heard, that my Lord JESUS di'd" (line 7), the second stanza begins. Who is speaking? and, to whom? To one, presumably, who has not heard, and thus still speaks? Is the voice of the first stanza, then, the voice of despair that has not heard its dismissal? Does, therefore, some voice other than the one of the first stanza now enter the poem? Or does despair enter, to answer that the Lord said to hear (in line 1) is, in fact, dead? Or, is the Lord of this line – the dead Lord – the same as the Lord that hears? Or, is the line spoken to him, to hear the death of this other Lord? Or, spoken to anyone in the position of hearing – for example, the reader? These questions play within the space of the opening within voice; an opening that could also be described as the displacement and replacement of the initial line, resituating its terms, respelling its elements.

From this opening, a speaker emerges to tell a story: "Then let me tell thee a strange storie" (line 8). Strange: foreign, not his own. The voice that emerges derives its authority (if it has any) from telling what has been told already, telling another's story, and telling it as strange/estranged.[29] A story outside the interiority of telling. "What verse/Can thy strange wayes rehearse?" (*Miserie*, lines 65-66); "He did descend, undressing all the way" (*The Bag*, line 12). The "way" described in *The Bag*: the story of the death of Christ, told as the story of, at once, creation (the descent of light) and incarnation. At once, the present of storytelling tells three stories at one time, an equivocal telling in which words require respelling; e.g. he "resolv'd to light" (line 11) = he dissolved into light (Let there be light); he decided to descend to earth (he was born; he died); he dissolved into (im)materiality, discarding/clothing. Making and unmaking the way. The "way" = the manifestations of the word as the world of traces, effaced tracks. The dissolving/resolving elements of the word/world. The being of the seen; the word makes visibility. "And when they ask'd, what he would wear;/He smil'd and said as he did go,/He had new clothes a making here below" (lines 16-18); the words-in-citation cite the world made text, the garment of style in which the world is wrapped, the exteriority that produces and dissolves the voice that voices/manifests his dispersal, scarcely keeping up with the transformative/annihilative way that he wears (away). The presence (of speech) is the aftereffect of an attempt to arrive at a present evaded in the motion that generates question and answer. Presence is the motion (the way) of becoming-absent.[30]

The death of Jesus, in which this story – and all utterance – occurs is the movement of words that do not arrive at final signification, and that (by telling three stories at once) derive from an origin in repetition that must, perforce, de-originate all utterance and replace/displace it within the already written. In this "strange storie" the very notions of fullness, origin, presence, and Being (of all that supposedly inheres in voice) are replaced by spacing (literally, the making of space), repetitive motion, tracing, dissolution, undoing: death. The "being" of writing.[31]

The story of the making/unmaking of spacing, and its effects of de-origination and depossession: the violence of the instrusion of the letter, its insistence, overwhelming the scene of speaking/hearing. As in what follows:

> When he was come, as travellers are wont,
>   He did repair unto an inne.
>   Both then, and after, many a brunt
>   He did endure to cancell sinne:
>   And having giv'n the rest before,
> Here he gave up his life to pay our score.
>
> But as he was returning, there came one
>   That ran upon him with a spear.
>   He, who came hither all alone,
>   Bringing nor man, nor arms, nor fear,
>   Receiv'd the blow upon his side,
> And straight he turn'd, and to his brethren cry'd,
>
> (19-30)

He comes, and then another one comes; he comes with "his spear" (line 14); he ("all alone") comes "to his brethren." Uncanny echoes, dissolve of pronoun, crossing of attributes, as he comes to give and receive, the cancellation that generates repetition; there is more beyond "the rest." Into which he comes "as travellers are wont," entering "unto an inne" that seems to have no exit, a fully receptive interiority. A reciprocal receptacle, "turn'd" as verse, the turns and returns of the open heart or the violence of the letter, "Christ-side-piercing spear" (*Prayer (I)*, line 6). The "straight" turns of the lines, coming and going. The dialogic space in which speech occurs, ventriloquized through other voices, other scenes. For it is to citation that the text turns finally, the rehearsal of another voice, the rehearsal (re-play and fore-play) of the way.

121

> If ye have any thing to send or write,
>> I have no bag, but here is room:
>> Unto my Fathers hands and sight,
>> Beleeve me, it shall safely come.
>> That I shall minde, what you impart,
> Look, you may put it very neare my heart.

(31-36)

The entrance of another voice makes explicit what has been implicit in the movement from stanza to stanza, and within the transfers that characterize the narrative. Entrance of other voices within the re-citation of the already written as the condition of utterance, even, as here, of the utterance of the master trope transformed into a letter box to receive on his heart (and thence on his tongue) what has been written. So he will have in mind this reminder, and tending these letters, minding them, he will also "minde" them as the violation of his (and anyone's) propriety. What is in mind (as conscience) is the internal scene of a Father who is all hands and eye, master proprietor of the simulacrum–of the space of writing.[32]

Christ's utterance declares his office: bearer of the letter. His "room" the space of (re)writing, the space of *The Temple*. Donne glosses: "the death of Christ is given to us, as a *Handwriting*, for when Christ nail'd that Chirographum, that first hand-writing [i.e. the law of the Old Testament; cf. Coloss. 2:14]... to his Crosse, *he did not leave us out of debt,* nor absolutely discharged, but he laid another *Chirographum* upon us, *another Obligation arising from his death*." Christ's death is "*as a writing... a Copy*, to learne by.... It is not onely given us to reade, but to *write over,* and practice."[33] The economy of death, or writing– or living ("practice"), reiteration as rewriting/effacement (writing over), without a final discharge. Ejaculation within the staying hand, the overseeing eye. Coming safely.

Ending, *The Bag* arrives at that threshold of the text beyond which *The Temple* does not move, staying and coming; a revolving door is the way of reinscription:

> Or if hereafter any of my friends
>> Will use me in this kinde, the doore
>> Shall still be open; what he sends
>> I will present, and somewhat more,
>> Not to his hurt. Sighs will convey
> Any thing to me. Harke, Despair away.   (37-42)

"Hereafter": the present of re-iteration. "Kinde": the only nature, textual violation, "not to his hurt," the dead letter. "Present": "somewhat more."

Presentation as re-presentation, supplementation. The still opening of the wound in Being and the existence of Being-in-death. "Sighs": the life-of-death (breath is nothing itself without the letter), the breath that conveys "any thing"–materialized, departicularized, meaningless. The dead letter the life of breath and voice. "Harke, Despair away": the text ends in a re-citation; who quotes whom? Is Despair commanded to depart or to continue? Who speaks in this dissolve of voices, in the text-in-quotation? In the very closure of the poem, an opening; no beginning or end but reiteration; no voice but other voices already written; no life but in the violence of the cancellation of all propriety, of ownership, authorship, self, meaning.

In *The Bag*, the new dispensation is death, voice is the death of voice, the animation of the dead letter, the life of substitution and reiteration that does not end (or ends in the death of Christ which is "the animation of the dead letter," etc.). The voice(s) of *The Bag* tells the already written voiced by the hearer who is a teller, a counter in this economy of exchanges, the encircling and enclosures of the open heart, the tablet of effacement and rewriting. A scene of writing within writing within. . . the productive mirror of auto-affection, voice as the echoing simulacrum of the seen of which there is no beyond in the "hereafter."[34]

Christ is the way, the door: the dead letter kept in circulation and kept from arrival at anything more or less than endless supplementation. This is the path of *The Temple* or *The Pilgrimage*, journey without arrival, without the solace of one's own, the lesson of *Obedience*. And so, by necessity, all poems in *The Temple* are about writing (there is nothing but), and of course, explicitly so often, in every register of the entrance of an Other–*Peace, Love Unknown, A true Hymne*–but as much so by being in language where all is copy (where all *copia* is), where all being is (boxed, sepulchred, already penned and yet to be written) the sweetness of ejaculation without the expense of spirit, written within the father's productive denial:

> *There is in love a sweetnesse readie penn'd:*
> *Copie out onely that, and save expense.*
>
> (*Jordan (II)*, 17-18)

6

Milton's warning voice: considering preventive measures

"I conceav'd my selfe to be now not as mine own person, but as a member incorporate into that truth whereof I was perswaded" (*Apology*, 1:871).[1] This sentence speaks of a "now," the present of a self-conceiving and a self-disowning: "now" marks the entrance into writing under the impress of persuasion, writing one's own "not as mine own," under rhetorical duress, sacrificing the "person" to be a "member" and, so dismembered, embodied, incorporated into the materiality of written truth. This is where Milton *is*, a place where he stands, waiting, positioned in a career always about to begin. Where, then, is voice located in this situation of waiting for one's own? What "member" speaks in the void of speech, in the figuration and disfiguration of a rhetorical truth, one's own disowned to speak in other words?

Milton waits for that other voice to overcome his; this is, crucially, *Milton's* story, the rhetoric of his truth, compelled, as he often says, by "bitter constraint, and sad occassion dear" (*Lycidas*, line 6)[2] to break into speech when "Silence, and Sufferance" (*Apology*, 1:871) are properly his. A self-conceiving of a self "not as mine own." This story of not being his own person is the poet's conception, his birth, an imagined beginning in which he gives birth to his own voice as not his own, a beginning for himself in "the truth which I had written" (*Apology*, 1:871). "To write," Maurice Blanchot comments, "is to make oneself the echo of what cannot stop talking." And hence, Blanchot says, the fundamental position for the writer is to be always before the work, in a beginning which is never terminated by writing. "The writer's solitude, then, this condition that is his risk, arises from the fact that in the work he belongs to what is always before the work."[3] Milton's career is stationed in this beginning. His being is language, already written.

In this position, his own is silence, speech is not his own; because, already written, the work in some way almost unfathomable *is* without its having been written, its existence (virtually no different than its nonexistence) renders him speechless and provides him with a voice, at once, in an intensely problematic "now" that defines his place in history, and in literary history as well. In the Miltonic text, the word for this enabling and disabling moment is *prevention*. Prevented by occasion from maintaining his own, he is compelled by occasion to an untimely, premature writing. As he represents it, writing impedes him from what he should be doing (studying, maturing, preparing) and compels him to foredate the moment when he would be ready to enter into the work and begin to write. He writes within the impediment, the forestalling; having been prevented, he speaks within the prevention, the blocked writer who becomes the great stumbling block for future writers. For, pre-vented, he comes before himself, lodges the voice within the antecedence in which, not being his own person, he can speak in the person of the truth that he conceives conceives him, the truth that he had written and which had written him.

There is no single beginning text for Milton; every text is a beginning again placed within prospect of the arrival at a beginning coincident with his own emergence into his own – maturity, ripeness, fruition. This is, as Edward Le Comte has so brilliantly documented, a poet whose central obsession and compelling dread is that he will never arrive at that beginning moment, and who represents that fear by predating himself, offering his texts as those from a before before the poet has any desire to own them as his works, deferring to the end his own beginning, his arrival into his own.[4] "O run, prevent them with thy humble ode" (*NO*, line 24), such is the preposterous (literally) gesture of one emergence (his twenty-first birthday and the birth of Christ), stationing – hastening – to occupy a position preoccupied by the "star-led wizards" (line 23) arriving beforehand at the preordained place. Humility no less than the overturning of history to allow a place for his prevented voice, to place that voice before; to prevent the preventers. (Poets are magi, too; at any rate, this one considers himself star-led.) Eve names that preventive voice as "our great forbidder"(*PL* 9:815), but the voice of prevention is also the desired voice: "O for that warning voice" (*PL* 4:1), for a voice that coming before would prevent what would come. Yet, there is dread in the desire: "Return Alpheus, the dread voice is past" (*Lycidas*, line 132). The dread voice of the past prevents and overcomes all beginnings, and it is within that dread that the desired voice is located. Hence, at the end, Milton can present Jesus about to "enter, and begin" (*PR* 4:635), he, too, "long choosing, and beginning late" (*PL* 9:26). (The true beginning is reserved for Samson's final act.) Deferring beginning, Milton is, from the start, belated, as he reports in a letter to the friend who admonishes "that the howres of the night passe on" (1: 319), sending him a copy of another beginning text with its familiar story of his belatedness, "How soon hath Time, the subtle thief of youth."

If we were to pursue now some of these beginning moments, entering into the preventive space in which Milton's voice is located, we would want to know the shape of the dread and the desire that preoccupies him, would want to arrive there and see it–represented; more we could not expect. If we were to put names in these preventive places (the name of the Father, we may grant, without naming), we might (we will) call them Shakespeare and Spenser, although self-conceiving will take us further, beyond. We might have as a preliminary example the entrance of the god of poetry in *Lycidas* so stunningly observed by Stanley Fish in "*Lycidas*: A Poem Finally Anonymous." From the moment Apollo's voice appears, Fish argues, there is no telling who is speaking, no way to know where one voice starts and another begins. Tenses tell, however, that whenever the god's voice began, it began before the voice we had assumed to be speaking first began. And this before, as Fish says, is the pretext in which the intelligibility of the text is secured–precisely because the moment has already been written before either voice was allowed its register in this text. The text tells its voices. "When Apollo plucks his trembling ear, he repeats an action already performed in response to another poet who also has dreams of transcending the pastoral conventions:

> When I tried a song of kings and battles, Phoebus
> Plucked my ear and warned. 'A shepherd, Tityrus,
> Should feed fat sheep, recite a fine-spun song.'
> (Virgil, *Eclogue 6*, trans. Paul Alpers)

Apollo, in short, puts Virgil in his place, and by doing so establishes a place (or commonplace) that is now occupied by the present speaker."[5]

On the title page of the 1645 volume of poems, the first poems to which he lent his name (another beginning), another Virgilian quotation appears: "Baccare frontem/Cingite, ne vati noceat mala lingua futuro" (*Eclogue* 7: 27-28), wreath my brows with foxglove, lest an evil tongue harm the bard to be.[6] Yet other tongues – evil tongues – compel him to speak, in the voice of a futurity he may come to occupy when he occupies the place which prevents him. He speaks of/in a future always yet to be and already written; the "now" in which he writes and is written, the future anterior in which "speech is the life of . . . death."[7]

"On Shakespeare" and Spenser

Milton first appears in print in the second Shakespeare folio (1632) as the anonymous author of "An Epitaph on the admirable Dramaticke Poet, W. Shakespeare," a poem later retitled "On Shakespeare" and redated 1630, foredating his beginning.[8] He begins in denial:

> What needs my Shakespeare for his honoured bones,
> The labour of an age in piled stones,
> Or that his hallowed relics should be hid
> Under a star-ypointing pyramid?
> Dear son of memory, great heir of fame,
> What need'st thou such weak witness of thy name?
>
> (1-6)

The anonymous poet refuses to erect a monument, denies Shakespeare a tomb or the memorialization of his name. The denial presumably reflects the sufficiency of Shakespeare's name – he has no need of such a "weak witness"; but the denial also carries attendant assertions through its refusals and by an appropriation of "my Shakespeare" that diminishes Shakespeare (indeed, as son and heir, is not Shakespeare entirely dependent – for a past as well as a future – on others?). Shakespeare, at any rate, is the name for a corpse – "honoured bones" – a sainted body ("hallowed relics"); and although he has a name (unlike the author of the poem, who nonetheless allows Shakespeare his name as he appropriates it), he is not named as an author of a corpus of works (except in the folio title excised in the 1645 volume of Milton's poems). The anonymous author appears to say that the appropriate tribute to one who has no need is not to give him anything; such is the condition for his own appearance. However, the denial exacts its cost upon the one who so gives. For the refusal to erect the tomb is also a refusal to write, a denial of the poem. Thus Horace proclaims himself through his labor: "Egexi monumentum aere perennius/regalique situ pyramidum altius," I have finished a monument more lasting than bronze and loftier than the Pyramids' royal pile (*Odes,* 3:30, lines 1-2); "Not marble nor the gilded monuments/Of princes shall outlive this pow'rful rhyme," is a familiar Shakespearian transcription (sonnet 55).[9] Milton refuses a "weak witness"; in l632, the phrase is "dull witnesse" – the text an unpolished, silent gravestone. Self-denial and self-denigration coincide with the refusal to give tribute to Shakespeare.

This opening poem – Milton's gesture towards a futurity that print can confirm, that the company of Shakespeare can assure – appears to prevent itself from appearing. What he denies to Shakespeare, he denies himself: and in that denial, the text of the poem – appropriating and disappropriating – appears.

In these countermoves of denial, voice – as echo – is at stake, a struggle over propriety is enacted, over a tomb. Is the text "On Shakespeare" a speaking stone or a silent one? Does it provide the voice of fame, an incarnation of Echo as the voice of futurity and preservation of the past?[10] Refusing to erect a "star-ypointing pyramid" does he nonetheless translate him to the skies, as the Lady wishes in her song to Echo in *Comus* (line 241), pointing there, if not arriving? In the mutual denials of the text are there not also identifications? No name for its author, but no witnessing of the name it names (but only as a name): "hallowed relics." "I cannot hallo to my brothers" (line 225), the Lady confesses before she attempts to invoke "Sweet Echo...that liv'st unseen" (line 229); does this text "On Shakespeare" hallo to its brother in its virtually printless identification in denial? To ask the question in the *Nativity Ode*: can it "afford a present" (line 16)? A voice "touched with hallowed fire" (line 28)? Or does the early rising poet need the stars to himself? He alone the morning star?

In the *Nativity Ode*, the preventive moment of emergence occurs in a "tedious" (line 239) time, within the protraction of the rising of the sun, interposing itself "now" in a present that "hath took no print of the approaching light" (line 20), fixing the stars despite the warning voice of Lucifer (line 74), finding voice in a voiceless infant, or in the song sung before by the "sons of morning" (line 119); the beginning poet sings within this dictum: "wisest fate says no,/This must not yet be so" (lines 149-50). In the denials of the weak/dull witness written "On Shakespeare" is the emergence of voice into printless print, the struggle over the space of inscription on a stone endowed with the echo of voice, the "live-long monument" that sounds the trope of life-in-death, "the fiction of the voice-beyond-the-grave" as Paul de Man puts it, considering Words-worth's recollection of Milton's "On Shakespeare."[11] The struggle over the tomb; the question, whose star is rising, the inscription – the dead letter that might strike one dead – "make us marble" – and its cost; writing, the present, and the death of being.

No one has written more suggestively about Milton's attachment to the stars than William Empson, tracing the strange sympathy that links morning and evening, Lucifer and Christ, that stillpoint of emergence in which the Miltonic voice – the Miltonic echo – arises.[12] When the Lady in *Comus* sings her song to Echo, she hopes to receive word "of a gentle pair/That likest thy Narcissus are" (lines 235-36), a curious doubling consonant with the echo effects Empson explores. And in the masque, the Lady's hallo fails to reach her brothers' ears; rather, it reaches another pair – shepherds, both – Comus testifying to the powers of a song that "would take the prisoned soul,/And lap it in Elysium" (lines 255-56); the Attendant Spirit, "wrapt in a pleasing fit of melancholy/To meditate my rural minstrelsy . . . was all ear,/And took in strains that might create a soul/Under the ribs of death" (lines 545-46, 559-61). The evocative voice summons up life-in-death; it functions as a virtual sepulchre. In Comus and the Attendant Spirit, the Lady catches the figures in the masque that John Guillory has aptly associated with Shakespeare and Spenser,[13] transfixing them in the moment of the masque coincident with Milton's delayed emergence. It is the moment when the stars bid the shepherds fold (lines 93, 541), plaiting the garlands of repose–the interruptive, inter-pelliate, preventive moment.

Milton's first printed poem points to a rising star; he meets Shakespeare in the "star-ypointing pyramid" that he refuses to erect, a monument that would translate him to the skies, echo denied; yet, as in the Lady's song, an echo is effected, hid in the "hallowed" tomb. Moreover, the rising star is a persistent trope for emergence and beginning through-out Milton's texts; it does not cease to point to Shakespearian associations even as it denies them. Echo triumphs in despite of, as a means to, Milton's voice. The relationship between the rival poets is enacted in syntactic marks of denial and (dis)engagement: "my Shakespeare" is initially objectified, third-person; then Shakespeare becomes the addressee for the remainder of the poem. As Benveniste has argued, the "I" in discourse exists only by virtue of its relationships to the categories of the third-person (the person that is not a person) and the second person (the thou that is not-I, but also complements the I); the plural privileges the "I" implicit in the "we."[14] Hence, this text does not say "I," but emerges buried in the otherness to which it consigns Shakespeare – and itself. Appropriated, objectified, as the recipient of voice–as auditor–the text places, displaces (dislodges–no tomb for those bones) its subject. But insofar as the denial of emergence is how Milton emerges, the stilled rival, the brother poet, remains his starry echo in the confraternity of con-*sidera*tion.

This "star-ypointing" relationship between Milton and Shakespeare is perhaps most obvious in "When I consider how my light is spent," as it recasts sonnet 15, "When I consider every thing that grows" (although we should not forget that the poem "On Shakespeare" is modelled on an epitaph that Milton might well have believed Shakespeare authored).[15] The opening of Milton's sonnet overtly signals and fully appropriates its Shakespearian counterpart, and even pairing those first lines suggests something of the transference enacted in the early poem "On Shakespeare" with its refusal of expenditure to one who seems to have no need. Here, too, the later poet would appear incapable of giving;

129

he is spent, a spent voice speaks. Considering "every thing," the earlier poet would perhaps need nothing; his star is hitched to an endless fecundity. Milton's, on the other hand, would seem to have gone out before it ever was.

> When I consider how my light is spent,
>   Ere half my days, in this dark world and wide,
>   And that one talent which is death to hide,
>   Lodged with me useless, though my soul more bent
> To serve therewith my maker, and present
>   My true account, lest he returning chide,
>   Doth God exact day-labour, light denied,
>   I fondly ask; but patience to prevent
> That murmur, soon replies, God doth not need
>   Either man's work or his own gifts, who best
>   Bear his mild yoke, they serve him best, his state
> Is kingly. Thousands at his bidding speed
>   And post o'er land and ocean without rest:
>   They also serve who only stand and wait.
>
> (Sonnet 16)[16]

Read against Milton's earlier poem "On Shakespeare," is there not also some strange victory here? To be spent, to be extinguished before–this is to displace Shakespeare even further, to deny, by occupying, his tomb. The echoes between "On Shakespeare" and Milton's "When I consider" multiply: it is "death to hide" the talent; hallowed relics should not be "hid"; "God doth not need" his labor; "What needs my Shakespeare . . ./The labour of an age"; "his state is kingly" and "kings for such a tomb would wish to die."

In these echoes, "When I consider how my light is spent" constitutes a reconsideration, a refiguration of the early poem "On Shakespeare"; it offers, as well, a reading of the Shakespeare sonnet, itself a text about the holding action that a poet performs in despite of time, and an assertion of power:

> When I consider every thing that grows
> Holds in perfection but a little moment,
> That this huge stage presenteth nought but shows
> Whereon the stars in secret influence comment,
> When I perceive that men as plants increase,
> Cheered and checked even by the self-same sky,
> Vaunt in their youthful sap, at height decrease,
> And wear their brave state out of memory,
> Then the conceit of this inconstant stay
> Sets you most rich in youth before my sight,

Where wasteful time debateth with decay
To change your day of youth to sullied night,
  And all in war with time for love of you,
  As he takes from you, I engraft you new.

(Sonnet 15, 1609 text modernized)[17]

Shakespeare's text represents an action taken to forestall the arrival of
the night in which Milton's poem is located; its action is to preserve the
rich sight of youth, while the latter, written "ere half my days," declares
the expungement of light, a buried talent that cannot grow in the dark.
Shakespeare's text co-opts the stars whose "secret influence" provides
a running commentary on the world's impermanence; for he, too, glosses
the war with time, and by entering into it ("in war with time") finds a
place in the "self-same sky." The generative principle of the text makes
him another star, cheering and checking to hold onto the "little moment,"
"this inconstant stay"–to hold *in* perfection (to refrain from the arrival
at the end, to write in the end). Milton's is the voice of the unproductive
laborer with his buried talent; Shakespeare engrafts, and the conceit he
has planted ("men as plants increase") generates the text, another leaf
in the forest of *silvae*.

It is precisely this productive territory that Milton's text reoccupies,
drains, and denies. The generativity of the "inconstant stay" of the
Shakespearian text is refigured in the preventive voice of patience that
comes to forestall the opening words of the poem. Whereas Shakespeare
forestalls the end by planting his voice in every thing that grows, Milton
occupies the tomb and buries his voice in quotation of Shakespeare, or
the chiding voice (only retrospectively owned as his own, but owned
and disowned at once–it is a foolish utterance), or within the voice of
preventive patience, whose reply anticipates all utterance (as Fish has
argued, finding here a moment analogous to the intrusion of Apollo in
Lycidas).[18] Whether patience ever stops talking, whether the voice first
heard (although declared spent), then silenced, returns, the text does
not mark. Locating "his" voice in one that anticipates his own and that
survives its end, Milton's "I" is sustained precisely by being denied.
Buried, it has become a monument. The Shakespearian text is all motion,
endless grafting, staying and going at once, a text whose slippages align
it with the text the stars create in their endless commentary on the rise
and fall of all things, a text that duplicates the world and outstrips it in
its generativity – it is a text made by an endless eye. Never prior, its
secondarity and supplementation of natural generativity with textual
generativity is its lease on life. Milton's text takes hold of death, and in
its denials it enters into the realm where nothing changes, achieves the
priority of death, the place where Comus and the Attendant Spirit were

131

caught, within the echo of the Lady's voice. Perhaps Milton does aim to be alone and always "heaven's youngest teemed Star" (*NO*, line 240).[19]

*

And what's her history?
A blank, my lord. She never told her love,
But let concealment, like a worm i'th'bud,
Feed on her damask cheek. She pined in thought;
And, with a green and yellow melancholy,
She sat like Patience on a monument,
Smiling at grief. Was not this love indeed?

(*Twelfth Night*, 2.4, 108-14)

*

Shakespeare engrafts; Milton engraves: an economy of death is what Milton claims from Shakespeare; his transformation of the Shakespearian text reaches that dead end in which he can locate an origin in prevention.

*

The scene of that transformation is spelled in the remaining lines of the folio poem, for the answer to the question about need replaces the sufficiency of the prior poet with the sufficiency of the later one, the sufficiency of the tomb: "Thou in our wonder and astonishment/Hast built thyself a live-long monument." Becoming blank, astonished . . . made stone, the Miltonic text can become the tomb on which an *initial* inscription is engrafted; stones before seeds, an excessive monument, a pyramid built to conceal what is buried within. This is the blank space of the Miltonic inscription: "For the book of knowledge fair/Presented with a universal blank/Of nature's works to me expunged and razed" (*PL* 3:47-49).[20]

The construction of this sepulchral echo chamber is the introduction of Echo in the text, an Ovidian scene that arises from the echoes in the opening lines "On Shakespeare." Between the reverberating repetition, "What needs . . . What need'st," there is the space of a tomb, uninscribed, the weak/dull witness, not speaking, blank. "Honoured bones" and "piled stones" sound the story of Ovid's nymph; refused her love, she pined away. Her cave became a tomb, without air and moisture, she became the air, mere voice, her body no more than bone. And the bones, as in the Miltonic text, became stones. "Vox tantum atque ossa supersunt:/vox manet, ossa ferunt lapidis traxisse figuram" (*Meta.* 3:398-99), only her voice and her bones remain: then, only voice; for they say that her bones were turned to stones.[21] Shakespeare denied Echo, or become Echo? The silent witness Narcissus transfixed by the (denying) image, or Echo transformed into rigid identification? Twin narcissi, Echo and Narcissus, Echo, the image of the voice of Narcissus, the *twin* of a rigidified identification, the literalization of astonishment, the voice in the stone that remains; in the tomb, in the flower. Seeds from stones; poetic progeny. The text as the statue of Patience.

> For whilst to the shame of slow-endeavouring art,
> Thy easy numbers flow, and that each heart
> Hath from the leaves of thy unvalued book,
> Those Delphic lines with deep impression took,
> Then thou our fancy of itself bereaving,
> Dost make us marble with too much conceiving;
> And so sepulchred in such pomp dost lie,
> That kings for such a tomb would wish to die.
>
> (9-16)

The tomb precedes the corpse, and the effect of Shakespeare's fecundity, the *scandal* of his shameful ease, is that slow-endeavouring art, lagging behind, comes before. The condition for its precedence is its emptiness, the blankness of a page upon which an impression can be imprinted, this sepulchral page which is the only room that contains the corpse of the fecund poet. The proprietary poet has relinquished his own to claim Shakespeare as his own; the first person has been dissolved in a plural, a kingly state. Spent himself, fancy bereaved, his emptiness is nonetheless a pompous sepulchre, the excessive pyramid that is also an empty tomb anticipating death, making death the end of desire. "If we are to take it as a truth that knows no exception that everything living dies for *internal* reasons – becomes inorganic once again – then we shall be compelled to say that '*the aim of all life is death*' and, looking backwards, that '*inanimate things existed before living ones*'."[22] To achieve priority, to write at the origin, to begin (as Milton always is beginning), the voice of the Miltonic text *is* when it can take as its own a founding and fundamentally (im)possible sentence, 'I am dead.' In *Speech and Phenomena*, Derrida draws from this sentence the fact that "the signifying function of the *I* does not depend on the life of the speaking subject," indeed, that "the anonymity of the written *I*, the impropriety of the *I am writing*, is . . . the 'normal situation.'" And, elsewhere, he adds, "I believe that the condition for a true act of language is my being able to say 'I am dead.' . . . 'I am dead' is not only a possible proposition for one who is known to be living, but the very condition for the living person to speak is for him to be able to say, significantly,

'I am dead.'"[23] That significant sentence is the Miltonic translation; when he considers everything that grows, his light is spent. He writes in the dark, in the tomb, in the blankness which (de)originates language and which is the sepulchral space of the page–even the written one. Such death is the 'being' of language, existence on the page, the twinning of repetition and denial, the fascinated stare that constitutes self and other in the echoing space of denial, in the hollowed cave of Echo.

That blank space–where the warning voice and prevention meet– is Milton's territory, and not only, as we have been seeing, when he becomes blind. He claims it as his own at every beginning. As in that early (1633) letter to a friend, enclosing "How soon hath Time": there, hearing in his friend a warning voice, the speaker a nameless "watch man" (another star?) admonishing "that the howres of the night passe on (for so I call my life as yet obscure)," he reports the other's warning in a voice which appropriates the warning and makes it his own–"so I call my life." But the warning voice is already in quotation, Christ speaking to the blind man at Siloah's brook, miraculously restoring his sight so that he can work in the light granted in darkness before the final darkness comes.[24] To the watchman's eyes, he offers the text of a poem in which, having no buds or blossoms to offer, no poem to show, he shows his blankness to an eternal eye. For he will not pursue "the emptie & fantastick chase of shadows" in ignorance of "the solid good flowing from due & tymely obedience to that command in the gospell set out by the terrible seasing of him that hid the talent" (1:320). More Shakespearian con-siderations.

The condition of writing–at first–is to have been granted a second sight that precedes first (and spent) sight, to have embraced an economy of death repudiating the generation of fancy, the "fantastick . . . shadows" of a Shakespearian creativity ("If we shadows have offended . . ." (*MND*, 5.1, line 412)). The poet who has no buds and blossoms to show in his late spring stands against "sweetest Shakespeare fancy's child,/Warbl[ing] his native wood-notes wild" (*L'Allegro*, lines 133-34), the easy poet of flowing numbers whose book of leaves so deeply impresses that fancy is bereaved–replaced by the all-preceding tomb, the ever-during dark. If Milton's text re-prints, his copy also preserves and takes precedence, a marble conception, the "useless" (dis)lodging of the "unvalued book," reinscribed on the blocking stone.[25]

The inscription is Delphic, obscured, cryptic, yet Apollo's. When we seek the scene of writing conveyed from the "unvalued book" of "Delphic lines," we find a wounded heart, a scene of interior inscription, the "deep impression" that makes seeds of stone. What are "those Delphic lines"? The devastating loves of Apollo sung by his shattered son Orpheus? Of Cyparissus, mourning endlessly his mortally wounded deer? Is that the scene of inscription in the heart? Or Hyacinthus, destroyed in loving contest? His death provokes Apollo . . . to write; the hand that authored death – "Ego sum tibi funeris auctor" (*Meta.* 10: 199) – now inscribes eternal mourning:

> Non satis hoc Phoebo est (is enim fuit auctor honoris):
> ipse suos gemitus foliis inscribit, et AI AI
> flos habet inscriptum, funestaque littera ducta est.

> (Phoebus, not satisfied with this – for 'twas he who wrought the honouring miracle – himself inscribed his grieving words upon the leaves, and the flower bore the marks, AI AI, letters of lamentation, drawn thereon.)

(Meta. 10: 214-16).

The flower is not enough; there must be words edging it, buds and blossoms, the flowers of rhetoric. The scene of writing on the heart and this marginal figuration are Delphic intrusions, like the voice of Apollo in *Lycidas*, preventing; the text, like the gown of Camus (another disruptive figure), the garment of nature that is itself a text, "Inwrought with figures dim, and on the edge/Like to that sanguine flower inscribed with woe" (*Lycidas*, lines 105-6).[26] Inwrought, inscribed: the internal incision in the wounded heart that produces the sheer exteriority of the marble tomb awaiting occupation; this overwrought text with its dim figurations and buried echoes locates the place of the buried talent, a seedbed of stone that appropriates and devastates the Shakespearian landscape, planting deadly seeds in those wild woods.

"Fancy of itself bereaving": the assault of Shakespeare is deflected, reflected. Other voices invade the Shakespearian: Ovidian . . . Spenserian. Why, after all, represent Shakespeare as a *pastoral* poet? Consider, for example, how the echo in the Lady's voice raises its Spenserian (and, inevitably, Virgilian) response: "Wrapt in a pleasing fit of melancholy/To meditate my rural minstrelsy,/Till fancy had her fill" (*Comus*, lines 545-47). The Lady's echo bereaves his fancy, too, displacing silence, too, an originary sound to which the spirit attends, "all ear" (line 559), to a voice that re-constitutes and pre-constitutes him, the preventive sound of a prior voice. "O poor hapless nightingale" (line 565): the price of such priority, to be the voice of nature the tongue must be sacrificed. The generative transference from the Lady's echo to the Attendant Spirit as echo rebounds with this Ovidian metamorphosis; both voices witness the bereaving of fancy; both are conceived within this bereaval, this sepulchral echo chamber that has no bounds. If Milton implicates the priority of Ovidian pastoral in the "Delphic lines" of the Shakespearian text, and thereby reduces Shakespeare to a Spenserian echo, his voice is also – in all these buried allusions, an inscription, too; does he preserve his talent in these strategies, or bury it further, expend it in the echo chamber, or seize hold upon the monumental? "Marble with too much conceiving": is this Echo rigidified as voice or Narcissus locked in the gaze? Fraternal considerations? Is the Shakespeare of "On Shakespeare" –Ovidian, Spenserian, biblical, pastoral–the image and echo of Milton?

We can look, for a moment, elsewhere, to another beginning and to a refiguration of these questions about fancy bereaved, fancy conceiving, Echo and Narcissus as our first parents, the poet's conception. Take Eve locked into the reflective gaze, fascinated, risking becoming fixed, and finding herself in a warning voice that leads her to another "where no shadow stays/Thy coming" (*PL* 4:470-71), Narcissus turned Echo:

> a voice thus warned me, What thou seest,
> What there thou seest fair creature is thyself,
> With thee it came and goes: but follow me,
> And I will bring thee where no shadow stays
> Thy coming, and thy soft embraces, he
> Whose image thou art.

(PL 4:467-472)

Adam dreams the narcissistic dream of the Miltonic text; "dazzled and spent" (*PL* 8:457), eyes shut, deep in the cave of fancy: "Mine eyes he closed, but open left the cell/Of fancy my internal sight" (lines 460-61). Eyes open, he sees her come, the embodied image, led by a voice.[27] There is no going back for her, no return to the dream, for she returns in his eyes whence she came, the wounded heart, her origin beneath the ribs of death, the cave where the fecund image is supplanted by the voice coming before. "Thou hast fulfilled/Thy words," Adam acknowledges (*PL* 8:491-92); Narcissus discovering the prescription in which he is written as an echo of the preventive voice. Words before images: the reproduction of images–internal or external–is replaced by the warning voice, refusing this first state of consciousness for the priority of a constitutive split: the priority of a voice not one's own. And this replacement plants, in Adam, the consciousness, "unfelt before" (*PL* 8:475), a sweetness in his heart, a desire for loss – replacing the wide wound; he is inspired, reborn in this creative loss, much as Eve is herself by being twice over an image. The master voice is a shaping hand: "The rib he formed and fashioned with his hands;/Under his forming hands a creature grew" (*PL* 8:469-70). The inscription of Apollo? The hand of Pygmalion?

This scene of bereaving and conceiving recalls the text "On Shakespeare," its productive marble – the surface of the text, the stumbling block of poetic transmission. Milton has "his" voice in the tomb, in the dark: blankness is his own, his the always blank page which prevents and blocks writing. The present afforded by the youngest teemed star, new born, new emptied. "The present cannot be produced except in the movement which retains and effaces it."[28] Produced on the block, the inscribed stone.

Maurice Blanchot writes of/in this moment, calling it the essential solitude, naming it as the fundamental dread, claiming the writer's territory as the right to death. "When I speak: death speaks in me." "When I first begin, I do not speak in order to say something, rather a nothing demands to speak, nothing speaks, nothing finds its being in speech and the being of speech is nothing."[29]

The lady whose voice is echo becomes a stone maiden, the tomb of patience, the blocking stone: the voice of prevention. "Watch therefore" (the voice of prevention says) "for ye know neither the day nor the hour wherein the Son of man cometh" (Matt. 25:13).[30] And when he returned, their lamps had gone out. Their light was spent. And the door was shut and there was no room. The talent was spent; it had not been used. But (preventing the warning voice, citing text against text), Milton tells his friend, with his warning (watching) voice, that "those that were latest lost nothing," that there is a penny–a talent–even for those called at the eleventh hour. "Is it not lawful for me to do what I will with mine own? Is thine eye evil, because I am good?" (Matt. 20:15). Answering the warning voice, Milton places one biblical text before another, reads the later text through the former one. The warning to act, the injunction to write, becomes this holding action, not spending the talent. "This very consideration," he continues, his star properly teamed, twinned Narcissus truly planted, "of that great commandment does not presse forward as soone as may be to undergo but keeps off with a sacred reverence & religious advisement how best to undergoe [,] not taking thought of beeing late so it give advantage to be more fit, for those that were latest lost nothing when the maister of the vinyard came to give each one his hire" (1:320). Prevention prevented.

And, so, "On Shakespeare," and its preventive consideration of the "unvalued" book, produced by the master, which takes its value from the tomb, the empty tomb that is, at once, interiority (built "in our wonder and astonishment," impressed on the heart) and exteriority (the pompous sepulchre awaiting inhabitation). The transference of writing –the flow of lines and leaves that becomes this new site of inscription –replaces the book with the absence of the book, the blankness of the already inscribed page produced by and preventive of the flow, the sequential disturbed by the Miltonic present in which the last will be first, in which the future will produce the past, the child will generate the parent. Shakespeare, the child of fancy, the son of memory, the heir of fame. Fancy bereaved, the productive tomb; "too much conceiving." The excess in which Shakespeare is produced as a name in Milton's text, the weak witnessing, the dull surface of a marble text, inscribed and illegible. No buds or blossoms – the press of leaves produces the echo chamber that precedes the possibility of transference. Denial perfected: there is nothing to read in Milton's text 'on' Shakespeare. Dead speech.

"Marble with too much conceiving": the text as statue, the impression of death. The Miltonic *Wunderblock* (Freud's Mystic Writing Pad?), a statue – standing and waiting – receiving impressions, fecund, empty – replete and void, awaiting inhabitation, a virgin surface (monumental patience) or a teeming mother, marble with too much conceiving. One T. C. C. in *Notes and Queries* finds Niobe in the image, and paraphrases the lines: "Shakespeare petrifies us by his imagination and deprives us of our own. The resultant blocks of marble make a sepulchre for him beyond any royal mausoleum!"[31] Excessive. Mark Pattison puts the scene of writing this way: "The elevation is communicated to us not by the dogma or deliverance, but by sympathy. We catch the contagion of the poet's mental attitude. He makes us bow with him before the image of Shakespeare, though there is not a single discriminating epithet to point out in what the greatness which we are made to feel consists."[32] Excessive, depleted – empty generation. T. C. C. glosses the marble monument of the poem "On Shakespeare" with *Il Penseroso*, line 42: "Forget thyself to marble," and John Carey reglosses: "The idea originates in the Niobe legend, employed in an epitaph by Browne . . .:'Some kind woman . . ./Reading this, like Niobe/Shall turn marble, and become/Both her mourner and her tomb."[33] The reader turned to stone. Sympathetic conception, the original seed, mortality, death before life. Paul de Man comments: "'Doth make us marble,' . . . cannot fail to evoke the latent threat that inhabits prosopopeia, namely that by making the death [*sic*] speak, the symmetrical structure of the trope implies, by the same token, that the living are struck dumb, frozen in their own death."[34]

*

Mine eye hath found that sad sepulchral rock
That was the casket of heaven's richest store,
And here though grief my feeble hands up lock,
Yet on the softened quarry would I score
My plaining verse as lively as before;
  For sure so well instructed are my tears,
That they would fitly fall in ordered characters.

(*The Passion*, 43-49)

A father comes to claim the body of his son and is told a story, even Niobe ate, "she of the lovely tresses . . . . She remembered to eat when she was worn out with weeping." And amid the nymphs who haunt her streams, "stone still, she broods on the sorrows that the gods gave her" (*Iliad*, 24:600-620).[35] A father comes to claim his son, to claim his son's memory, a son who sees his mother "like Niobe, all tears" (*Hamlet*, 1.2, line 149)–mourning *whose* death?–and the son wipes the slate clean to receive the new impression. A poet comes to present himself–signing himself for the first time (as a poet–in prose: *The Reason of Church-Government*), burdened with the "scantest measure" (1:801) given him "even to a strictnesse," a gift which must be spent, words "which would be a terror, and a torment . . . to keep back" (1:804). He writes in a "preventive fear" (1:806), articulating a voice within–the considerations of his "Secretary conscience" (1:822), writing at his dictates–what he writes is the promise to dispense, he writes of "intentions which have liv'd within me ever since I could conceiv my self any thing worth" (1:820). Conscience is the voice of the Church, his mother–his mother tongue. That voice has "pluckt" from him his "abortive and foredated discovery," the still birth of a beginning yet to come. He writes in the book which he has consumed, "that mysterious book of Revelation which the great Evangelist was bid to eat, as it had been some eye-brightning electuary of knowledge, and foresight," the wisdom, he goes on to say, like that of blind Tiresias when Oedipus called him before him. And he rewrites the lamentation of Jeremiah: "*his word was in my heart as a burning fire shut up in my bones, I was weary with forbearing, and could not stay*"(1:803). The fire within–the "hallowed fire" (*NO*, line 28) of the hallowed reliquary of voice, touching his lips, burning his heart, searing his eyes, burning his belly, bearing the word, the stony seed.

"Marble with too much conceiving."

What stories are in these stones? So many at once, a petrifying conflation. Echo, Niobe, the productive sepulchre. In this beginning, multiple scenes of writing and reading, sight and blindness, seeing with other eyes. To the echoes, add then the story of Perseus the eyestealer, who can only gaze at Medusa by looking in the mirror, and who brandishes her snaky head like the shield of Athena, goddess of knowledge, thence turning all gazers to stone, the dismembered head a mirror.[36] After Perseus rescues Andromeda, their wedding feast is interrupted when her forebetrothed returns; to end the battle, Perseus resorts to the head of the Medusa, to make them all marble. And, at last, he gives what he can: a great gift: "quin etiam mansura dabo monimenta per aevum" (*Meta.* 5:227), a monument that will last forever. They are made their own monuments, turned into statues. The gift that Perseus gives is the gift of the Medusa. Herman Rapaport sums up the scene: "the *blanc* of the Miltonic text, the place where it is not seen, renders to Milton the power of a Medusa in the Freudian sense, that is, as a traumatizing figure who terrifies because her potency, her symbolic phallus, is imagined as being cut off."[37]

"Then thou our fancy of itself bereaving,/Dost make us marble with too much conceiving": the poet as Medusa . . . or Orpheus bereaved of Eurydice, conceiving (in his gaze) the work? As in Spenser's *October* eclogue and its allusion to Orpheus:

> Seemeth thou dost their soule of sence bereave,
> All as the shepheard, that did fetch his dame
> From *Plutoes* balefull bowre withouten leave.
>
> (27-29)[38]

At whom has the star been pointing–*ypointing*–if not to Spenser? His the signature assembling these texts commemorating Shakespeare, the more meant than meets the ear. To read this text against its echoes–the scenes of writing from Ovid and Virgil–to read this poem as the deathly pastoral raised in the tomb, what is this if not to read it as if it were a Spenserian poem? And to confirm the propriety of this outrageous reading, this putting Shakespeare in his place by taking on the voice of Spenser (just the reverse occurs in *Comus*, and at the end, the voice of the Attendant Spirit, Spenserian vehicle, exits translating Spenserian materials into the sounds of Puck–or Comus), the insistent echo of Orpheus, singer of so many of the songs buried in this text, surfaces in an echo that is not simply buried allusion but virtual transcription; Spenser is allowed his line as the Delphic utterance. And the association of a generative bereaving with Orpheus, singer in loss, is an authentic Spenserian sound. In *Virgils Gnat*, too, Orpheus figures in the economy of elegiac replacement: "And the shrill woods, which were of sense bereav'd,/Through their hard barke his silver sound receav'd" (lines 455-56). The echo of leaf against leaf, silver sylvan *silvae*: in Milton the conception becomes marble, the surface ready for inscription, the block. This preventive surface, where Milton's voice "is": the wounded place of echo, an opening for voice between the antecedent voices–Spenser and Shakespeare–raised to cancel each other, to allow and block the emergence of the poet who is always beginning, the poet singing always already in the dark, hoarding and spending his useless talent.

And so, from "On Shakespeare" to the famous error in *Areopagitica*, Guyon sent into the Cave of Mammon under the tutelage of the Palmer.

For we should add to it the error in "On Shakespeare," the ungrammatical "ypointing," a Spenserism that would never be found in Spenser. And, to these, a lapse in *Il Penseroso* (beautifully examined by John Hollander);[39] alluding to Spenser, silvan poet of the mysterious echo of leaves, "Of forests, and enchantments drear,/Where more is meant than meets the ear" (lines 119-20), allusion suddenly becomes contagion, and the poem's discretely rhymed tetrameter couplets succumb to a Spenserian desire to prolong the close: the rhyme repeats, a line becomes hypermetrical: "Thus Night oft see me in thy pale career,/Till civil-suited Morn appear" (lines 121-22). "The howres of the night passe on (for so I call my life as yet obscure, & unserviceable to mankind) & that the day with me is at hand wherin Christ commands all to Labour while there is light" (1:319). The Miltonic night: Spenserian territory where the buried treasure is to be found, held – at what cost.

Harold Bloom sums up the Miltonic strategy we have been pursuing: "Milton's aim is to make his own belatedness into an earliness."[40] Of the *Areopagitica* error itself, he says that Milton's forgetting of Spenser is his defense against him, increasing the distance from him – for Guyon is Milton's precursor. Milton in the Cave of Mammon, where the buried treasure is lodged with him useless, used and prevented. As in *The Reason of Church-Government* where the talent is displayed to a preventive voice, prevented in a covenant with the reader, the promise of a future expenditure. Where what is expended is also denied, work of the left hand, produced in a shady, pastoral bower, produced because occasion demands an entrance, because the future must be prevented by this entrance so that the future can be preserved. And what is displayed and withheld is treasure, the talent a heap of riches, those "summes of knowledge and illumination, which God hath sent him into this world to trade with" (1:801), "truths of such an orient lustre as no diamond can equall" (ibid.), "treasure inestimable without price" (1:802). Such is the talent (as Paul Goodman points out, being one it is unique – virtually priceless;[41] and also the least of God's gifts; not spent, it is withheld, not used he preserves its value) – useless, the "unvalued book," supremely valuable, and worthless, upon which he draws, which he reserves.

For Guyon is a poet in the Cave of Mammon, and the defense against his strangely passive power is Milton's misreading, misremembering: he splits Guyon by giving him the company of the Palmer. And Milton's place then becomes the occupation of the split, regaining a unity that he has shattered. Eve and the image, Adam and the dream: occupying the place of the truth of the warning voice. Guyon *is* a poet in the Cave of Mammon:

141

As Pilot well expert in perilous wave,
   That to a stedfast starre his course hath bent,
   When foggy mistes, or cloudy tempests have
   The faithfull light of that faire lampe yblent,
   And cover'd heaven with hideous dreriment,
   Upon his card and compas firmes his eye,
   The maisters of his long experiment,
   And to them does the steddy helme apply,
Bidding his winged vessell fairely forward fly:

So *Guyon* having lost his trusty guide,
   Late left beyond that *Ydle lake*, proceedes
   Yet on his way, of none accompanide;
   And evermore himselfe with comfort feedes,
   Of his owne vertues, and prayse-worthy deedes.

                                       (*FQ* II. vii. 1-2. 1-5)

A star-led poet guiding his poetic vessel, and his lamp goes out, and he is blind, and the world is dark, yet he can see what his taskmaster appoints, read a guiding text, a map, find it within himself, the book that feeds his eyes, feeds himself. In that scene of writing blind, Guyon emerges alone, on the way to the Cave where all the world's riches lie. That scene, almost transparently, is the buried text "On Shakespeare," lying beneath all considerations of expenditure. *Areopagitica*, where the error of his ways emerges into full light, *is* Milton's rewriting of the Cave of Mammon, his appropriation of Guyon's career in that dark and illuminating night.

To see his secret store.
(*FQ* II. vii, argument)

My plenty poure out unto all.
(vii. 8. 3)
   exceeding store,
As eye of man did never see before.
(vii. 31. 4-5)

riche heapes...doest hide apart
From the worldes eye, and from her right usaunce.
(vii. 7. 3-4)

God...powrs out before us ev'n to a profusenes all desirable things.
          (*Areop.* 2:528)
seek for wisdom as for hidd'n treasures...the hardest labour in the deep mines of knowledge.
          (*Areop.* 2:562)
Truth and understanding are not such wares as to be monopoliz'd.
          (*Aerop.* 2:535)

heapes of gold, that never could be spent.	our richest
(vii. 5. 2)	Marchandize, Truth
	(*Areop.* 2:548)
wordly mucke doth fowly blend.	To the pure all things
(vii. 10. 5)	are pure.
never eye did vew,	(*Areop.* 2:512)
Ne toung did tell.	What needs my
(vii. 19. 6-7)	Shakespeare.
All that I need I have.	God doth not need.
(vii. 39. 3)	That he might see and
	know, and yet abstain.
	(*Areop.* 2:516)

To have all one needs, all that one lacks, neither to claim as one's own, nor to reject: that path Guyon follows, not falling into the stream of the endless desire of Tantalus, nor the endless washing off of the one who always laves, Pilate, the great denier. His ship flies another course, sailing right on. Nothing is forbidden, everything is allowed, yet nothing is taken, everything is denied. This is the position Milton occupies in *Areopagitica* . . . and after: "Milton himself . . . offers the opposing aspects of a being so unified, self-sufficient and given to quietude *as to need no successors,* and yet also of being so diverse, self-transcendent and fecund *as to compel generous imitation.*"[42] In the Cave, Guyon views all the riches which are the matter of poems, the buried gold "Woven with antickes and wild Imagery" (4.6), the ingots fired at Vulcan's forge (36), the loaded rifts (which Keats took to be an image of the poetic process) beneath the weaving of Arachne (28), the Garden of Proserpina (53), a garden of death which is the place of the immortal text, golden apples that never drop except to produce heroic offspring, Troy, Hercules, Ovidian tales (54-55). In Milton, that apple is the single one to which the twins good and evil cleave, and its seeds are the dragon teeth sown by Cadmus:

> For Books are not absolutely dead things, but doe contain a potencie of life in them to be as active as that soule was whose progeny they are; nay they do preserve as in a violl the purest efficacie and extraction of that living intellect that bred them. I know they are as lively, and as vigorously productive, as those fabulous Dragons teeth; and being sown up and down, may chance to spring up armed men.
>
> (*Areop.* 2:492)

From them arise "brotherly dissimilitudes" (2:555),"neighboring differences, or rather indifferences" (2:565). Indifferences: to the pure all things are pure. He has absorbed the lesson of Jesus: nothing defiles when it enters the mouth, only when it comes out. So . . . promiscuous reading is in order (2:517). So . . . Milton takes license speaking against license (2:493), aims at reforming reformation (2:553), suppressing the suppressers (2:568). Denying himself so much, he allows himself everything: preventive measures.[43]

Taking everything in, he cannot go into everything: such entrance would violate the sufficiency of nature, the excessive profusion of God's creativity, poured out in abundance, but not, therefore, to be had: "Untroubled Nature doth her selfe suffise" (*FQ* vii. 15. 4); self-sufficiency, to feed on what one has – what is *seen* – is to suffice on what one needs, what one lacks. Not to trouble is to have Guyon's imperturbability, his willingness to confess his lack of worth. Such confession is what can be given to the one that does not need. Such having exceeds those who have (who have desire) by its privation. Such having leaves those who have intact, yet also robbed. They have been robbed of what they have by the one who has what he needs and does not need what they have. The one, that is, who prevents himself from having and who yet has all that he needs.

What is not to be had, not to be possessed, Guyon represents to Mammon, is his "great Grandmother" (17.2); not to be had, is what Mammon represents to Guyon as the sum of art and of his doing, his daughter. Abstaining from one is abstaining from the other.

> Then gan a cursed hand the quiet wombe
> Of his great Grandmother with steele to wound,
> And the hid treasures in her sacred tombe,
> With Sacriledge to dig. Therein he found
> Fountaines of gold and silver to abound,
> Of which the matter of his huge desire
> And pompous pride eftsoones he did compound.
>
> (*FQ* vii. 17. 1-7)

"A good Booke," Milton will gloss, "is the pretious life-blood of a master spirit, imbalm'd and treasur'd up on purpose to a life beyond life" (*Areop.* 2:493). Licensers are grave marauders, raking "through the entralls of many an old good Author, with a violation wors then any could be offer'd to his tomb" (2:503). Bereaving conceiving: licensers stifle "the issue of the womb" (2:505). The book that Milton conceives is, as ever, a fruitful grave, womb and tomb.

And when Guyon agrees not to violate the great Grandmother earth, Mammon addresses him as son (18.1): the Palmer replaced. And a scene of instruction follows, Mammon reminding Guyon that he "that dost live in later times" (18.4) – the latecoming poet – does not live in the golden age but in an age of gold. Guyon responds with questions of ownership;

once in the Cave, Mammon will pacify him "with reason" (43.1) when he disdains Disdayne. The sufficiency of Guyon is his sonship; no Oedipus he, he has no designs on the mother, nor on the daughter. He wants his own. He leaves ownership untroubled.

And it is into his own that Milton arrives. For there is one provision in the licensing act that he will not oppose; he says at first (2:491), he says at the end (2:570): the provisions for copyright, "the just retaining of each man his severall copy, which God forbid should be gainsaid" (2:570). Owning his text as his own. Having, like Guyon, denied himself the desire to violate the treasure and have as his own what he must have only to deny–the lifeblood drawn from the womb/tomb of nature/books, mothers and master spirits–*Areopagitica* is a declaration of his independence from patriarchal licensers whose permissions turn teachers into puny pupil teachers (2:533)–like Guyon with the Palmer, his independence of the Roman yoke beneath which his manhood suffers–for under it fathers have the right to kill their sons (2:559). The Truth that is his treasure cannot be bound. She invites him to follow her scattered limbs throughout the world, to pursue the wake of her seed, to embrace her in all her shapes – to enter into the schism. The assurance of this promiscuity is that such liberty is also subscription, to the yoke with which Christ made us free, to "*that hand writing nayl'd to the crosse*" (2:563). St Paul guides Milton to liberty; Mammon quotes St Paul: "eye hath not seen . . ." (1 Cor. 2:9).

What primal scene of inscription has been generated here, this conjunction of Mammon and Milton, Milton and Spenser, these dutiful sons making their peace at the expense of the mother, of the buried treasure that is their source, the matter of their huge desire–not to desire and to write? Is it perhaps figured too in Milton's text "On Shakespeare," when he assigns him his parents, female both, memory (Urania) and fame? What is this, if not, once again, to confuse Shakespeare and Spenser, to raise the pastoral poet to epic as he lowers him into the empty space of his awaiting tomb? Leaving him alone the Muse herself that Orpheus bore? At the end of *Areopagitica*, Milton anticipates the fall of license in a prior fall, when the Star Chamber fell to the revolution, "fall'n from the Starres with *Lucifer*" (2:570). And then he closes, his copyright secure. His star aloft. Wishing only for a king to bury. His territory, the tomb, all conceiving, all marble: where the muse and his mother meet.[44]

*

One more beginning: the first poem, a translation of Psalm 114 ("When Israel went out of Egypt"), done, he claims, at age 15. There is nothing sacred about the sequence of scripture. Conflate. There is nothing sacred about the sacred words. Supplement. Generate. "When the blest seed of Terah's faithful son,/After long toil their liberty had won" (*Paraphrase*, lines 1-2). The struggle to be born. The difficult beginning. "Shall a child be born unto him that is a hundred years old? and shall Sarah, that is ninety years old, bear" (Gen. 17:17). Ere half my days. Egypt and the pyramid. The empty letter. The mourning muse. The son that generates his mother. The muse that Orpheus bore.

> So may some gentle muse
> With lucky words favour my destined urn,
> And as he passes turn,
> And bid fair peace be to my sable shroud.
> For we were nursed upon the self-same hill,
> Fed the same flock; by fountain, shade, and rill.
>
> (*Lycidas*, 19-24)

Twin brothers; narcissi; consider . . . who would not sing for . . . the self one does not have . . . generative seeds. "The trace is the erasure of selfhood, of one's own presence, and is constituted by the threat or anguish of its irremediable disappearance, of the disappearance of its disappearance. An uneraserable trace is not a trace, it is a full presence, an immobile and incorruptible substance, a son of God, a sign of parousia and not a seed, that is, a mortal germ."[45]

Sarah Milton died in April 1637, several months before Edward King perished in the Irish Sea.[46] From the blood of the Medusa Pegasus was born–"my adventurous song,/That with no middle flight intends to soar" (*PL* 1:13-14)–from Pegasus' hoofprint the Hippocrene stream arose, in the grove of the muses. Beginning: preventive adventure. Flying. Petrified. Primal scenes.

Letter to a friend: "& heere I am come to a streame head copious enough to disburden it selfe like Nilus at seven mouthes into an ocean, but then I should also run into a reciprocall contradiction of ebbing & flowing at once . . ."(1:320).

Reciprocal conditions: Echo evoking the brothers. Shakespeare and Spenser, a stream "copious enough" in its "reciprocall contradiction." The copious text: the parable of the talents and the value of withheld expenditure, not pressing forward, but keeping off, "not taking thought of beeing late" (ibid.). And thinking of nothing else. Text against text.

The streamhead of copy, endless text. The flow of Nilus, the flood from the mouth of Error, disgorging books (*FQ* I. i. 20), disburdening, giving birth. The words in which the poet is conceived. "Hail native language" ("At a Vacation Exercise," line 1). Born in language. To which, after two years, he finds his way, it finds its way, "Driving dumb silence from the portal door,/Where he had mutely sat two years before" (lines 5-6). Second birth: in language. Passage through the mouth. Letting the treasure emerge. Blocked speech. A banquet. A wardrobe: "clothe my fancy" (line 32). Outside in, inside out: "I have some naked thoughts that rove about/And loudly knock to have their passage out" (lines 23-24). "And the door was shut" (Matt. 25:10). "Some graver subject" (line 30). Conceiving/bereaving. "Deep transported mind" (line 33). Marble self-forgetting: coming into one's own. Up or down? "Secret things . . . Nature in her cradle" (lines 45-46). Always beginning again. "Rivers arise" (line 91): beginning in the copious text, Spenserian. "Thy easy numbers flow": Shakespearian. "God . . . powrs out before us ev'n to a profusenes all desirable things" (*Areop.* 2:528). "Greatest god below the skye,/That of my plenty poure out unto all,/And unto none my graces do envye" (*FQ* II. vii. 8.2-4). Milton in the mines. Minding mine: muck, mother, muse.

Warning voice.

Yet once more

Once more unto the breach, dear friends, once more.

(Henry V, 3.1, 1)

*

Always beginning again. Beginning in repetition. Twins. Essential resemblance. The "original" split. Resemblance "before" being. "Original" repetition. Narcissus and Echo. Narcissus and the mirror. The mirror state, standing only: "the correspondences that unite the *I* with the statue in which man projects himself."[47]

*

Editors have noticed that Milton's final sonnet, "Methought I saw my late espoused saint," opens with a phrase derived from Ralegh's poem stationed in the anteroom to *The Faerie Queene*, quite literally *coming before*. The Miltonic echo thus, once more, aligns its futurity to a preventive past in choosing the poem by Ralegh for imitation. The choice raises anew the question of the itinerary that leads to such a choice, one that can be framed this time by considering that final sonnet. If, by pursuing that question, we can regard Milton beginning again, perhaps now, moving beyond Shakespeare and Spenser, we can arrive at the scene of writing in which his career is written. First, the poem by Ralegh:

Me thought I saw the grave, where *Laura* lay,
Within that Temple, where the vestall flame

Was wont to burne, and passing by that way,
To see that buried dust of living fame,
Whose tombe faire love, and fairer vertue kept,
All suddenly I saw the Faery Queene:
At whose approch the soule of *Petrarke* wept,
And from thenceforth those graces were not seene.
For they this Queene attended, in whose steed
Oblivion laid him downe on *Lauras* herse:
Hereat the hardest stones were seene to bleed,
And grones of buried ghostes the heavens did perse.
Where *Homers* spright did tremble all for griefe,
And curst th'accesse of that celestiall theife.[48]

This scene of poetic history takes place in a grave, and the newly arrived poem – "the Faery Queene" – displaces the earlier one. In the glance of Ralegh's poem, he looks askance ("passing by") in a tomb where the virginal purity of a text exists so long as no new text comes to displace it; displaced, he regards the displacement of prior poems and their replacement, their virtual disappearance ("were not seen") and "oblivion." Oblivion lies where Laura lay, and oblivion thus accompanies the new text. For it, too, is a shade, another occupant of a tomb. This scene of death is, thus, the scene of the life of texts, their past, present, and future within the tomb, "the buried dust of living fame," "buried ghosts." This scene we know from "On Shakespeare," or *Areopagitica*: "A good Booke is the pretious life-blood of a master spirit, imbalm'd and treasur'd up on purpose to a life beyond life" (2:493). Milton fears the grave marauders because they would occupy his position: first in the tomb, the priority of a beginning that must always be renegotiated, preventing the preventers, coming before the texts that come before, priority no different, then, than repetition.

What haunts this scene, in Ralegh, is the image of the text as the corpse of a woman, Laura or the fairy queen; and the buried, weeping poet. That scene, however, is implicated in the Miltonic texts we have considered; the corpse as easily might be called Niobe or Echo or Patience. In the final sonnet, it is the dead wife. Writing her, Milton inscribes the image – like Orpheus memorializing the loss of Eurydice. The scene of inscription is the tomb, writing in stone, an eternizing and memorializing haunted by oblivion and effacement. In Ralegh, the stones bleed, the author weeps. Signs of the mourning that is writing. Signs of the materializing of the text. For the eternal text will fade, and the living tomb dies; the author who lives in the text is buried alive; texts are mortal remains, images. Inscribed death is not immortality, but mortality. In the Miltonic rewriting of "Me thought I saw," the text presents itself in the image of Alcestis, the wife who dies for her husband, and who returns. It is the return of the image as what remains that we must regard, keeping in mind other scenes as we contemplate this one, Narcissus and Echo, or Narcissus and the image in water.

> Methought I saw my late espoused saint
> Brought to me like Alcestis from the grave,
> Whom Jove's great son to her glad husband gave,
> Rescued from death by force though pale and faint.

In Euripides' *Alcestis*, Admetus confronts the impending death of Alcestis, imagining, like a poet, what he will do after she is dead.[49] Mourning forever, he proposes making an image of her, so that he could worship it, and hold it, instead of her, close to his heart (lines 348-51). Cold consolation of the image. Better, he thinks, if she could come to him in dreams: the image internalized; that would be, he imagines, more comforting if less substantial (lines 354-56). Best, if he could, like Orpheus, sing his way to hell and bring her back (lines 357-63). But, since none of these solutions is tenable, he asks only for her to wait for him in the grave. Thus, he ends with the final solution of Orpheus, for the song or the image is possible only in loss, as Blanchot has argued in "The Gaze of Orpheus," and there is no solution in life to the dilemma Admetus confronts. There is, however, in the play, for Alcestis is (thanks to Hercules) restored from the grave. She returns, however, as the very *likeness* of herself, so like that Hercules urges the husband to touch the wife. Stretching his fingers towards this wife–this *living image of herself* who remains silent all the while–Admetus says, "I feel like Perseus killing the gorgon" (line 1118). Is this a reunion in life? Or in a life-in-death, a return possible only in the text? "Be stone no more," as Paulina says to the statue Hermione, adding immediately, "strike all that look upon with marvel" (*The Winter's Tale*, 5.3, lines 99, 100). Scenes of astonishment.

Is this not the shape of a Miltonic dream, once more, on Shakespeare and Spenser, and here refigured in the image of the "late espoused saint," his Eve, his other–the text? The wife who prevents her husband's death, who precedes him into the grave and returns. The poet's life-in-the-text appears as this dreadful dream of desire; for the scene in Milton's sonnet is one of prevention–the touch denied–and fascination–life only is in the denying figure. The horror of the realization of writing, of living in the corpse that returns, can be seen in Admetus, fearing what fascinates him, that he will be turned to stone in the touch that he desires; he shrinks from touching his wife (recall Samson with Dalila); does he fear to find her dead, or fear being turned to stone by her life? What he articulates is a moment of triumph, Perseus killing the Medusa, averting her

149

petrifying gaze. Yet the triumph of Perseus over the Medusa is his acquisition of her power. Renaissance mythographers regularly read Perseus as a figure for the triumph of reason over sensuality.[50] Admetus's response to the image of his wife–or Milton's to his–testifies to a meeting of desire and denial, to have her alive again by killing her, or his desire for her; a reunion that splits the subject, and that raises a scene in a mirror, rendering all *being* within the spectre of the image.

*

Recall Ovid's account of Perseus and the Medusa: stealing an eye, Perseus travels to where the Medusa dwelt, passing by those who had been turned to stone in her gaze. He looks at her, but in a mirror, and drives in his glancing blade (*Meta*. 4.765-86). Perseus lives – from then on – in the mirror, has power in her power, the power of the petrifying image. Brandishing her head, he comes upon Andromeda; looking at her, "he would have thought her a marble statue" (4.675), so fascinating; for a moment he hangs still, oblivious in the air, forgetting to move his wings, chained in love. In Andromeda, he marries the image of his dreaded desire. And when Phineus comes to disturb the wedding, Perseus enacts his desire, turning all before his eyes into marble statues, Phineus becoming, in a further displacement, a solace for the eyes of Andromeda (5.229), another lover caught in a fascinating glance. The very tears freeze upon the cheeks of the former lover, turned to stone, eternally mourning. Another image of enthrallment and the power of resemblance. Even Athena *could not look* at the Medusa, and transferred her image to her shield, protective reflection.

*

What does the Medusa mean to poets? The question, raised by the astonishment in "On Shakespeare" or by the Euripidean scene (its rewriting in *The Winter's Tale*) and refiguration in Milton's final sonnet, is not exhausted by the Spenserian milieu of Ralegh's poem, for it disseminates a Petrarchan trope for the monumental text. The hearse of Laura is an apt image for the poet who found his own name written in stone–literally, etymologically. And, as John Freccero has suggested, his images of petrification, in turn, go back to Dante's *Commedia* and his early *rime petrose* with their stony lady. In Dante, the Medusa is what must not be looked at, the fascination of the letter that kills, of desire that is death.[51] Narcissistic idolatry, in short. And for Petrarch, the figure of an unavoidable and deeply ambivalent desire. Laura is explicitly the Medusa, and he a stone, fascinated by her: "Medusa et l'error mio m'àn fatto un sasso," Medusa and my error have made me a stone, he writes in the last of the *rime sparse* (366: 111), inscribing an ultimate shape for the desire that he refigures, as Robert Durling has pointed out, through repeated Ovidian scenes.[52] Echo and Narcissus haunt the *rime sparse* and one mirror scene mirrors another. As Freccero argues, Petrarch's legacy to poetry is the image of "an eternally weeping lover"; "the petrified idolatrous lover is an immutable monument to Petrarch," he continues;[53] the monument, or the reified text, the mirror whose reflections offer in the twinned images of Laura and the poet "an autonomous universe of autoreflexive signs," *being*-in-language. That the Medusa should be the figure for the poet's language can perhaps be glossed through a comment by Coluccio Salutati in *De laboribus Hercules*, 3:42;[54] the head of the Medusa, he writes, signifies the power of rhetoric to make men *oblivious* of what they formerly believed ("Medusa autem oblivionem significare vult, quod est sine dubitatione rhetorice, que mutans affectus hominum priores conceptus oblivisci facit"). The Medusa, he concludes, is eloquence. What other commentators took to be her overwhelming, sensual beauty, Salutati takes as an image of language at its most artifical and most persuasive. The horror, then, is that hers is a power the poet desires and which must undo him; like Perseus, the poet is enthralled. The text remains as the testament to a desire that ends in oblivion and which exerts, without the poet's own powers, its petrifying fascination. All writing, as Derrida would have it, inscribes significantly the sentence, 'I am dead.' This is the end of the desire for *being*-in-the-text. And perhaps, its beginning, once again.

For the Medusa, as wife, as muse–as the figure for (as the image of the image of) a forbidden sight–testifies to an inescapable fascination. She figures the desire for being and the recognition that being is mortal, that existence and origin are rooted in secondarity, mirror states. In a word, the desire for self-generation and its haunting by an other, Echo, language, secondary effects that prevent original ones. The Other, the Mother. Maurice Blanchot speculates: "Perhaps the power of the maternal figure derives its brilliance from the very power of fascination, and one could say that if the Mother exerts this fascinating attraction, it is because she appears when the child lives completely under the gaze of fascination."[55] Euripides' Admetus tells his father that Alcestis is truly his *mother*, for by dying for him, she has given him life (line 667).

*

We can return to the "fancied sight" (line 10) in Milton's "Methought I saw my late espoused saint." Take notice now of a strange, specular identification in the mirroring syntax of "me like Alcestis" (line 2), a *likeness* that works in two directions. Who is in the grave? Another scene of the buried talent, unburied, reburied: "fancied sight" – the image in the mirror, in the mind, on the page, confirmed and denied, likeness and difference at once. We might, with this "fancied sight" in mind, return to the poem "On Shakespeare," pausing to note some textual variants: in 1632, line 13 reads, "Then thou our fancy of her selfe bereaving"; in the 1640 text (in some respects unauthoritative but nonetheless supplying, for the first time, the author's initials, and introducing changes adopted in Milton's 1645 text), the line reads, "Then thou our fancy of our selfe bereaving"; finally, in 1645 we have, "Then thou our fancy of itself bereaving." Fancy: female, plural, neuter. Mothering muse ("Sweetest Shakespeare fancy's child"), or mother of us all, all devouring, all-conceiving, or the very neutrality of the specular remains in the mind, what we could claim as our own. Fancy: Shakespearian territory, or the place of the text in the mind, locus of the image, and with it all the ambivalence of Admetus' deadly desire. The tomb again, and the mine: familiar territory.

Ovidian review: the place of stone, where the gaze is transcribed; between the eye and the mirror, the image appears. Narcissus looks in the pool, hanging in speechless wonder "like a statue carved from Parian marble" (*Meta.* 3:419): Milton's response to the text of Shakespeare–or the response to the Medusa (or Alcestis), and the powers of rhetoric. Narcissus, whose name, Comes notes, derives from the Greek for stupefaction and lack of feeling.[56] Narcosis, petrifaction. What Narcissus sees, Echo becomes, the stone, or the image of voice–or the Medusa's head (the shield of Athena). The stone that freezes seeing in the rigidity of fascination transcribes and blocks the gaze. The self is seen as an *image*. The gaze is broken–there is no return to self save as image, only as echo. This is what returns in the Miltonic dream (the dream of Admetus as Perseus with the power of the Medusa, which is Alcestis, the living image) "rescued from death by force though pale and faint" (line 4). Here, too, syntax reverses, and we may ask *who* is pale and faint? Whose force accomplishes these returns, the rebounds of the image? For ultimately, what is "brought back" is "my night" (line 14). Once again, the encompassing circle of Night's "pale career" (*Il Penseroso*, line 121), the night that as early as the letter to his nameless friend, watching and warning, is the Miltonic day, in which he fears that he has given up himself "to dreame away my Yeares in the armes of studious retirement like Endymion with the Moone" (1:319). Embracing shadows.

The sun to me is dark
And silent as the moon,

When she deserts the night
Hid in her vacant interlunar cave.

(*SA*, 86-89)

No embrace of the image – except in the interlunar cave, the gap *between*: the tomb, the text.

What is the space of the Miltonic text, the interlunar cave of Echo constituted in "Methought I saw my late espoused saint," if not the place between me and thought, the space opened in thinking or revery, in which the dream image (the text) appears and withdraws, brought to "me like Alcestis from the grave"? Between the 'I' and the image the imaginary is transcribed through the simulacra of *likeness* including the agency of Hercules and the allusion to Alcestis and Admetus and their Ovidian echoes–Narcissus, Perseus, Orpheus–echoes of the return of voice-in-stone, or the blocking image.

The sonnet moves to what is "mine," and the image eludes the grasp, the syntax gapes on a space that cannot be embraced, the vacancy of a petrifying place:

Mine as whom washed from spot of childbed taint,
   Purification in the old Law did save,
   And such, as yet once more I trust to have
   Full sight of her in heaven without restraint,
Came vested all in white, pure as her mind:

Likeness and allusion produce the text in the mirror whose only truth is similitude: "as" is where this text is, "as . . . washed," "as yet once more," "as her mind"; similes continue to the end: "as in no face" (line 12), "as to embrace" (line 13). The place of *as*: where transformation is frozen into the image, where the delay of the return (the suspension of grammar) constitutes and impedes the text–and where the text is, and is the impediment. A place, in short, of "restraint," a dream both had and censored (within the dream and by awakening as well). Having "mine" is deferred to a future when "yet once more I trust to have," the hope of a beyond when the gap will be crossed, the wound closed, when 'I' and the reflection will unite. The text does not produce that return but the place of its transcription, in the block, in the impediment, the stone between where writing takes place.

And the beyond itself, the place of the hope, may itself be "yet once more" a place of repetition. Perhaps the dreamed of beyond and the hoped for return are the illusions that the image not only blocks but gives access to? Perhaps it is the place where origin and end are transcribed, held; perhaps, then, the image is the *truth* of origin and end, the truth of repetition, similitude – and thus, truth simulated.

153

The text transcribes what Blanchot (and Lacan) call the imaginary; indeed, Blanchot's essay, "Two Versions of the Imaginary" reads as a virtual gloss on Milton's final sonnet; for its image of the return of the ghost of his wife (of mine in the mirror) responds to Blanchot's opening question about the image: what is a cadaver? What, if not the occupant of a space neither of the dead or the living, a space defined when we say of the cadaver, how *like* it is the one who died, how true-to-life. That likeness, Blanchot argues, is the simulacrum of the image, its truth. The "essence" of the cadaver is its resemblance, its preservation of resemblance and, thus, its intimation of an endurance beyond and before mortal limitation; yet a preservation preserved in the mortal remains. What remains and endures is the image. Through the image absence is mastered, loss is secured. Yet the image is of what is absent and lost and never to be had as it was; mortal remains remain. The image, Blanchot writes, "inclines towards the intimacy of what still continues to exist in the void";[57] it reveals the "being" of nothing. At the end of Milton's sonnet, the image "inclines," too, to an embrace which would be fatal, a claiming of the tomb. Refused, declined, the image establishes its presence and absence, the day and night, weakness and strength that the text can claim for itself, standing between the 'I' and the other, between "me" and "mine." *Fort! Da!* The game that Orpheus and Eurydice play in the grave. For what is intimate, Blanchot intimates, is the very impersonality and distance which the image opens up and occupies, the strange space in which it is neither living nor dead, not a person nor dead matter either. The impersonality, that is, of the enduring stone, the monument, the eternal resemblance. "Man is made in his own image."[58]

After the blocking and accumulation of "as's" that clog the center of Milton's text, it proceeds, in the end, to the meeting of 'I' and other in the shifting and slipping, the full ambiguity and uncanniness of having and losing, of day and night, seeing and blindness–the more than subtle displacement of logical categories, of temporal sequence–"I waked, she fled"–as dream and reality slide into the terrain of the text, occupy the place of "as" where such sliding can be solidified into the truth of essential resemblance. That place, Blanchot notes, is where dissimulation – the imaginary – establishes its primacy, "the fact that – before the beginning–nothingness is not equal to being, is only the *appearance* of the dissimulation of being, or else that dissimulation is more "original" than negation."[59] That place might also be called, or so Blanchot hints in a final note to "The Essential Solitude," *literature*: "in literature, doesn't language itself become entirely image, not a language containing images or putting reality into figures, but its own image, the image of language –and not a language full of imagery–or an imaginary language, a language no one speaks–that is to say, spoken from its own absence–in the same way that the image appears on the absence of the thing, a language that is also addressed to the shadow of events, not to their reality."[60] Shadows, fancy's realm: the echo of voice, a language no one speaks, a language in which the text speaks.

This beginning "before" beginning, this transcription on stone, this writing of the corpse is where Milton *is* in his texts. This space between opens up on that beginning. And in the dream of return that is the space of the image, the other comes and goes, identified and rejected, purified. This beginning, Julia Kristeva argues, poets find; she locates the site of the Medusa as the horrific place of abjection.[61] It blocks the Miltonic text as soon as "mine" appears, "Mine as whom washed from the spot of childbed taint." Milton's text is Kristeva's when she turns to the semiotics of Biblical abomination, the chapters on defilement and purification in Leviticus. Defilement, she argues, is rooted "in the cathexis of maternal function – mother, women, reproduction" (91), and purification is necessary since "the body must bear no trace of its debt to nature: it must be clean and proper in order to be fully symbolic" (102). The attachment to the mother is the origin in the imaginary, the state of primary narcissism in which there is no distinction between I and other, mother and child bound together in an inseparable union. But that union thus also represents (at least retrospectively) a threat when the I emerges into the oedipal/symbolic state. It evokes, then, horror, it provokes abjection, the repudiation of the abject that one is at the beginning, when one is not (is not, that is, a subject, an I, an ego). Then, the mother's body that one was, that is one's origin, becomes the object of self-loathing, and to purify the self, to split it off from the original dyad (we were not one at first but two, locked in the mirror of resemblance), it must be seen as defilement, and must be purified. The defilement that one *is*, "the death that 'I' am" (25). The loathing of the mother's body as the place of death that gives birth, that gives mortality, that signifies the frailty of the ego that emerges from the dyad. The splitting of the I that occurs in the entrance to the symbolic is the splitting off of the pre-ego that was joined to the mother by bonds of pleasure and pain (they were then indistinguishable, for there were no boundaries in the "original" state of twoness, there was no securing of the I).

To that dark night, Kristeva argues, poets are drawn and repelled: "The abject confronts us . . . with our earliest attempts to release the hold of *maternal* entity even before ex-isting outside of her, thanks to the autonomy of language" (13). The abject testifies to our constitutive loss, it speaks of the need for exclusion. It speaks, then, to the condition represented by Guyon–the twinning of writing with the repudiation of

155

desire. It testifies to the union of writing and death, "*a drive economy in want of an object*" (35). In Milton's final sonnet that pre-object, abject and identified, is the corpse that returns, purified and silent, the dead wife that like Alcestis is also the mother: "washed from spot of childhood taint." The mother that is "mine" and that witnesses origin, the originary voice (voiceless) that makes voice echo.

So that when he considered how his light was spent he discovered Patience preventing him, displacing him, speaking before he spoke. So that when he reaches out to the vision of return he finds himself blocked by the image that displaces and stands before, like a statue. So that the text is the body of inscription, Niobe and Echo and Medusa. Petrifying sight.[62]

Freud reads the Medusa as castration;[63] Kristeva reads the castration complex, the entrance into the oedipal/symbolic as rooted in the abjection of the imaginary state, the repudiation of the mother. As Lacan argues, man needs to posit woman as loss to cling to the illusion of his entirety.[64] But Milton bears on his eyeballs the trace of that illusion, the sign of his entrance into the symbolic. Bears it – and always (from the letter to the friend) – desired it as the sign of his exclusion. In the twin sonnet to "Methought I saw," "To Mr Cyriack Skinner Upon his Blindness," the connection of blindness and his mother's body is made. If she has been "washed from spot of childhood taint," his eyes are "clear/To outward view, of blemish or of spot" (lines 1-2). (In Leviticus, chapter 12 on the purification of women is followed by one on the blemishes of the body.) His eyes have been purified. Without spot: immaculate conception. Milton has seen the unseeable, looked where one may not, and, frozen, petrified, he produces the text where he conceives himself.[65] "I conceav'd my selfe to be now not as mine own person, but as a member incorporate into that truth whereof I was perswaded, and whereof I had declar'd openly to be a partaker. Whereupon I thought it my duty, if not to my selfe, yet to the religious cause I had in hand, not to leave on my garment the least spot, or blemish in good name so long as God should give me to say that which might wipe it off" (*Apology*, 1:871).

A membership in the Truth of resemblance where he conceives himself not as a self (his good name his anonymity) but a partaker, pen "in hand," wiping the garment clean – the garment of language (compare "At a Vacation Exercise"), mother tongue, mother church. Printless writing. Pure and white. "He, waking early (as is the use of temperate men), had commonly a good stock of verses ready against his amanuensis came; which if it happened to be later then ordinary, he would complain, saying *he wanted to be milked*."[66]

*

The dark and vicious place where thee he got
Cost him his eyes.

(King Lear, 5.3, 173-4)

*

He can scarcely begin to tell the story of his life, whenever he tells it –
in *Reason of Church-government*, in the *Second Defence* – without
pronouncing "my father"(1:808, 4:612). Sarah Milton is so rarely
mentioned that it provokes Erik Erikson's question about Luther, did the
man have a mother?[67] She is mentioned in the *Second Defence*, "my
mother a woman of purest reputation, celebrated throughout the
neighborhood for her acts of charity" (4:612). A mother unspotted as
his eyes (yet Aubrey recalls that her eyes were weak), profuse in her
generosity–the bounty of nature poured forth in profusion. *Ad Patrem*
shows the oedipal struggle, the struggle to repay a debt he does not want;
from his lips, from his heart, flows the Pierian stream that originates in
the twin peaks (lines 1-3); "still govern thou my song,/Urania" (*PL* 7:30-
31), "nor could the Muse defend/Her son" (7:37-38). When Jesus recalls
his life (so uncomfortably like Milton's, as editors regularly note), his
mother's voice enters his, and, yet once more, one cannot tell when one
stops and the other starts (see *PR* 1:230ff.). This, in the penultimate poem,
opening in the affirmation that it, at last, is the poem he covenanted to
write (and *Paradise Lost* merely the pastoral prelude); *Paradise Regained*
closes, however, by preventing that assertion, the career has not yet
begun, a return, yet once more, to his mother's house. And then, at last,
Samson Agonistes, the son finally paying the debt to his father, the poem
that finally moves forward to the only place that the writer seeks–death,
when, finally, as Blanchot says, the work exists and the author is dead.
In that beginning is his end.

The imagination is like Adam's dream, Keats wrote, he awoke and found
it true. "Methought I saw,/Though sleeping, where I lay . . . wide was the
wound . . . I waked/To find her, or for ever to deplore/Her loss" (*PL*
8:462-80).

When out of hope, behold her, not far off
Such as I saw her in my dream, adorned
With what all earth or heaven could bestow
To make her amiable: on she came,
Led by her heavenly maker, though unseen,
And guided by his voice.

(PL 8:481-86)

157

Adam awakes to separation and loss, to the necessity of repetition, to the wound within now without. Adam awakens indeed to the truth of the imagination, the truth of the image. Original resemblance. The block that separates and on which the poet transcribes the primal loss, the loss of primacy, always beginning again.

*

Where does human history occur if not within the prohibition. What is the prohibition? "Sole daughter of his voice" (*PL* 9:653), the biblical name for Echo.[68] Or the place of the Miltonic text. Preventive space. Preventing birth. Preventing death. Coming before oneself.

Notes

1 Terminals:

1 Telephone relays are antecedents of the voice terminal, but the name has encouraged an image of vocal immediacy; consider, too, a series of advertisements for AT&T widely broadcast in the last few years: "reach out and touch someone" is the message, and juxtaposed screens show each party on the telephone. Both phenomena – telephone and voice terminal – would fall under Jean Baudrillard's condemnation of the obscenity of modern communication: "All functions abolished in a single dimension, that of communication. That's the ecstasy of communication. All secrets, spaces and scenes abolished in a single dimension of information. That's obscenity" in "The Ecstasy of Communication," in Hal Foster, ed., *The Anti-Aesthetic: Essays on Postmodern Culture* (Port Townsend, Washington: Bay Press, 1983), p. 131.

2 "Marvell's Nymph and the Echo of Voice" appeared originally in *Glyph 8: Johns Hopkins Textual Studies* (Baltimore: Johns Hopkins University Press, 1981), pp. 19-39.

3 On simulation as the woman's truth–an issue related to the choice of the nymph as voice–see Jacques Derrida, *Spurs: Nietzsche's Styles/Eperons: Les Styles de Nietzsche*, trans. Barbara Harlow (Chicago: University of Chicago Press, 1978, 1979), esp. pp. 60-61, 66-71.

4 Elizabeth Story Donno, ed., *Andrew Marvell: The Complete Poems* (Harmondsworth: Penguin Books, 1972), p. 246. For a discussion of the historical moment implicit in Marvell's lyrics, see Barbara Everett, "The Shooting of the Bears: Poetry and Politics in Andrew Marvell," in R. L. Brett, ed., *Andrew Marvell: Essays on the Tercentenary of his Death* (Oxford: Oxford University Press, 1979). The Nymph, she argues, is caught "in a moment of real time" and voices the knowledge "that something is finished" (p. 96).

5 On the historicity of Milton's "subject-position," see Anthony Easthope, "Towards the Autonomous Subject: *Milton On His Blindness*," in Francis Barker, ed., *1642: Literature and Power in the Seventeenth Century*, Proceedings of

the Essex Conference on the Sociology of Literature, July 1980 (Colchester: University of Essex, 1981), pp. 301-14, and Francis Barker, *The Tremulous Private Body: Essays on Subjection* (London: Methuen, 1984), pp. 41-52.

6 Milton's texts are quoted from *The Poems of John Milton*, ed. John Carey and Alastair Fowler (London: Longman, 1968; New York: W. W. Norton, 1972).

7 Jacques Derrida, *Dissemination*, trans. Barbara Johnson (Chicago: University of Chicago Press, 1981), p. 304.

8 Spenser's texts are quoted from *The Poetical Works of Edmund Spenser*, ed. J. C. Smith and E. de Selincourt (London: Oxford University Press, 1912).

9 *Dissemination*, p. 329.

10 The proverb appears in *Lingua* and is quoted by Terence Cave, *The Cornucopian Text: Problems of Writing in the French Renaissance* (Oxford: Clarendon Press, 1979), pp. 164-65.

11 Shakespeare, *Hamlet*, ed. Willard Farnham (Baltimore: Penguin Books, 1957), 1:5, 99-101.

12 Jacques Lacan, *Le Séminaire, livre XX: Encore* (Paris: Seuil, 1975): "Je ne puis ici que supposer que vous évoquerez mon énoncé qu'il n'y a pas d'Autre de l'Autre. L'Autre, ce lieu où vient s'inscrire tout ce qui peut s'articuler du signifiant, est, dans son fondement, radicalement l'Autre" (p. 75).

13 Milton, *Reason of Church-Government*, ed. Ralph A. Haug, in *Complete Prose of John Milton*, ed. Douglas Bush *et al.* (New Haven: Yale University Press, 1953), 1:815.

14 Herbert's texts are quoted from *The Works of George Herbert*, ed. F. E. Hutchinson (Oxford: Clarendon Press, 1941).

15 Edward Said, *Beginnings: Intention & Method* (Baltimore: Johns Hopkins University Press, 1975), p. 210. Cf. Jacques Derrida, "D'un ton apocalyptique," in *Les fins de l'homme: à partir du travail de Jacques Derrida* (Paris: Galilée, 1981), esp. pp. 469-71.

16 Geoffrey Hartman, "Adam on the Grass with Balsamum," in *Beyond Formalism: Literary Essays, 1958-1970* (New Haven: Yale University Press, 1970), p. 125.

17 Geoffrey Hartman, *Saving the Text: Literature/Derrida/Philosophy* (Baltimore: Johns Hopkins University Press, 1981), p. 49.

18 *Cornucopian Text*, p. 124. For some suggestions about *copia* and grammatological invention, see Gregory L. Ulmer, *Applied Grammatology: Post(e)-Pedagogy from Jacques Derrida to Joseph Beuys* (Baltimore: Johns Hopkins University Press, 1985), pp. 150, 180-81.

19 ibid., p. 151.

20 John Freccero, "The Fig Tree and the Laurel: Petrarch's Poetics," *Diacritics* 5 (1975): 34.

21 *Dissemination*, p. 309.

22 Thomas M. Greene, *The Light in Troy: Imitation and Discovery in Renaissance Poetry* (New Haven: Yale University Press, 1982), p. 45.

23 Lawrence Lipking, *The Life of the Poet: Beginning and Ending Poetic Careers* (Chicago: University of Chicago Press, 1981). The progressive–teleological–plot, its demarcation into rationalized stages, the autonomized "being" of poets-in-

poems, are all implicit in Lipking's guiding questions: "How does an aspiring author of verses become a poet? How does a poet, once established, face the challenge of refreshening and deepening his work, instead of being content to write the same poem over and over? What is the legacy a poet leaves?" (p. vii). Cf. "A poet who wants to grow must learn to read his own early works, to explore its secret life and hidden meanings" (p. 15); poets, it seems, have been to a school of New Criticism.

24 Maurice Blanchot, "The Essential Solitude," in *The Gaze of Orpheus*, trans. Lydia Davis (Barrytown, New York: Station Hill Press, 1981), p. 66. Blanchot's point is that the writer *writes* the work, which is not the same as reading it, that in order for the writer to go on writing he cannot become a reader. Blanchot's writer always begins again, and does not see the totality of the work; the reader constructs such a totality. The writer faces an abyss.

25 These are the terms–contingency, materialism, impertinence–of Alan Singer's *A Metaphorics of Fiction: Discontinuity and Discourse in the Modern Novel* (Tallahassee: Florida State University, 1983), a deconstruction of the naturalism of novels through an examination of the motivating tropes (particularly catachresis) of modern fiction.

26 *Saving the Text*, p. 14.

27 "Translator's Introduction," pp. xvi-xviii. To these qualities, one might add a relentless and repetitive habit of reading, almost talmudic in style. The effect of these clashing styles has been likened to collage by Gregory L. Ulmer in "The Object of Post-Criticism" (in *The Anti-Aesthetic*); he asks, "Will the collage/montage revolution in representation be admitted into the academic essay, into the discourse of knowledge, replacing the 'realist' criticism based on the notions of 'truth' as correspondence to or correct reproduction of a referent object of study?" (p. 86).

28 Emile Benveniste, "Active and Middle Voice in the Verb," in *Problems in General Linguistics*, trans. Mary Elizabeth Meek (Coral Gables, Florida: University of Miami Press, 1971), p. 146.

29 ibid., p. 148.

30 "Subjectivity in Language," in *Problems in General Linguistics*, pp. 226, 224. See also "Relation of Person in the Verb" and "The Nature of Pronouns" in the same volume.

31 See, for example, "Excommunication," in *The Four Fundamental Concepts of Psycho-Analysis*, trans. Alan Sheridan (New York: W. W. Norton, 1978), pp. 11-12.

32 This is Derrida's argument in "Le Facteur de la Vérité" (in *La Carte Postale* (Paris: Flammarion, 1980), trans. in part as "The Purveyor of Truth," *Yale French Studies*, 52 (1975), 31-114). His position has been analyzed by Barbara Johnson in "The Frame of Reference: Poe, Lacan, Derrida," *Yale French Studies*, 55-56 (1978): 457-505, revised version in *Psychoanalysis and the Question of the Text*, ed. Geoffrey H. Hartman (Baltimore: Johns Hopkins University Press, 1978).

33 Jacques Derrida, *Positions*, trans. Alan Bass (Chicago: University of Chicago Press, 1981), pp. 28-29.

34 Cf. *Dissemination*, " The Double Session," pp. 177ff. The jotting by Mallarmé

quoted below is reproduced on p. 275.

35 In *Beyond Formalism*, pp. 337-55. The passage is discussed on pp. 337-38; the chart appears on p. 353. For Derrida's shuttle (*la navette*), see *Glas* (Paris: Galilée, 1974), pp. 232-33.

36 In "Adam on the Grass," *Beyond Formalism*, p. 146.

37 On catachresis, see Singer, *A Metaphorics of Fiction*, pp. 41-45, 58. The trope is also used by Derrida to explore the meaning of philosophy's truth in "White Mythology: Metaphor in the Text of Philosophy," in *Margins of Philosophy*, trans. Alan Bass (Chicago: University of Chicago Press, 1982).

38 John Hollander, *The Figure of Echo: A Mode of Allusion in Milton and After* (Berkeley and Los Angeles: University of California Press, 1981). Hollander's densely elegant book offers a discussion of the acoustic phenomenon of echo; a history of the mythological representations of the figure; a study of acoustic echo phenomena in verse; and a study of the figure-as-figure, including an appendix on the history of metalepsis. The book is invaluable.

For some further detail on the history of echo–and Echo–in classical literature, see Joseph Loewenstein, *Responsive Readings: Versions of Echo in Pastoral, Epic, and the Jonsonian Masque* (New Haven: Yale University Press, 1984). Loewenstein's elusive argument for the authority, autonomy, and anachrony of Echo (as the voice of the poet), although at times finely tuned to the complexities "of voice radically without presence" (p. 103), more often absorbs the resistances (especially of the political and historical) to a poetics of allusion as "a literary locus amoenus" (p. 130), an empire of the ear.

39 Quintilian, *Institutes*, III. vi. 37-39, cited in *The Figure of Echo*, p. 135.

40 Cf. *Dissemination*, t.n. 9, p. 182 and pp. 212-13.

41 Bacon, *De dignitate et augmentis scientarum*, II, xiii, cited in *The Figure of Echo*, p. 10; the telling of Echo's story depends on the chapter entitled "Echo Allegorical."

42 Geoffrey H. Hartman, "Evening Star and Evening Land" in *The Fate of Reading* (Chicago: University of Chicago Press, 1975), p. 163.

43 ibid., p. 161-62.

44 "Wordworth and Goethe in Literary History," in *The Fate of Reading*, pp. 195-96.

45 Jacques Derrida, *Speech and Phenomena*, trans. David B. Allison (Evanston, Illinois: Northwestern University Press, 1973), p. 77. Cf. "The Pit and the Pyramid: Introduction to Hegel's Semiology," in *Margins*, p. 95.

46 Jacques Derrida, "Qual Quelle: Valéry's Sources," in *Margins*, p. 287.

47 *Dissemination*, p. 323.

48 Derrida examines the passages from Aristotle's texts in "White Mythology," in *Margins*, pp. 236-41. The Platonic text–and with it the concept of mimesis–is studied in "The Double Session" in *Dissemination*.

49 Virgil, *Eclogue 1*, in vol. 1 of the Loeb edition, trans. H. Rushton Fairclough (Cambridge, Mass.: Harvard University Press, 1953).

50 For a bibliography of the *silva* tradition, see Alastair Fowler, "The Silva Tradition in Jonson's *The Forrest*," in *Poetic Traditions of the English Renaissance*, ed. Maynard Mack and George deForest Lord (New Haven: Yale University Press,

1982), pp. 163-66.
51 *The Figure of Echo*, p. 61.
52 *Dissemination*, p. 306.
53 ibid., p. 299.

2   Marvell's nymph and the echo of voice

1   All citations from *The Poems and Letters of Andrew Marvell*, ed. H. M. Margoliouth, vol. 1 (Oxford: Clarendon Press, 1952). To these examples might be added the song in "Bermudas," which may rebound from heaven to "Eccho beyond the *Mexique Bay*" (line 36), especially in light of Barbara Everett's description of the poem in "The Shooting of the Bears: Poetry and Politics in Andrew Marvell," in R. L. Brett, ed., *Andrew Marvell: Essays on the Tercentenary of His Death* (Oxford: Oxford University Press, 1979): "The boat moves, it is unclear where, and the song rises, it is unclear from whom or to whom–indeed, it seems unclear to the singers themselves, whoever they are . . ." (p. 100). On the vault in "To His Coy Mistress" and its marking "a mute limit of the penetrative capacity of the male voice" (p. 93), see Francis Barker, *The Tremulous Private Body* (London: Methuen, 1984), pp. 85-94 *passim*.

2   I place the word *about* in quotations marks to indicate that the function of language in "The Nymph complaining" is not mimesis. Most criticism of this poem has foundered in believing that the voice in the text belongs to a dramatic character (a character created in "her" language) who is then judged problematic or defective since, at times, the language of the poem goes beyond the character imagined to be speaking (for example, with "*Deodands*" or the "*Heliades*"); at other times, it seems naive or inhuman. Thus, for example, Rosalie Colie condemns the nymph as self-regarding, myopic, irrational and overly emotional in "*My Ecchoing Song*": *Andrew Marvell's Poetry of Criticism* (Princeton: Princeton University Press, 1970), pp. 87-88, 127. Like many other critics faced with the dilemma of the voice of the poem, Colie attempts to assess these excesses and lapses in relation to the poet, and she wavers between seeing the nymph as a poet and the nymph as an ironic relation of the real and "feeling" poet (pp. 113, 119, 125); she ends by trying to have it both ways: "Clearly, though he deplores the nymph's narrowness of vision, he appreciates her sweetness and her taste, and makes us acknowledge the power and appeal of her aesthetic sensibility" (p. 132). Colie is alive to the many generic and allusive elements in the text (although she faults them for failing to cohere) and, as she says well, "*Something* is exhausted in this poem; but I am not quite sure what it is" (p. 61).

Other critics have tried to rescue the poem by centering it on some allusive pattern – biblical or classical – or on the reality of some psychological process supposedly independent of the poem. This is the argument, for example, in Phoebe S. Spinrad, "Death, Loss, and Marvell's Nymph," *PMLA* 97 (1982): 50-59, whose pluralistic stance declares all prior readings true – and inadequate – since the poem is about an "ageless and universal" (p. 53) pattern of the mind and depicts a psychological process that points to themes shared by "all art"

(p. 59). Spinrad, without quite offering an *ego* in the poem, offers the text as a piece of ego-psychology; her "universal" frame is, however, an unnoted text, Elizabeth Kübler-Ross's anatomy of the stages of mourning; Spinrad makes Marvell's nymph the purveyor of an upbeat moralism. As a critical position, Spinrad offers pop psychology; everyone is all right. Rather than the "reality" of the mind, John J. Teunissen and Evelyn J. Hinz, in "What is the Nymph Complaining For," *ELH* 45 (1978): 410-28, offer the reality of the body; the fawn (as its etymology suggests) is a foetus; Sylvio's crime was a literal seduction. The poem is really "about" this "external" event.

My "about" means to avoid such presuppositions about inside and outside and about representation and its relation to some reality other than that of the text; language speaks here in a site of excess and not through a speaker who owns language. The critical position I assume is thus indebted to Derrida's grammatological investigations and to Lacanian psychoanalysis. Historically, the argument can be assimilated to the Renaissance "prose of the world" described by Michel Foucault in *The Order of Things* (New York: Vintage, 1970), language in an infinite regress, not regulated by what Foucault calls the "classical" conditions of representation. One further note: my "about" does not indicate a return to New Critical formalism, with its declarations of the contained, art-for-art's sake text. I do not assume (or describe) a closed text, nor one bounded by authorial control or intention.

3 "'The Nymph Complaining for the Death of Her Faun': A Brief Allegory," in *Beyond Formalism* (New Haven: Yale University Press, 1970), pp. 173-92. For the reasons noted above, I do not subscribe to the religious allegory that Hartman offers in the second half of the essay.

4 Jacques Derrida, *Of Grammatology*, trans. Gayatri Chakravorty Spivak (Baltimore: Johns Hopkins University Press, 1974, 1976), p. 7. In other words, the nymph as, simultaneously, demimythical consort of a faun and a young woman is not a name which signifies a signified, but a name which is already written into a chain of signifiers without a final determination. Hence, the notion of the text as a dramatic monologue falls in the play of the word, a play continued in the "object" of speech, the faun/fawn/h[e]art.

5 *The Collected Poems of Sir Thomas Wyatt*, ed. Kenneth Muir (Cambridge, Mass.: Harvard University Press, 1950). Cf. no. 26, "I fynde no peace and all my warr is done," for a typical Petrarchan enumeration of the lover's antitheses.

6 Silvia is the owner of the pet stag that Ascanius murders in *Aeneid* 7: 475-509. The episode has frequently been cited as an allusion; what has not been noted is the transformation in name. The circuit that produces the nymph passes through Silvia, the voteress of Diana in Tasso's *Aminta*, and Silvio, the chaste hunter and enemy of love in Guarini's *Il Pastor Fido*. This final, witty repositioning of Sylvio functions as both a reversal and an identification; is the nymph's name "really" Sylvia? Such an argument might be supported by Harry Berger Jr.'s presentation of the nymph as a study in narcissism, in "Andrew Marvell: the Poem as Green World," *Forum for Modern Language Studies* 3 (1967): 290-309, although his focus is on the identification of nymph and fawn,

which he also likens to the story of Pygmalion, but played in two directions, so that the nymph is both the artist-maker, as well as the statue (pp. 291, 297).

Spenser's Sylvio is the Sylvanus of *The Faerie Queene*, I. vi. 15ff.; all citations from *The Poetical Works of Edmund Spenser,* ed. J. C. Smith and E. de Selincourt (London: Oxford University Press, 1912). Seeing Una, an echo of remembrance leads Sylvanus to "His ancient love, and dearest *Cyparisse,*/And calles to mind his pourtraiture alive,/How faire he was, and yet not faire to this,/And how he slew with glauncing dart amisse/A gentle Hynd, the which the lovely boy/Did love as life, above all worldly blisse" (I. vi. 17. 2-7). As Hugh Maclean notes in *Edmund Spenser's Poetry* (New York: W. W. Norton, 1968), p. 68, Spenser re-casts Ovid, *Metamorphoses* x. 10:106-42 along lines suggested by Natalis Comes's *Mythologiae*. In Ovid, Cyparissus is both the lover and murderer of the deer; Sylvanus's love for Cyparissus is, in Comes, an explanation of his attribute (the cypress) in Virgil (see Natalis Comes, *Mythologie*, trans. J. de Montlyard, ed. J. Baudouin (Paris, 1627; New York: Garland Publishing, 1976), IV. xi, p. 328; V. xi, p. 450). Harry Berger, Jr. comments on Spenser's Sylvanus: "Half goat, half man, a deity of woods and gardens, he is truly a god of boundaries: mere nature emerging into human nature, or, conversely, human nature tending toward its lower origins," in "Spenser's *Faerie Queene*, Book I: Prelude to Interpretation," *Southern Review* 2 (1966): 34. Spenser's account of the relation of Sylvanus and Cyparissus crosses another boundary, as well, since "he" (I. vi. 17. 5) may refer to either of them as the deerslayer.

7   Roland Barthes, *S/Z*, trans. Richard Miller (New York: Hill and Wang, 1974), pp. 176-77.

8   Lines cited above: from Sidney, *Astrophil and Stella*, *Fourth Song* refrain, *The Poems of Sir Philip Sidney*, ed. William A. Ringler, Jr. (Oxford: Clarendon Press, 1962); Wyatt, no. 66; John Donne, "Wilt thou forgive the sinn, where I begunn," *The Poems*, ed. H. J. C. Grierson (Oxford: Clarendon Press, 1912), 1: 370. The refrain (lines 5-6, 11-12) can finally be stopped (lines 17-18) by depleting the voice (" I have noe more") and replacing the endless word ("done") in the endless Word ("thou hast done").

9   See Ovid, *Metamorphoses*, 3: 339-510. In the account that follows, I depend on the following episodes in the story, which I retell here to point up the echoes. Echo first sees Narcissus netting a deer (line 356); alone, Narcissus calls out: "'ecquis adest?' et 'adest' responderat Echo" (line 380); when she is repulsed, Echo turns to stone (line 397). Narcissus retiring to a tree-circled pool (line 412) loves the image in the water; staring at it, transfixed like a statue ("ut e Pario formatum marmore signum" (line 419)), beautiful as a god mingling red and white (lines 420-24), he desires a form that moves forward and backward and yet eludes his grasp (lines 425-36). At the moment that he reports that he cannot hear the words in the mirror (lines 461-62), he realizes whom he loves: "inopem me copia fecit" (line 466), he cries out – in a line that may echo through Renaissance discussions of *copia*. Desiring somehow to separate himself from the image, he dies, and with him the image, both gone in a single breath (lines 467-72); he dies, beating his breast ruddy with his pallid hands (lines 480-85),

crying out, and Echo resounding (lines 494-501). Citations from the Loeb edition, ed. F. J. Miller (Cambridge, Mass.: Harvard University Press, 1960). For summaries of further texts, see Louise Vinge, *The Narcisssus Theme in Western Literature up to the Early Nineteenth Century* (Lund: Gleerups, 1967).

10   Sigmund Freud, *Beyond the Pleasure Principle*, trans. James Strachey (New York: W. W. Norton, 1961), ch. 2, pp. 8-9. Jacques Derrida's reading of chapter 2 of *BPP*, "Coming into One's Own," trans. James Hulbert, in *Psychoanalysis and the Question of the Text*, ed. Geoffrey H. Hartman (Baltimore: Johns Hopkins University Press, 1978), emphasizes the *Fort! Da!* as the scene of writing, of writing *BPP*. (The argument is extracted from Derrida's "Spéculer–Sur 'Freud'," in *La Carte Postale* (Paris: Flammarion, 1980).) Derrida acutely notices that the reel is inserted and withdrawn from a curtained bed, and goes on to say (using terms developed as well in "The Double Session," in *Dissémination*, trans. Barbara Johnson (Chicago: University of Chicago Press, 1981)): "This I call the *hymen* of the *fort:da:* The veil is the interesting thing about the bed and the *fort:da* of all these generations" (p. 130). In my reading, I too am assuming that the text is about writing itself, that in the Renaissance the veiled mode is allegory, that the movement of the fawn (the "it") is a movement of text–what Derrida might call its iterability, a term developed, for example, in "Signature Event Context," in *Margins of Philosophy*, trans. Alan Bass (Chicago: University of Chicago Press, 1982); that within the text it serves–as does the child's reel in Freud–as a replacement for the lost-absent-beloved (a critical commonplace about the poem) *and* as an image for the self who disappears and reappears in a mirror–Narcissus, or what Lacan calls the mirror-stage; see Jacques Lacan, "The Mirror Stage as Formative of the Function of the I," in *Ecrits: A Selection*, trans. Alan Sheridan (New York: W. W. Norton, 1977); the "it" I discuss also bears comparison with Lacan's "The Freudian Thing." Marvell's text, like Freud's, is generated in the *Fort! Da!*, as the multiple senses of "Race" (at line 66; cf. "The Garden," line 28) suggest, and as the "print" reinforces. Freud's text, insofar as it touches on questions of eros, loss, mourning, pleasure, death, and repetition, seems necessary to bear in mind reading "The Nymph complaining." The pertinence of psychoanalysis to Marvell's poem is suggested, too, when Geoffrey Hartman describes the therapeutic scene this way: "the analyst is attracted to and therefore protects himself from the ecstatic message, the heart of darkness in the patient, that is, in himself. He hunts the wounded hart as in some spiritual chase, but only to build on it (strange rock that weeps) . . .": in "Psychoanalysis: The French Connection," in *Psychoanalysis and the Question of the Text*, pp. 89-90; reprinted in *Saving the Text* (Baltimore: Johns Hopkins University Press, 1981), pp. 98-99.

11   To tabulate the twenty-six appearances of "it" or a form of it in lines 55-92: occurrences at lines 56, 57, 58, 59, 60, 63, 64, 66, 67, 68, 69, 73, 76, 78 (twice), 79, 80, 82, 83, 84, 85, 87, 88, 89, 91 (twice). Iteration joins the fawn and the garden in the voice.

12   Marsilio Ficino, "Five Questions Concerning the Mind," trans. Josephine L. Burroughs in *The Renaissance Philosophy of Man*, ed. E. Cassirer, P. O. Kristeller,

and J. H. Randall (Chicago: University of Chicago Press, 1948), pp. 200-1.

13   In the midst of a not surprising rationalizing and moralizing interpretation of Narcissus and Echo, George Sandys, in *Ovid's Metamorphosis Englished Mythologiz'd And Represented* (1632), comments on "The image of the voice so often rendred, is as that of the face reflected from one glasse to another; melting by degrees, and every reflection more weake and shady then the former. *Ausonius* makes *Eccho* thus speake to the Painter that would have drawne her; Fond Painter, why wouldst thou my picture draw?/An unknowne Goddesse, whome none ever saw./Daughter of aire and tongue: of iudgement blind/The mother I; a voice without a mind./I only with an others language sport;/And but the last of dying speech retort./Lowd Ecchos mansion in the eare is found:/If therefore thou wilt paint me, paint a sound" (p. 104). Sandys' *image of voice* is a veritable Derridean "mise en abŷme," the heraldic term glossed by James Hulbert's note to "Coming Into One's Own" as "a structure in which the whole is represented in miniature in one of its parts" (pp. 147-48). John Hollander explores the *image of voice* as *The Figure of Echo* (Berkeley and Los Angeles: University of California Press, 1981), pp. 9ff., *et passim*.

14   *The Works of Geoffrey Chaucer*, ed. F. N. Robinson (Boston: Houghton Mifflin, 1957), *General Prologue* to *The Canterbury Tales*, lines 5-6. For some examples of Petrarch's ubiquitous puns on Laura, see "Di pensier in pensier, di monte in monte" (no.129), "L'aura celeste che 'n quel verde lauro" (no.197), "L'aura che 'l verse lauro et l'aureo crine" (no.246), "Rotta è l'alta colonna, e 'l verde lauro" (no.269); these are connected, as Robert M. Durling argues in the "Introduction" to his edition of *Petrarch's Lyric Poems* (Cambridge, Mass.: Harvard University Press, 1976), to Ovidian metamorphoses – including the Narcissus/Echo story (pp. 26-33). For the reciprocity of the lady made by the poet and the poet made (laureated) by the lady, and for the radical fragmentation implicit in the punning disseminations of Laura, see John Freccero, "The Fig Tree and the Laurel: Petrarch's Poetics," *Diacritics* 7 (1975): 34-40. Spenser, of course, takes the allegorical implications in this dissolve as a key feature in his poetry; his diction is Chaucerian, his narrative models Ovid and the Bible. These texts are "in" the voice of Marvell's text.

15   For the etymology, as well as the brief description offered here, I depend on Angus Fletcher, *Allegory: The Theory of a Symbolic Mode* (Ithaca: Cornell University Press, 1964). The argument is extended in my *Endlesse Worke: Spenser and the Structures of Discourse* (Baltimore: Johns Hopkins University Press, 1981).

16   Paul de Man, "The Rhetoric of Temporality," in *Interpretation: Theory and Practice*, ed. Charles S. Singleton (Baltimore: Johns Hopkins Press, 1969), p. 191. De Man's argument is about Rousseau, but contextualized in a discussion that alludes back to St Augustine and Petrarch.

17   Geoffrey Hartman beautifully documents the epigraphical form of the poem in his essay in *Beyond Formalism*, esp. pp. 177-80. Poems are written upon occasions, upon objects, but, in any case, texts are situated in relationship to something which is not there and which the text replaces. The strange "being"

of texts, as the memorial of loss, is complicated as well by the fact that texts are written "upon" other texts, an act at once foundational and obliterative (an echo effect). In "The Nymph complaining," the place of writing is the difference generated in the Sylvio/*Silvae* pun, a boundary marking the passage nature/art. Illumination on this troping is shed by Rensselear W. Lee, *Names on Trees: Ariosto into Art* (Princeton: Princeton University Press, 1977), which traces the motif of writing-on-trees in Renaissance texts back to classical sources and the medieval *liber naturae*. Lee remarks that when a lover, like Orlando in *As You Like It*, wounds the bark, the tree is treated as a blank page now written "with the thought of lovers" (p. 6). Marvell's witty inversion of this trope in "The Garden" attempts a collapse of this turn of the trope back into some "original" form, and his tautology (Pan loving Syrinx as a reed and all the tree-lovers in that generation) permits the *différance* nature-as-text/text-as-nature by making the writing of tree *on* the tree an indication of the secondarity of all signifiers. This verge (of nature/art) is, obviously, a crucial one–it is Lévi-Strauss's nature/culture boundary (also undecidable), and the margin of representation. It is also a privileged demonstration in structuralist linguistics, Saussure having chosen (not so accidentally) to represent the signifier/signified relationship with an image of a tree and the word "Arbor" below it; see Ferdinand de Saussure, *Cours de Linguistique Générale* (Paris: Payot, 1967), p. 99, a metaphysical "naturalism" scrutinized by Derrida in *Of Grammatology*, and by Lacan in "The Agency of the Letter in the Unconscious," *Ecrits*, p. 151.

18   And so perhaps the body of the text is, in Roland Barthes's terms, "the Zambinellan body . . . real . . . only insofar as it descends from a body already written by statuary (Ancient Greece, Pygmalion). . . ." (*S/Z*, pp. 114-15). More radically, the statue, as Maurice Blanchot suggests, images the "being" of the text–its "objective" status; see, for example, "Reading," in *The Gaze of Orpheus*, trans. Lydia Davis (Barrytown, N.Y.: Station Hill, 1981), p.94.

For the already written statue behind Marvell's, see, for example, Spenser's *Aprill* eclogue in *The Shepheardes Calender*. Colin's lay in praise of the incomparable Eliza refuses and engages this superlative: "I will not match her with *Latonaes* seede,/Such follie great sorow to *Niobe* did breede./Now she is a stone,/And makes dayly mone,/Warning all other to take heede" (lines 86-90). The passage is also discussed in chapter 3 below; Niobe is further investigated in chapter 6.

19   "Mourning," lines 33-36.

3   Consuming texts: Spenser and the poet's economy

1   All citations from *The Poetical Works of Edmund Spenser*, ed. J. C. Smith and E. de Selincourt (London: Oxford University Press, 1912). My account of *The Shepheardes Calender* is indebted to Harry Berger Jr.'s treatment of disjunctiveness in this text implicit in "A Secret Discipline," in *Form and Convention in the Poetry of Edmund Spenser*, ed. William Nelson (New York: Columbia University Press, 1961) and developed in "Mode and Diction in *The*

Shepheardes Calender," *MP* 67 (1969): 140-49, an account of the "variety of perspectives" (p. 140) that are criticized in the poems. Berger concludes his essay by noting that eclogues are, etymologically, *fragments*, and that Spenser's are, at once, dessicated and excessive (p. 149). These observations can be aligned to Michel Beaujour's description of the Renaissance book as "nonnarrative, nonmimetic . . . the disconnected entries (or fragments) of a virtual encyclopedia-to-be. . . . The titles under which these texts were published imply an apologia for their shapelessness: essays, *sylva*, timber, *bocage*, *bizarrures*, anatomy, meditations, etc." ("Genus Universum," *Glyph* 7(1980), p. 27). The range of allusions that Spenser's book (as book) makes has been explored by Ruth Samson Luborsky, in "The Allusive Presentation of *The Shepheardes Calender*," *Spenser Studies* 1 (1980): 29-67. Michael McCanles has associated E. K.'s role in the book as a gesture towards making it a classic text with typical editorial apparatus, in "*The Shepheardes Calender* as Document and Monument," *SEL* 22 (1982): 5-19. Richard Newton has compared the miscellany, as a type of Renaissance book that diffuses the author into fragmentary texts, with the claims to narrative continuity that the sonnet sequence makes or the critical consistency of Ben Jonson's stance, in "Poems Becoming Texts," forthcoming.

2   In "Authorship, Anonymity, and *The Shepheardes Calender*," *MLQ* 40 (1979): 219-36, David L. Miller reads anonymity as part of a cultural tradition that reveals Spenser's intention to make his poem a classic text that offers itself as "the fiction of a self-made poem" (p. 225). He suggestively notes Sidney's *fathering* role of this orphaned text (p. 225). His Colin is a negative exemplar (pp. 233-36), a position voiced in a number of recent essays, for example by Louis Adrian Montrose in "'The perfecte paterne of a Poete': The Poetics of Courtship in *The Shepheardes Calender*," *Texas Studies in Literature and Language* 21 (1979): 34-67, who reads Colin as Spenser's projection of a failed career, Immeritô as his projection of the author of the poem; Spenser is neither of these personae. Miller has extended his arguments to Spenser's entire career in "Spenser's Vocation, Spenser's Career," *ELH* 50 (1983): 197-231, arguing for the tensions in a platonic poetics of a social/spiritual transcendence. His reading of social relations draws upon Montrose as well as Richard Helgerson's important essay, "The New Poet Presents Himself: Spenser and the Idea of a Literary Career," *PMLA* 93 (1978): 893-911, incorporated into *Self-Crowned Laureates: Spenser, Jonson, Milton, and the Literary System* (Berkeley and Los Angeles: University of California Press, 1983). Harry Berger Jr. enunciated the "paradise principle" in "Mode and Diction" as "a single restrictive ideal" that underlies and limits the escapist and reforming stances articulated in the poem (*MP* 67 (1969), p. 142). He has extended his argument in "The Aging Boy: Paradise and Parricide in Spenser's *Shepheardes Calender*," in *Poetic Traditions of the English Renaissance*, ed. Maynard Mack and George deForest Lord (New Haven: Yale University Press, 1982), "Orpheus, Pan, and the Poetics of Misogyny: Spenser's Critique of Pastoral Love and Art," *ELH* 50 (1983): 61-81, "The Mirror Stage of Colin Clout: A New Reading of Spenser's *Januarye* Eclogue," *Helios* n.s. 10 (1983): 139-60.

3   Paul Alpers, *The Singer of the Eclogues: A Study of Virgilian Pastoral* (Berkeley

and Los Angeles: University of California Press, 1979), p. 128. Citations from Virgil are from the Loeb edition, ed. H. Rushton Fairclough (Cambridge, Mass.: Harvard University Press, 1953); translations depend upon Alpers and C. Day Lewis, *The Eclogues and Georgics of Virgil* (Garden City, N.Y.: Doubleday, 1964).

4   The mixing of *dulce* and *utile* is a Horatian doctrine: "Aut prodesse volunt aut delectare poetae/aut simil et iucunda et idonea dicere vitae," *Ars Poetica*, ed. H. Rushton Fairclough (Cambridge, Mass.: Harvard University Press, 1961), lines 333-34; "omne tulit punctum qui miscuit utile dulci,/lectorem delectando pariterque monendo" (lines 343-44).

Citations from Sidney's *Defence of Poetry*, ed. Jan Van Dorsten (Oxford: Oxford University Press, 1961).

5   For this digestive metaphor, see Thomas M. Greene, *The Light in Troy: Imitation and Discovery in Renaissance Poetry* (New Haven: Yale University Press, 1982); he documents the Senecan tradition. Erasmian *copia* is explored in Terence Cave's *The Cornucopian Text: Problems of Writing in the French Renaissance* (Oxford: Clarendon Press, 1979); see especially the section on "Imitation." See also G. W. Pigman, III, "Versions of Imitation in the Renaissance," *Renaissance Quarterly* 33 (1980): 1-32; I have also consulted Jacqueline T. Miller's (unpublished) "Creative Imitation in the Renaissance."

Petrarch, *Letters from Petrarch*, trans. Morris Bishop (Bloomington, Indiana: Indiana University Press, 1966), p. 184; Erasmus, *De Copia*, in *Collected Works*, ed. Craig R. Thompson (Toronto: University of Toronto Press, 1978), 24: 348-54.

6   George Chapman, "To my admired and soule-loved friend," lines 125-26, in *The Poems*, ed. Phyllis Brooks Bartlett (New York: Russell & Russell, 1962), p. 383. Cf. John Donne, "T'have written then," "*Nothings*, as I am, may/Pay all they have, and yet have all to pay" (lines 7-8), in *The Satires, Epigrams and Verse Letters*, ed. W. Milgate (Oxford: Clarendon Press, 1967). Perhaps no poet of the English Renaissance plays on the food/poetry equation as insistently as Ben Jonson; for him, a cannibalistic audience consumes his metaphoric dishes, as Don K. Hedrick argues in "Cooking for the Anthropaphagi: Jonson and His Audience," *SEL* 17 (1977): 233-45.

7   The meeting of Statius, Dante, and Virgil occupies cantoes 21 and 22 of the *Purgatorio*. Statius is saved by Virgil's text: "Per te poeta fui, per te cristiano," (22, line 73; ed. John D. Sinclair (New York: Oxford University Press, 1961)). Virgil first avoids meeting Statius with a silent look (21, line 104), and then greets him. Life to one poet is not life to the other, and the terms of this extraordinary meeting are an extreme version of the Spenserian situation.

8   "Orpheus, Pan, and the Poetics of Misogyny," *ELH* 50 (1983): 28; Spenser's interpretation of Orpheus, Berger argues, "maintains Virgil's realistic *sadness* . . . as a yardstick against which to measure Ovid's 'victory of art'" (p. 32). Ovid's 'victory,' as argued below, is somewhat bleaker than Berger admits.

9   Maurice Blanchot, "The Gaze of Orpheus," in the volume of the same title, trans. Lydia Davis (Barrytown, N.Y.: Station Hill Press, 1981), p. 101. The entire essay offers a remarkable study of the gaze that constitutes writing-as-loss.

10 Ovid, *Metamorphoses*, trans. Frank Justis Miller (Cambridge, Mass.: Harvard

University Press, 1964), 11, line 7. The account offered draws mainly upon books 10 and 11 in Ovid, although the repeating of Eurydice's name occurs in Virgil's *Georgics*, 4, lines 525-27.

Spenser's three-line version of the story of Orpheus ascribes to him a task of Hercules, perhaps rooted in Ovid's comparison of Orpheus, numbed by the loss of Eurydice, as if faced by the triple-headed Cerberus (10, lines 64-68). The songs of disastrous love sung by Orpheus are those of Apollo and Cyparissus (10, lines 106ff.), Jove and Ganymede (lines 155ff.), Apollo and Hyacinth (lines 162ff.), Pygmalion (lines 220ff.), Cinyras and Myrrha (lines 298ff.), the mother of Adonis, born from a tree, told by Venus the tale of Atalanta (lines 560-707). Orpheus sings forbidden love and the satisfactions that stories offer. His audience is the lovers transformed into trees and stones. When the Maenads attack, their weapons are the audience: stones and trees alternate (cf. 11, lines 1-2, 9-10). Similarly, Eurydice is bitten by a snake (10, line 10), and Orpheus's head menaces a snake (11, lines 56-60). The whispered farewell of Eurydice (10, lines 62-63) is answered by the ludic replay of that loss (11, lines 62-63). Orpheus knows the story of Persephone (10, lines 26-29); the union in hell prefigures his own.

For Orpheus as the father of pederasty, see 10, lines 83-85. Socrates, of course, is a pederast, and his dialogues are as much seduction as philosophical discourse. Citations from the *Phaedrus*, trans. W. C. Hembold and E. G. Rabinowitz (Indianapolis: Bobbs-Merrill Co.,Liberal Arts Press, 1956). Paternity is crucial to the dialogue, as Jacques Derrida argues in "Plato's Pharmacy," in *Dissemination*, trans. Barbara Johnson (Chicago: University of Chicago Press, 1981). I depend upon his knowledge of the Greek text for the pattern identifying poison, remedy, love and writing, a pattern of oppositions comprehended in the term (*pharmakon*) that appears to constitute one side of the opposition and which thus exceeds and undermines the opposition; hence "*pharmakon* cannot simply be assigned a site within what it situates, cannot be subsumed under concepts whose contours it draws" (p. 103).

11 The Argus story is told in *Meta*. 1:621-723.

12 The grasshopper's tale is Aesopian, hoarding and then being depleted; Socrates's story, like the meeting of Statius and Dante in the *Purgatorio*, finds depletion in the confluence of avarice and prodigality. For the grasshopper in literary history, see D. C. Allen, *Image and Meaning* (Baltimore: Johns Hopkins Press, 1960), pp. 80-92.

13 Citations from Freud in the text are from *Three Essays on the Theory of Sexuality*, trans. James Strachey (N.Y.: Avon Books, 1962). See also, "On Narcissism: An Introduction," reprinted in *General Psychological Theory*, ed. Philip Rieff (New York: Collier Books, 1963).

The question of psychic economy in relation to its mechanical and biological dimensions, and the problematic of "propping" and "slippage" involved in moving from the vital order to the psychic register, receive acute examination in Jean Laplanche's *Life and Death in Psychoanalysis*, trans. Jeffrey Mehlman (Baltimore: Johns Hopkins University Press, 1976); see esp. pp. 106-24. Narcissism, especially in relation to the image, is central to Julia Kristeva's work;

see, for example, "Motherhood According to Giovanni Bellini," in *Desire in Language*, ed. Leon S. Roudiez (New York: Columbia University Pres, 1980), or *Powers of Horror: An Essay on Abjection* (N.Y.: Columbia University Pres, 1982), discussed in chapter 6 below.

14 On the biblical resonance of the metaphor of milk/word, see Stanley Fish, *The Living Temple* (Berkeley and Los Angeles: University of California Press, 1978), pp. 59-60.

15 For a reading of Sidney's *Defence* as a narcissistic strategy, see Margaret W. Ferguson, *Trials of Desire: Renaissance Defenses of Poetry* (New Haven: Yale University Press, 1983).

16 *Meta.*, 6: 385: "Quid me mihi detrahis?" This image of the poet's economy is favored by Renaissance painters and philosophers too, as Edgar Wind argues in *Pagan Mysteries in the Renaissance* (New York: W. W. Norton, 1968), pp. 171-76.

17 The argument about the relations between poetry and power draws on "The Authority of the Other," in my *Endlesse Worke: Spenser and the Structures of Discourse* (Baltimore: Johns Hopkins University Press, 1981). Thomas Cain has analyzed the *Aprill* eclogue in the context of a discussion of the Renaissance Orpheus in *Praise in The Faerie Queene* (Lincoln: University of Nebraska Press, 1978), pp. 11-36. Cain sees Orpheus as a model for poetic self-proclamation and complaints about attrition on pp. 29-36. Harry Berger has argued against the idealistic bias in Cain's account in "Orpheus, Pan, and the Poetics of Misogyny," *ELH* 50 (1983): 27ff., pointing to the connection between Orpheus's failures as a lover and his poetic achievement, brilliantly likening his enduring monuments to those produced by the Medusa, and attaching the name of *Elisa* to *Elisium* (p. 37). The politics of *April* are central to Louis Montrose's "'Eliza, Queen of shepheardes' and the Pastoral of Power," *English Literary Renaissance* 10 (1980): 153-82.

Cain's reading stumbles over the allusion to Niobe: "This passage strikes an odd sour note. . . . We may also note that, in spite of Spenser's refusal to 'match her with Latonaes seed' (Apollo and Diana) he has already made precisely these comparisons" (p. 18). In "Authorship, Anonymity, and *The Shepheardes Calender*," *MLQ* 40 (1979), David L. Miller reads Niobe as "an emblem for the dangers of artistic presumption" (p. 231).

The relationship between E. K.'s gloss and Colin's lay is complicated by the fact that the gloss depends upon a different organization of the stanzas of the poem, one in which the allusion to Niobe comes close to the end, rather than in the middle. Although this situation may simply point to a reorganization of the poem after the writing of the gloss, the effect of the gloss is a rewriting of the lay to end in an apotheosis of the shattering power of memorialization. Niobe, as "was feigned of the Poetes," became a sepulchral stone, a memorial to her children. The shepherd fears the "like mysfortune." E. K. follows this gloss with one on "the conclusion. For having so decked her with prayses and comparisons, he returneth all the thanck of hys laboure to the excellencie of her Maiestie" (p. 435). The conjunction of the poet's fearful projection and his drawing back from the comparisons in which he has constituted Eliza thus seems to suggest a shattering reading of the lay.

One remarkable linkage of the queen to death has been suggested in Judith H. Anderson's reading of Belphoebe as an "ensample dead" (*FQ*, III. v. 54, line 9) in "'In living colours and right hew': The Queen of Spenser's Central Books," in *Poetic Traditions of the English Renaissance*, pp. 47-66, esp. 54ff.

18 See, for example, Richard F. Hardin, "The Resolved Debate of Spenser's 'October'," *Modern Philology* 73 (1976): 257-63, for a reading that finds Piers's humanistic views central; for the view that regards the dialogues as resolved elsewhere, see Patrick Cullen, *Spenser, Marvell, and Renaissance Pastoral* (Cambridge, Mass.: Harvard University Press, 1970), pp. 69-76 *et passim*. Montrose and Berger sustain a dialectical approach.

19 "Signature Event Context," in *Margins of Philosophy*, trans. Alan Bass (Chicago: University of Chicago Press, 1982), p. 318.

20 Harry Berger has noted one echo uniting Piers and Palinode in *Maye*, in "Mode and Diction," *MP* 67 (1969): 145. His "paradise principle" locates characters as stationed at stages along a continuum; but the circular and dialectical relations between characters also leads Berger to notice how the "same" character may have stepped into another's place; see, for example, his striking remarks in "The Aging Boy," pp. 37-38, on the "mirror inversion" by which Colin ages and Thenot becomes younger in the course of the *Calender*.

21 Cuddie's aspirations can be contextualized through the arguments presented in Anthony Esler's *The Aspiring Mind of the Elizabethan Younger Generation* (Durham, N.C.: Duke University Press, 1966). Esler claims that Marlowe is the voice of this generation, and we might take Tamburlaine's progress from shepherd to king as the tragic counterpart to the Virgilian pattern of ascent; it is perhaps to be attached to the paradigm as it is articulated in *October*, and especially in Cuddie's theatrical aspirations. An echo of Marlowe and Spenser has been elucidated by Stephen Greenblatt in *Renaissance Self-Fashioning: From More to Shakespeare* (Chicago: University of Chicago Press, 1980), pp. 222-24. Greenblatt argues that Marlowe subverts a Spenserian text; however, Spenser's text so fully problematizes itself that one might read Marlowe's transportation of *FQ* I. vii. 32 to Tamburlaine as a reading of Spenser that deconceals something already written in the text.

22 In "'The perfecte paterne of a Poete'," Montrose reads Colin's appearances as a developing story; this seems to me to falsely narrativize his role and to homogenize the aspects of the poet's economy–his singing for others (in others' voices, for the audience of Rosalind, Eliza, or the shepherds) – distributed throughout the text. I do not mean to endorse the opposite reading of Colin that finds him the same in *Januarye* and *December*, an idealistic reading that treats the entire poem as a closed circle. Its structure is perhaps more like a mobius strip. The prevailing view in recent criticism (Berger, Miller, McCanles) that Colin represents a position that Spenser repudiates can only be sustained in the recognition that it remains a repudiated view throughout the career, that is, a view of the poet-as-repudiated, as in *Colin Clouts Come Home Againe*, or

in the disturbed vision in book VI of *The Faerie Queene*. A distinction thus must be drawn between the representation of repudiation and repudiation itself.

23 *Dissemination*, p. 149. This is not solely a Derridean perspective. In his commentary on the *Phaedrus*, Ficino emphasizes the distinction between false and true writing. See Michael J. B. Allen, *Marsilio Ficino and the Phaedran Charioteer* (Berkeley and Los Angeles: University of California Press, 1981), pp. 210-12.

24 Joel Fineman has explored this tradition in "Shakespeare's 'Perjur'd Eye'," *Representations* 7 (1984): 59-86.

25 *Muiopotmos* demonstrates the importance of the Arachne story for the Spenserian text. For a reading of the poem in the light of its Ovidian and Virgilian textuality and its social import, see Robert A. Brinkley, "Spenser's *Muiopotmos* and the Politics of Metamorphosis," *ELH* 48 (1981): 668-76.

26 The literature on the comparison of the arts is vast. "Ut pictura poesis" is line 361 in Horace's *Ars Poetica*; the comparison occurs in *Phaedrus* 275. The importance of the paragone for painting is treated by Rensselaer W. Lee in *Ut Pictura Poesis: The Humanistic Theory of Painting* (New York: W. W. Norton, 1967); for literature by Jean Hagstrum, *The Sister Arts* (Chicago: University of Chicago Press, 1958); in Sidney, by Forrest G. Robinson, *The Shape of Things Known* (Cambridge, Mass.: Harvard University Press, 1972); in relation to a hermetic philosophy of the image, by Frances A. Yates, *The Art of Memory* (Chicago: University of Chicago Press, 1966).

27 For the place of the mazer within the exchange system of the *Calender*, see Harry Berger Jr., "Orpheus, Pan, and the Poetics of Misogyny," *ELH* 50 (1983), pp. 40-41. With E. K.'s gloss, cf. the Argument to *Februarie*, describing the tale there as "so lively and so feelingly, as if the thing were set forth in some Picture before our eyes." The woodcut for *October* could be compared to the *November* cut; on one side it represents the funeral of Dido (recounted in the text); on the other side, the poet is crowned, something that happens nowhere in the text. Indeed, in that case, the image represents a virtual counter-argument to the text.

28 See, for example, Paul de Man, *Allegories of Reading* (New Haven: Yale University Press, 1979), pp. 12, 17.

29 The *March* eclogue offers a description of Eros with "spotted winges like Peacocks trayne" (line 80), a counter-reading to the immortality of E. K.'s gloss, and more in line with the pattern of Orpheus.

30 This "friendship" of Bacchus and Apollo destroys Orpheus. The deconstructive reading of Nietzsche's *The Birth of Tragedy* in De Man's *Allegories*, pp. 79-102 could be offered in support of the treatment of the figures in *October*. Edgar Wind has argued for a Renaissance tradition in which these gods are mutually entailed in *Pagan Mysteries*, pp. 171-90, and Ficino finds them proximate in his *Phaedrus* commentary, "Phebus enim Baccho proximus" (*Phaedran Charioteer*, p. 144; cf. p. 139).

31 Ovid, *Fasti*, 6, lines 5-6, ed. Sir James George Frazer (Cambridge, Mass.: Harvard University Press, 1941). The tag has been dropped in the one-volume Oxford edition of Spenser but does appear in the three-volume set.

174

4 Shakespearian characters: the generation of Silvia

1 On the destination of the letter, see Barbara Johnson, "The Frame of Reference: Poe, Lacan, Derrida,' *Yale French Studies* 55/56 (1977): 457-505, the revised version of her essay in Geoffrey H. Hartman, ed., *Psychoanalysis and the Question of the Text* (Baltimore: Johns Hopkins University Press, 1978), and the texts from Derrida's *La Carte Postale* and Lacan's *Ecrits*, to which she refers. In the pages that follow, the differences between Derrida and Lacan are not engaged, in part because of the persuasiveness of Johnson's arguments, in part because such texts as Derrida's *Eperons* and Lacan's *Encore* suggest some reconciliation of their positions regarding phallogocentrism.

2 All citations from *William Shakespeare: The Complete Works*, ed. Alfred Harbage (Baltimore: Penguin Books, 1969).

3 See *A Defence of Poetry*, ed. J. A. Van Dorsten (Oxford: Oxford University Press, 1966), pp. 74-75. Among the others would figure the Shakespearian sonnet; for a history of the trope and its uses, see J. B. Leishmen, *Themes and Variations in Shakespeare's Sonnets* (New York: Harper & Row, 1963), pp. 25-91.

4 All citations from the Loeb edition, trans. Frank Justus Miller (Cambridge, Mass.: Harvard University Press, 1960).

5 All citation from the Loeb edition of Virgil's *Eclogues*, trans. H. Rushton Fairclough (Cambridge, Mass.: Harvard University Press, 1953).

6 On the inescapable pastoral of *The Two Gentlemen of Verona*, see Richard Cody, *The Landscape of the Mind* (Oxford: Clarendon Press, 1969), esp. pp. 83-84, 92, and his useful reminders that Tasso's *Aminta* and Guarini's *Il Pastor Fido* figure in Silvia's name.

7 Joseph A. Porter, "Mercutio's Brother," *South Atlantic Review* 49 (1984): 31-41. The *OED* provides the literal meanings of valentine.

8 The phrase is Paul Alpers', *The Singer of the Eclogues: A Study of Virgilian Pastoral* (Berkeley and Los Angeles: University of California Press, 1979), discussed above in Chapter 3.

9 The Lacanian texts would include the seminar on "The Purloined Letter," partially translated in *Yale French Studies* 48 (1973): 38-72, and "The Agency of the Letter in the Unconscious," in *Ecrits: A Selection*, trans. Alan Sheridan (New York: W. W. Norton, 1977).

10 "The Agency of the Letter," p. 167.

11 In *Unredeemed Rhetoric: Thomas Nashe and the Scandal of Authorship* (Baltimore: Johns Hopkins University Press, 1982), Jonathan V. Crewe discerns a similar figure in Nashe's history of the page, Jack Wilton; see, for example, pp. 69-70.

12 This is another instance of what Derrida calls the violence of the letter and its violation of limits, propriety, boundaries, and origin; see, for example, *Of Grammatology*, trans. Gayatri Chakravorty Spivak (Baltimore: Johns Hopkins University Press, 1974, 1976), pp. 101-64.

13 Jacques Lacan, "On Structure as an Inmixing of an Otherness Prerequisite to Any Subject Whatever," in *The Structuralist Controversy*, ed. Richard Macksey

and Eugenio Donato (Baltimore: Johns Hopkins University Press, 1970, 1972), pp. 193-94.

14   "The Agency of the Letter," p. 147.

15   All citations from Angel Day, *The English Secretorie (1586)* (Menston: Scolar Press, 1967).

16   For an elegant argument about character that focuses on the early plays and answers the traditional charges, see Barry Weller, "Identity and Representation in Shakespeare," *ELH* 49 (1982): 339-62. Weller argues that characters are not seeking themselves but *self-representation* (p. 343), and that the truth of character coincides with representation. This involves refiguration within a variety of matrices – others' perceptions, social prescriptions (e.g. the dictates of love and friendship in *The Two Gentlemen of Verona*); the "being" of character, from this perspective, is its metamorphic capacity, discontinuous change as its "essence." "The protean character of humanity may be essentially resistant to the termination of process, that is, to the translation of man from something which becomes to something which is" (p. 350). Weller concludes his discussion by gesturing in the direction taken in this study: "the most comprehensive name for the otherness through and against which the self struggles to proclaim its uniqueness is language, and discussion of identity in the early comedies requires a supplementary interrogation of the sources of language" (p. 358). The approach in these pages is also encouraged by Stephen Greenblatt's use of Lacan in the analysis of *Othello* in *Renaissance Self-Fashioning: From More to Shakespeare* (Chicago: University of Chicago Press, 1980), pp. 244-45 and by the work of Joel Fineman, especially "Fratricide and Cuckoldry: Shakespeare's Doubles," in *Representing Shakespeare*, ed. Murray M. Schwartz and Coppélia Kahn (Baltimore: Johns Hopkins University Press, 1980) and "Shakespeare's 'Perjur'd Eye'," *Representations* 7 (1984): 59-86. The discussion of the sonnets that follows runs parallel to many of Fineman's concerns although it does not schematize the poems in his visual/linguistic dichotomy.

17   See, for example, Mary L. Fawcett, "Arms/Words/Tears: Language and the Body in *Titus Andronicus*," *ELH* 50 (1983): 261-77 and S. Clark Hulse, "Wresting the Alphabet: Oratory and Action in *Titus Andronicus*," *Criticism* 21 (1979): 106-18.

18   Fawcett sees Lavinia's mouth as a *vagina dentata*, Hulse sees fellatio in the scene.

19   Ann Thompson summarizes some points of contact in "Philomel in *Titus Andronicus* and *Cymbeline*," *Shakespeare Survey* 31 (1978): 23-32.

20   See *Phaedrus* 259.

21   The titillating pictures in the chamber are described in Act 2, Scene 4.

22   All citations from *The Overburian Characters*, ed. W. J. Paylor (Oxford: Basil Blackwell, 1936). "What a Character Is" (p. 92) appeared first in 1615. On the etymology, see Warren Anderson's introduction to *Theophrastus: The Character Sketches* (Kent State University Press, 1970), pp. xv-xvi. The most usual meaning for 'character' in Greek texts is an impression stamped on a coin. On that etymology, see Marc Shell, *The Economy of Literature* (Baltimore: Johns Hopkins University Press, 1978), p. 64. For some further discussion of the

implications of the term for the depiction of character, see Warren Ginsberg, *The Cast of Character: The Representation of Personality in Ancient and Medieval Literature* (Toronto: University of Toronto Press, 1983), pp. 14-19.

23 *Profitable Instructions*, cited in Marion Trousdale, *Shakespeare and the Rhetoricians* (Chapel Hill: University of North Carolina Press, 1982), p. 8. Trousdale's demonstrations of the rhetorical placement of character in text is assumed in this discussion. Texts, as Trousdale argues, offer "a verbal structure in which possible relationships between different pieces of action are suggested by rhetorical elaboration" (p. 134); the locus of action is thus rhetorical *place*, copiously filled and refilled, fully and endlessly textualized: "one text is structured by another and . . . such . . . activity necessarily creates discontinuous discourses, . . . a plurality of views" (p. 160). The speech of characters is their (re)placement within the troping of text upon text.

24 All citations from the Scolar facsimile edition (Menston, 1970).

25 *Micro-Cosmographie*, ed. Edward Arber (London, 1869), p. 21.

26 *The Works of Joseph Hall*, 12 vols (Oxford, 1837), 6:88. The standard history of the form is Benjamin Boyce, *The Theophrastian Character In England to 1642* (Cambridge, Mass.: Harvard University Press, 1947). For some connections between the character and visual epistemology, see Forrest G. Robinson, *The Shape of Things Known* (Cambridge, Mass.: Harvard University Press, 1972), pp. 206-14. For an Ovidian character book, see *A Strange Metamorphosis of Men, Transformed in a Wilderness* (London, 1634). The Shakespearian analogue might be found in *As You Like It*; e.g. "These trees shall be my books,/And in their barks my thoughts I'll character" (3.2, lines 5-6).

27 Letter of 23 Jan. 1614, quoted in John Carey, "Donne and Coins," in John Carey, ed., *English Renaissance Studies Presented to Dame Helen Gardner* (Oxford: Clarendon Press, 1980), p. 154. See also J. Eric Engstrom, *Coins In Shakespeare: A Numismatic Guide* (Hanover, N.H.: Dartmouth College Museum Publications, 1964), for an index to uses of coins in the Shakespearian text.

28 Derrida considers the relationships between phonetic alphabets and hieroglyphs in *Of Grammatology*, e.g. pp. 74-81; see also, "The Theater of Cruelty," in *Writing and Difference*, trans. Alan Bass (Chicago: University of Chicago Press, 1978), pp. 240-47. For a discussion of the significance of hieroglyphics for grammatology, see Gregory L. Ulmer, *Applied Grammatology: Post(e)-Pedagogy from Jacques Derrida to Joseph Beuys* (Baltimore: Johns Hopkins University Press, 1985), pp. 16-19.

In "George Herbert's Pattern Poems and the Materiality of Language: A New Approach to Renaissance Hieroglyphics," *ELH* 50 (1983): 245-60, Martin Elsky argues for the effect of neoplatonic allegorizations of letters upon humanistic ideas of writing as the transcription of voice (p. 246); the usual ascription of the origin of writing in the Egyptian hieroglyph lent symbolic and material density to the alphabet, and letters exceeded mere phonetic transcription. Elsky thinks this is to be seen in Herbert, rather than in sixteenth-century English theorists like Mulcaster. The evidence presented below, however, suggests otherwise, although it does not endorse any allegorization of the materiality of the letter. Rather, its materiality is representational, as a passage from Lomazzo, cited by Elsky, on writing as originary painting, would indicate: "Characters and the use of writing were first invented to preserve the memory of the Sciences, . . . Painting is an instrument under which the treasury of memory is contained, insomuch as writing is nothing else, but a picture of *white* and *black*" (p. 247). The movement of the Overburian definition, from phonetic to hieroglyphic character, passes through the "shadowing" of black and white.

29 Cf. A. Bartlett Giamatti, "Proteus Unbound: Some Versions of the Sea God in the Renaissance," in *The Disciplines of Criticism*, ed. Peter Demetz, Thomas Greene, and Lowry Nelson, Jr. (New Haven: Yale University Press, 1968), pp. 437-57.

30 George Sandys, *Ovid's Metamorphosis Englished Mythologiz'd And Represented* (1632), p. 104.

31 Booth comments on sonnet 122 on pp. 412-15 of his edition of *Shakespeare's Sonnets* (New Haven: Yale University Press, 1977).

32 In "Freud and the Scene of Writing," in *Writing and Difference*; cited passages appear on pp. 226-27.

33 *Theaetetus*, trans. Francis MacDonald (Indianapolis: Bobbs-Merrill, 1957). Similar passages from the *Phaedrus* are analyzed by Derrida in "Plato's Pharmacy," and from the *Philebus* in "The Double Session," in *Dissemination*, trans. Barbara Johnson (Chicago: University of Chicago Press, 1981). *La Carte Postale de Socrate à Freud et au-delà* (Paris: Flammarion, 1980) traces the path from the representation of Socrates as writer (in a medieval illustration to a fortune-telling book) to the Freudian scene of writing.

34 "The Subversion of the Subject and the Dialectic of Desire in the Freudian Unconscious," in *Ecrits: A Selection*, p. 305.

35 "The Agency of the Letter in the Unconscious," in *Ecrits: A Selection*, p. 172.

36 "The Subversion of the Subject," pp. 304-5. Cf. Lacan's description, in "The Function and Field of Speech and Language in Psychoanlysis," of the subject speaking: "In this labour which he undertakes to reconstruct *for another*, he rediscovers the fundamental alienation that made him construct it *like another*, and which has always destined it to be taken from him *by another*" (*Ecrits: A Selection*, p. 42).

37 See, for example, "Force and Signification," in *Writing and Difference*, pp. 19-20, or *Positions*, trans. Alan Bass (Chicago: University of Chicago Press, 1981), 35-36. Derrida reviews his quarrel with Lacan in *Positions*, pp. 111-13, n.44; see also p.113, t.n. 47, 48.

38 Lacan's designation of the symbolic as the name of the father (e.g. in "Function and Field of Speech," p.67), and his association of the symbolic with the phallus (e.g. in "The Signification of the Phallus," in *Ecrits: A Selection*, pp. 281-91) are not necessarily the phallogocentric endorsements that Derrida finds; see the witty exposition of Jane Gallop, *The Daughter's Seduction: Feminism and Psychoanalysis* (Ithaca: Cornell University Press, 1982), which emphasizes that Lacan's is the mother's phallus. Derrida inscribes the Freudian scene in the primal scene in "Freud and the Scene of Writing," *Writing and Difference*, p. 229.

39 On the impossible sentence, see Jacques Derrida's exchange with Roland Barthes, in *The Structuralist Controversy*, pp. 155-56; on iterability, see Derrida, "Signature Event Context," in *Margins of Philosophy*, trans. Alan Bass (Chicago: University of Chicago Press, 1982).

In *The Tremulous Private Body* (London: Methuen, 1984), Francis Barker takes Hamlet as a figure anticipatory of the bourgeois consciousness exemplified later in the seventeenth century; among his most provocative observations is his characterization of interiority as "a *doubling of the surface*" (p. 28); "at the centre of Hamlet, in the interior of his mystery, there is, in short, nothing. The promised essence remains beyond the scope of the text's signification: or rather, signals the limit of the signification of this world by marking out the site of an absence it cannot fill" (p. 37).

5 The dead letter: Herbert's other voices

1 Roland Barthes, *S/Z*, trans. Richard Miller (New York: Hill & Wang, 1974); for the question, 'who is speaking,' see p. 41; for the use of *voice* for textual code, see pp. 203-11; for reading as the voice of the reader inserted in the text, see pp. 151-52; for the voice of the castrato–as the sexual lure of the text–see pp. 109-10.

2 For an exemplary review of modern criticism, see Barbara Harman, *Costly Monuments: Representations of the Self in George Herbert's Poetry* (Cambridge, Mass.: Harvard University Press, 1982), pp. 1-38. Harman's indirect "self" invested in lapsing representations may be contrasted with the regenerate "self" in Richard Strier's *Love Known: Theology and Experience in George Herbert's Poetry* (Chicago: University of Chicago Press, 1983). Strier's low church emphasis–Herbert's theology is allied to Luther's views on free will–opposes the more usual Anglican accounts, for example, of Joseph Summers, *George Herbert: His Religion and Art* (Cambridge, Mass.: Harvard University Press, 1954); Rosemond Tuve, *A Reading of George Herbert* (Chicago: University of Chicago Press, 1952), with its liturgical emphases; and Heather A. R. Asals, *Equivocal Predication: George Herbert's Way to God* (Toronto: University of Toronto Press, 1981), a somewhat more latitudinarian study and valuable for its emphasis on the significance of writing in *The Temple*.

3 Harman believes that the representation of self in Herbert manages to achieve an opacity that forestalls the threat of a dissolution of the text into the already-written; it is the argument here, however, that that opacity is already textual, that representation takes place within the *copia* of the biblical pretext. This position resembles Stanley Fish's argument, for example, in "Letting Go: The Dialectic of the Self in Herbert's Poetry," in *Self-Consuming Artifacts* (Berkeley and Los Angeles: University of California Press, 1972), that the self is an ontologically insecure category in the poems always overwhelmed by the demands of faith. Fish dissolves voice into a transcendental unity that refuses the category of the individual self; the argument here is that such transcendence never escapes textualization, that dissemination, not unity, is the matrix in which the self is (dis)located. For the voice-in-quotation, see the arguments about

iterability in Jacques Derrida, "Signature Event Context," in *Margins of Philosophy*, trans. Alan Bass (Chicago: University of Chicago Pres, 1982), e.g.: "Every sign, linguistic or nonlinguistic, spoken or written (in the usual sense of this opposition), as a small or large unity, can be *cited*, put between quotation marks; thereby it can break with every given context, and engender infinitely new contexts in an absolutely nonsaturable fashion. This does not suppose that the mark is valid outside its context, but on the contrary that there are only contexts without any center of absolute anchoring. This citationality, duplication, or duplicity, this iterability of the mark is not an accident or an anomaly, but is that (normal/abnormal) without which a mark could no longer have a so-called 'normal' functioning" (pp. 320-21). For such iterability (mimesis as re-marking) in relation to the "normal" functioning of the literary, see "The Double Session" in *Dissemination*, trans. Barbara Johnson (Chicago: University of Chicago Press, 1981).

4   All citations from *The Works of George Herbert*, ed. F. E. Hutchinson (Oxford: Clarendon Press, 1941); some of the questionable procedures in this edition are examined by J. Max Patrick, "Critical Problems in Editing George Herbert's *The Temple*," in *The Editor as Critic and The Critic as Editor* (University of California, Los Angeles: William Andrews Clark Memorial Library, 1973); the typographical features of the 1633 edition have been preserved for their authoritative value.

5   Richard Strier reviews various readings of the poem in *Love Known*, pp. 204-5; his view, that "'supplie the want' is a joke," and that "Herbert is not in any way claiming that God actually wrote the final word of his poem," seems a desperate move to "save" the poem by denying it; Asals also "saves" the poem–and writing in Herbert, in general – by seeing it as the equivocation of a finer and final signature endurably written elsewhere, a locus that is an act of faith; see *Equivocal Predication*, pp. 24-25.

6   Readings of *The Collar* are legion, but insofar as they all tend to secure the rebellious account in its closure, they are answered by the provocative reading in Harman's *Costly Monuments*, pp. 64-88, indebted, as she notes, to Fish; Harman reads the past tense of the poem as a sign of a retrospection in which the speaker-as-duplicator achieves some coherent view of his life; thus, the final lines do not secure this view, although they do not entirely shatter it (as Fish claims). What Harman discounts is that the "coherence" is already undermined by the final voices-in-quotation which cannot be privileged as some extraordinary disruption.

7   Derrida's rehearsal of the role of *Speech and Phenomena* in *Positions*, trans. Alan Bass (Chicago: University of Chicago Press, 1981), pp. 4-5. All citations from *Of Grammatology*, trans. Gayatri Chakravorty Spivak (Baltimore: Johns Hopkins University Press, 1974, 1976).

8   For further arguments about the ideality of voice, see *Speech and Phenomena*, trans. David B. Allison (Evanston: Northwestern University Press, 1973), pp. 74-79, and "The Pit and the Pyramid: Introduction to Hegel's Semiology," in *Margins of Philosophy*, pp. 69-108, esp. pp. 88ff.

9   In *Image-Music-Text*, trans. Stephen Heath (London: Fontana/Collins, 1977), p. 145. For Benveniste, see chapter 1, above.

10 In *Language, Counter-Memory, Practice*, trans. Donald F. Bouchard and Sherry Simon (Ithaca: Cornell University Press, 1977), pp. 113-38; see esp. pp. 124-27 for the emergence of the modern 'author-function' as a man of property and the general conditions to which it corresponds. For the "sovereign" author in Derrida, see "Freud and the Scene of Writing," in *Writing and Difference*, trans. Alan Bass (Chicago: University of Chicago Press, 1978), pp. 226-27, and the discussion above in "The Inscription of Character."

11 For writing on the heart, see Asals, *Equivocal Predication*, ch. 1, esp. pp. 25-29; Strier, *Love Known*, ch. 6 and 7, esp. pp.168ff. on the *empty* cosmos and the space of inscription.

12 "On Narcissism: An Introduction," in *General Psychological Theory*, ed. Philip Rieff (New York: Collier Books, 1963), pp. 75-76. The entire third section of the essay deals with relationships between castration and narcissism.

13 For the critical problem of the unity of *The Temple*, see the opening chapter of Stanley Fish, *The Living Temple: George Herbert and Catechizing* (Berkeley and Los Angeles: University of California Press, 1978); Fish relocates the (de)constructive strategies of the book within the reader's activity of reading; the argument here embraces much in Fish's account but would locate the reader, too, within the problem of the book; see, on that issue and its relationship to the authoritative book that underwrites Herbert's, Derrida, "Edmond Jabès and the Question of the Book," in *Writing and Difference*, pp. 64-78; Maurice Blanchot, "The Absence of the Book," in *The Gaze of Orpheus*, trans. Lydia Davis (Barrytown, N.Y.: Station Hill, 1981), pp. 146-60, esp. pp. 155ff. on first and second writing within the Bible and the relationship of writing to exteriority.

14 Cf. *A Priest to the Temple*, describing the parson who "ever begins the reading of the Scripture with some short inward ejaculation, as, *Lord, open mine eyes, that I may see the wondrous things of thy Law*" (*Works*, 229), a citation of Psalm 119: 18. For ejaculation as the emission of fluid, seed, light–from the eye, words, see OED for seventeenth-century usages.

15 For the sexual implications of 'come' (usual only after the nineteenth century), see *Much Ado About Nothing*, Act 5, scene 2, in which Benedict urges Margaret to bring Beatrice to him, promising to write a sonnet in her praise "that no man living shall come over it; for in most comely truth thou deservest it" (5.2, lines 5-6); to which Margaret responds, "To have no man come over me?"; after some (s)wordplay, Margaret agrees to call Beatrice, "who I think hath legs" (line 21); "And therefore will come," Benedict replies.

16 Cf. Asals, *Equivocal Predication*, p. 85, for the relation of 'character' to the "ruling sentences" that write Herbert.

17 For the writing of Herbert's life through his texts, see David Novarr, *The Making of Walton's Lives* (Ithaca: Cornell University Press, 1958) and the biographical speculations in Jonathan Goldberg, "Herbert's *Decay* and the Articulation of History," *Southern Review* 18 (1985): 3-21. On such textual intercalation or collation, see Asals, *Equivocal Predication*, ch. 5, esp. pp. 101ff. on the terms.

18 For an argument about the materiality of the letter, see Martin Elsky, "George Herbert's Pattern Poems and the Materiality of Language: A New Approach to Renaissance Hieroglyphs," *ELH* 50 (1983): 245-60; on leaves as words in traditional psalm commentary, see Asals, *Equivocal Predication*, p. 49; on the echo of *Heaven*, pp. 29ff.; for the relation of echo to the catechismic discourse of *The Temple*, see Fish, *The Living Temple*, pp. 17-18.

19 Cf. Michel Foucault, "The Father's 'No'," in *Language, Counter-Memory, Practice*, pp. 68-86; the punning Lacanian term signals the castrating entrance into the symbolic; it is most fully explicated in the postscriptum to "On a Question Preliminary to Any Possible Treatment of Psychosis," in *Ecrits: A Selection*, trans. Alan Sheridan (New York: W. W. Norton, 1977), pp. 215-21.

20 On the reverberations of 'sweet' within *Vertue*, see Jonathan Goldberg, "Reading (Herbert's *Vertue*) Otherwise," *Mississippi Review* 33 (1983): 51-64, written, in part, to answer the domestication of 'sweet' in Helen Vendler's *The Poetry of George Herbert* (Cambridge, Mass.: Harvard University Press, 1975), pp. 9-24. For the dissemination of 'sweet,' the concordance remains the best critical guide.

21 For a reproduction of the 1674 page, see the frontispiece to Mary Ellen Rickey, *Utmost Art: Complexity in the Verse of George Herbert* (Lexington: University of Kentucky Press, 1968); in my copy of the ninth edition (1667), someone has inscribed a crude doorway around the text of SUPERLIMINARE, using the printed line as a threshold.

22 In *Ecrits: A Selection*, p. 150.

23 Freud, *Inhibitions, Symptoms, and Anxiety*, cited by Derrida, "Freud and the Scene of Writing," in *Writing and Difference*, p. 229. One might further remark the sexual connotation of Herbert's 'tool'.

24 Fish provides a fine account of the disequilibrium of reading *Jesu*, in *The Living Temple*, pp. 30-35, but the lesson he reads–that Christ is everywhere–is curiously not connected to his later remark (p. 67) on Jesus as the *embodiment*, and not resolution, of contradiction. That embodiment is the literality and materiality of the word rewritten in *The Temple*. Fish's infinite regress (p. 167) is, literally, grounded *en abŷme*, not sublated.

25 Although not a favored object of critical attention, *The Bag* has nonetheless a critical context to justify this re-marking; on the one hand, Tuve, in *A Reading of George Herbert*, p. 129, supplies the liturgical bag-as-trope, and thus the assumption that the poem is fully accounted for as a normative Christian utterance; on the other hand, Vendler, in *The Poetry of George Herbert*, pp. 173-78, produces a naive articulation as the voice of *The Bag* as the vehicle for a "personal" solution; something of the troublesome nature of the poem is recorded by Vendler, p. 292 n.14, Robert Graves's reading of it as a sexual allegory of spear and wound.

26 Cf. Susan Stewart, *On Longing* (Baltimore: Johns Hopkins University Press, 1984).

27 See n.4 above; "each stanza begins and ends with a long line. Between them, four lines begin further in, so that the hole remains on the left side, graphically representing the "bag" in Christ's side" (p. 22).

28 Cf. *The Church-Porch*, "In time of service seal up both thine eies,/And send them to thine heart" (lines 415-16). Cf. *The Glance*, on the eye taken into the heart, "a sugred strange delight" (line 6) not least *strange* by its ability to cut and "seal" (line 18).

29 More *Outlandish Proverbs*? "Life still pressing/Is one undressing/A steadie aiming at a tombe" (*Repentance*, lines 4-6); "Outlandish looks may not compare:/For all they either painted are,/Or else undrest" (*The British Church*, lines 10-12).

30 Cf.   *Ana*-(MARY)*gram*
                              (ARMY)
How well her name an *Army* doth present,
In whom the *Lord of Hosts* did pitch his tent!

Tent: wound; the disseminative and generative space/presence of the re-spelled word, all grams anagrams.

31 Cf. *Speech and Phenomena*, pp. 93-97, on the dependence of the "life" of writing on death.

32 "Covetousnesse breaks the bag," *Herbert's Remains* (*Works*, p. 358, *Jacula Prudentum*, 1071). Prudent ejaculation remains.

33 Sermon on Lamentations 3.1, cited in Asals, *Equivocal Predication*, p. 23.

34 Cf. *The Size*, and its "more hereafter" (line 3); "close again the seam,/Which thou hast open'd:. . . /Call to mind thy dream,/An earthly globe,/On whose meridian was engraven,/*These seas are tears, and heav'n the haven*" (lines 42-43, 44-47); a further inscription of the dividing line, the closed seam of an engraved internal writing/printing.

6 Milton's warning voice: considering preventive measures

1 All quotations from Milton's prose are taken from the Yale edition, *Complete Prose Works of John Milton*, 10 vols (New Haven: Yale University Press, 1953-83). Stanley Fish discusses this passage in "*Lycidas*: A Poem Finally Anonymous," *Glyph 8: Johns Hopkins Textual Studies* (Baltimore: Johns Hopkins University Press, 1981), pp. 5-6. The Miltonic 'present' (including self-presentation, the text as offering, the *being* of the text – its presence and its place within literary history) are read, in the pages that follow, within the Derridean problematic: the temporality of spacing; the becoming-trace of the present.

2 All quotations from Milton's poems are taken from *The Poems of John Milton*, ed. John Carey and Alastair Fowler (London: Longman, 1968; New York: W. W. Norton, 1972)

3 Maurice Blanchot, "The Essential Solitude," in *The Gaze of Orpheus*, trans. Lydia Davis (Barrytown, N.Y.: Station Hill Press, 1981), pp. 69, 66.

4 See Edward Le Comte, "Milton *versus* Time," in *Milton's Unchanging Mind* (Port Washington, N.Y.: Kennikat Press, 1973), pp. 5-68; e.g. p. 32 for a summary of Milton's central preoccupation, "worrying that he has not matured fast enough . . . and . . . predating himself in order to assuage his fears." On this subject, see also Edward W. Tayler, *Milton's Poetry: Its Development in Time* (Pittsburgh:

Duquesne University Press, 1979), e.g. p. 124: "The principle of Milton's poetic being seems to have been delay, deferment of the full release of those powers that, in the parable that haunts his prose and verse, it is death to hide."

5 Stanley E. Fish, "*Lycidas*: A Poem Finally Anonymous," *Glyph 8*, p. 9.

6 All citations from the Loeb edition of Virgil, ed. and trans. H. R. Fairclough (Cambridge, Mass.: Harvard University Press, 1953).

7 Maurice Blanchot, "Literature and the Right to Death," *The Gaze of Orpheus*, p. 46.

8 In the second folio, Milton's is one of two unsigned poems; the other, opening "Spectator, this life's shadow is," addresses the need to "turn reader" (line 3) to give "life" (line 8) to the otherwise dead image of Shakespeare. The conceit resembles Milton's marble conception, not least in presenting the life that the reader confers as a "truer image" (line 2). Among the other prefatory poems in the Shakespeare folios is, of course, Ben Jonson's, and its concluding asterism – "Shine forth, thou Starre of Poets" – must be read in conjunction with the Miltonic pyramid.

   Milton's poem also appears (initialled I. M.) in the 1640 edition of *Poems: Written by Wil. Shake-speare. Gent.*; among the commendatory poems is one signed W. B. that is worth comparison with Milton's since its setting is a tomb:

   > Renowned *Spenser* lie a thought more nigh
   > To learned *Chaucer*, and rare *Beaumont* lie
   > A little neerer *Spenser* to make roome,
   > For *Shakespeare* in your three-fold, foure-fold Tombe:
   >
   > (1-4)

   and it concludes by assigning Shakespeare "an unshar'd Cave/ . . . Lord, not Tennant of thy Grave" (lines 13-14). The poem is alluded to in Jonson's tribute, "My Shakespeare, rise; I will not lodge thee by/Chaucer, or Spenser, or bid Beaumont lye/A little further, to make thee a roome"; it was also printed in 1637, and survives in at least two manuscript versions – clearly it was written soon after Shakespeare's death (for bibliographical information, see R. Warwick Bond, ed., *The Poetical Works of William Basse* (London: Ellis & Elvey, 1893)).

9 Horace cited in the Loeb edition of *Odes and Epodes*, ed. and trans. C. E. Bennett (Cambridge, Mass.: Harvard University Press, 1954). Citations of Shakespeare from *The Complete Works*, ed. Alfred Harbage (Baltimore: Penguin, 1969).

10 For Echo as Fama, see Joseph Loewenstein, *Responsive Readings: Versions of Echo in Pastoral, Epic, and the Jonsonian Masque* (New Haven: Yale University Press, 1984); although it is only literally true that the Lady's song in *Comus* fails to arouse Echo, it is nonetheless valuable to see the masque, as Loewenstein does, as "a masque of delay" (p. 139) demonstrating "the difficulty of rendering action timely" (p. 140).

11 In "Autobiography as De-facement," *MLN* 94 (1979): 919-30, reprinted in Paul de Man, *The Rhetoric of Romanticism* (New York: Columbia University Press, 1984); see pp. 77-78 for a discussion of the Miltonic lines suppressed by Wordsworth and their haunting of the claims for the (poet's) life in the text.

Richard Macksey has pursued this scene of inscription in "Keats and the Poetics of Extremity," *MLN* 99 (1984): 845-84 through Oscar Wilde's contemplation of the tomb of Keats beside the Roman pyramid to the Keatsian text "into which the poet's voice has inscribed him" with "a kind of life as elegiac fiction" (p. 882). The tomb and pyramid resonate against the Hegelian scene of inscription explored by Jacques Derrida in "The Pit and the Pyramid: Introduction to Hegel's Semiology," in *Margins of Philosophy*, trans. Alan Bass (Chicago: University of Chicago Press, 1982); see also "Fors," *Georgia Review* 31 (1977): 64-120. Milton's textual scene, to anticipate the final pages of this essay, resounds in a Flaubertian conceit recorded by Derrida in "An Idea of Flaubert: 'Plato's Letter'," *MLN* 99 (1984): 748-68; "'my mother is a statue that weeps . . .'; 'my eyes are as dry as marble'; 'I was as tearless as a tomb-stone'" (p. 768).

12 William Empson, "Milton and Bentley," in *Some Versions of Pastoral* (Norfolk, Conn.: New Directions, 1952), pp. 149-91. He sums up his thematic point this way: "Christ . . . counts as the sun, but in *Paradise Regained* (i.294) he becomes Our Morning Star, who is Lucifer, who is Satan; the doubt about the symbolism fits Milton's secret parallel between the two" (pp. 182-83). That parallel establishes strange echoes and identifications in the text – it points to a range of influences and replacements and shifts in points of vision that are also shifts in historical consciousness.

13 John Guillory, *Poetic Authority: Spenser, Milton, and Literary History* (New York: Columbia University Press, 1983), pp.68-93; see, for example, p. 73: "The *Maske*, in its continuous allusions to a literary past already partially organized in "L'Allegro" and "Il Penseroso" further develops an implicit dichotomy between two types of poetic aspiration that can be represented, artificially but not inaccurately, by Shakespeare and Spenser." He links these questions to the stars on pp. 83ff.

14 Emile Benveniste, *Problems in General Linguistics*, trans. Mary E. Meek (Coral Gables, Florida: University of Miami Press, 1971); see "Relationships of Persons in the Verb." As he argues in "Subjectivity in Language," "*I* refers to the act of individual discourse in which it is pronounced, and by this it designates the speaker . . . . The reality to which it refers is the reality of the discourse. . . . And so it is literally true that the basis of subjectivity is in the exercise of language" (p. 226). Discourse, as Benveniste defines it, is precisely that set of structural coordinates in which 'I' is related to 'you' and 'it'.

15 The epitaph on Sir Edward Stanley can be found in A. S. P. Woodhouse and Douglas Bush, eds, *A Variorum Commentary on the Poems of John Milton*, 2:1 (New York: Columbia University Press, 1972), p. 208.

16 The text here is Carey's–except that I have removed the textually unwarranted capitalization of "patience."

17 I provide a less pointed version of sonnet 15 to allow for the openness of the text. Shakespeare's sonnet 16 continues, reconsiders, and refigures the materials in sonnet 15, a demonstration of Shakespeare's teeming textuality and refusal of closure. It is Milton who supplies the tomb.

18 See Stanley Fish , *Is There a Text in this Class?* (Cambridge, Mass.: Harvard

University Press, 1980), pp. 156-57. Cf. Tayler, *Milton's Poetry*, pp. 141-44, on the relationship of patience and prevention.

19   Cf. Elegy 6, "Canimus caelesti semine regem" (line 81), singing the heaven-sowed king.

20   Cf. *PL* 9:889-90, describing Adam "amazed,/Astonied stood and blank." His blankness signals receptivity to the story that Eve tells, and which will soon be his own.

21   Ovid's *Metamorphoses* cited in the Loeb edition, trans. Frank Justus Miller (London: William Heinemann, New York: G. P. Putnam's Sons, 1929). In *Ovid's Metamorphoses. Englished, Mythologiz'd and Represented in Figures* (London, 1632), George Sandys records a version of the story in which Narcissus has a twin sister who dies and for whom he pines, gazing in the fountain "as not beholding his owne shaddow, but the image of his dead sister" (p. 106).

22   Sigmund Freud, *Beyond the Pleasure Principle*, trans. James Strachey (New York: W. W. Norton, 1961), p. 32.

23   The sentence is Poe's and cited as the epigraph to *Speech and Phenomena*, trans. David B. Allison (Evanston, Illinois: Northwestern University Press, 1973); citation from p. 97; Derrida returns to the sentence in response to Roland Barthes, "To Write: An Intransitive Verb?" in *The Structuralist Controversy*, ed. Richard Macksey and Eugenio Donato (Baltimore: Johns Hopkins University Press, 1970, 1972), p. 156. Barthes had instanced that sentence as an impossible utterance (p. 143); in making it the "founding" possibility of utterance, Derrida points to a number of things, most insistently the status of the *I* in discourse and, more pointedly, one's "being" in language. No one lives in texts and that is where we all are. This condition – in which the "present" is inscribed in iterability, is examined in "Signature Event Context," in *Margins of Philosophy*; see, for example, p. 316.

24   John 9.4: "I must work the works of him that sent me, while it is day: for the night cometh, when no man can work." Cf. *PL* 1:11.

25   "The double import of *usure*: erasure by rubbing, exhaustion, crumbling away, certainly; but also the supplementary product of a capital, the exchange which far from losing the original investment would fructify its initial wealth" (Jacques Derrida, "White Mythology: Metaphor in the Text of Philosophy," in *Margins of Philosophy*, p. 210).

26   Milton's use of "inwrought" is the first recorded in the OED.

27   On the (poetic) consciousness represented by Adam's awakening, see the brilliant essay by Geoffrey Hartman, "Adam on the Grass with Balsamum," in *Beyond Formalism* (New Haven: Yale University Press, 1970), pp. 124-50, esp. 142-45, an extraordinary discussion of the ways in which Adam's sight becomes voiced, a pivoting of inward and outward, a complex figuration that catches the sidereal echo of Christ and Lucifer, morning and evening – figuration, then, taking place in the wound that is consciousness. Patricia Parker's discussion of Milton in *Inescapable Romance* (Princeton: Princeton University Press, 1979) is suspended in this pendancy.

28   Derrida, responding to Barthes, *Structuralist Controversy*, p. 155.

29   "Literature and the Right to Death," in *The Gaze of Orpheus*, p. 43.

30   Matthew 25 contains two parables, of the wise and foolish virgins and the talent; these are read by Milton in counterpoint; moreover, their countermessages – should the Lord's oil be stored and kept while his coin should be invested? – are pre-empted by the parable of the servants in the vineyard whose rewards were equal whether they were called early or late (Matt. 20).

31   T. C. C., "Milton: Marble for Thinking," *Notes and Queries* 184 (1943): 314.

32   *English Poets*, quoted in *A Variorum Commentary*, 2:1: 204.

33   Browne's poem is an epitaph for Sidney's sister; see Gordon Goodwin, ed., *Poems of William Browne*, Muses's Library edition, 2 vols (London: George Routledge & Sons, n.d.), 2:294; in his epitaph on his wife (*c.* 1614), Browne says to her, "thou need'st no tomb" because "thou art engrav'd so deeply in my heart,/It shall outlast the strongest hand of Art" (2:293).

34   *The Rhetoric of Romanticism*, p. 78.

35   Trans. Richmond Lattimore (Chicago: University of Chicago Press, 1951). Niobe's epithet in *The Iliad*, "she of the lovely tresses" (24:602), may point to a further connection with the Medusa, since it was the hair that attracted Neptune and that became the ultimate snaky horror. Are there connections, too, between Niobe's eating and Proserpina's? Her story is recounted in the grove of the Muses beside the Hippocrene stream produced by Pegasus – the genealogy of the story (told, we are told, by Calliope, the mothering muse of Orpheus) goes back to the Medusa; her blood produced Pegasus.

36   Tobin Siebers considers the roots of magical thinking in fascination in *The Mirror of Medusa* (Berkeley and Los Angeles: University of California Press, 1983), and draws connections between Medusa and Narcissus in terms of the communal uses of figures of isolation and self-absorption. The connections between Narcissus and Medusa in Ovid are explored in a forthcoming study by Leonard Barkan.

37   Herman Rapaport, *Milton and the Postmodern* (Lincoln: University of Nebraska Press, 1983), p. 214. Rapaport argues for a connection in castration between the Medusa and the tangles of Naerea's hair (p. 119), and suggestively proposes that Dalila, as the publisher of the secrets of the symbolically castrated Samson, is a figure for Milton writing (see pp. 150-52, 210 ff.); the blank is a figure for the blind spot.

38   Spenser is quoted from *The Poetical Works of Edmund Spenser*, ed. J. C. Smith and E. de Selincourt (London: Oxford University Press, 1926).

39   John Hollander, 1984 lecture for the Tudor and Stuart Club, Johns Hopkins University; see also Loewenstein, *Responsive Readings*, p. 146.

40   Harold Bloom, *A Map of Misreading* (New York: Oxford University Press, 1975), p. 131; the error is discussed on pp. 127-28.

41   Paul Goodman, *The Structure of Literature* (Chicago: University of Chicago Press, 1954), p. 205. Goodman's comments (p. 206) on the grandiose *I* needed to counter a wicked God are Empsonian anticipations of great acuity; also provocative is a brief remark on the styleless quality of Milton's sonnets, an 'expression' of neutralization, as he terms it (p. 215).

42 Bloom, *A Map of Misreading*, p. 87. With the Spenserian scene, compare *Hamlet* 3.2, lines 80-81: "my imaginations are as foul/As Vulcan's stithy."

43 Cf. Christopher Kendricks, "Ethics and the Orator in *Areopagitica*," *ELH* 50 (1983): 655-91, a discussion of the ways in which a rhetorical subject is produced in the treatise, self-validating and 'autonomous' in its absolutizing, an effect, Kendricks argues, of the Imaginary, and an ideological incursion marked by the commodification of Truth. For an incisive discussion of the Miltonic subject in *Areopagitica*, see Francis Barker, *The Tremulous Private Body* (London: Methuen, 1984); e.g. pp. 46-47, on self-discipline as an indirect "ideological control implanted in the new subjectivity," bourgeois consciousness, or, as he sums up the argument, "the more profound strategy of domination which is achieved not by *post hoc* intervention from without, but by the pre-constitution of the subject in its subjection" (p. 60).

44 Cf. the forbidden scene at which Jacques Derrida arrives in "Freud and the Scene of Writing," in *Writing and Difference*, trans. Alan Bass (Chicago: University of Chicago Press, 1978), pp. 196-231. On the significance of copyright in *Areopagitica*, cf. Barker, *Tremulous Private Body*, pp. 49-50.

45 "Freud and the Scene of Writing," p. 230.

46 The connection between Sarah Milton's death and the writing of "Lycidas" is stressed in Parker's biography, and William Kerrigan builds on it in *The Sacred Complex: On the Psychogenesis of Paradise Lost* (Cambridge, Mass.: Harvard University Press, 1983). Kerrigan posits the break between the early and middle portions of the career around the death of Milton's mother, regarding the early poems as those in which a narcissistic/feminine identity is entertained as a way of keeping himself intact (see pp. 50 ff.); in the oedipal solution that Kerrigan names the sacred complex (a sublimation of the oedipal by replacing the earthly father with the heavenly one), Milton reinvests himself, Kerrigan argues, in the mother ("the son as mother, materializer" p.189). Pages 177ff. are particularly provocative on questions of narcissism, dreaming, the mother-muse and the regaining of origins. On occasion, Kerrigan has anticipated some of my arguments, although the psychological model that I am working with is less dependent upon the oedipal complex than his is.

47 Jacques Lacan, "The Mirror Stage as Formative of the Function of the I," in *Ecrits: A Selection*, trans. Alan Sheridan (New York: W. W. Norton, 1977), p. 2.

48 I quote the text of Ralegh's poem as printed in *The Poetical Works of Edmund Spenser*.

49 All references are to Euripides, *Alcestis*, trans. Richmond Lattimore in *Euripides 1*, ed. David Grene and Richmond Lattimore (Chicago: University of Chicago Press, 1955).

50 See, for example, Natalis Comes, *Mythologie*, trans. Jean Baudouin (Paris, 1627) (New York: Garland Publishing, 1976), 2:761-65.

51 See John Freccero, "Medusa: The Letter and the Spirit," *Yearbook of Italian Studies* 2 (1972): 1-18.

52 Introduction to *Petrarch's Lyric Poems* (Cambridge, Mass.: Harvard University Press, 1976), pp. 26-33.

53 John Freccero, "The Fig Tree and the Laurel: Petrarch's Poetics," *Diacritics* 5 (1975): 34-40; cited passages p. 34.

54 I am grateful to Nancy J. Vickers for this citation, as well as for illuminating discussions of her work on Cellini's Perseus.

55 "The Essential Solitude," in *The Gaze of Orpheus*, p.76.

56 Comes, *Mythologie*, 2:1026: "Le nom de Narcisse vient d'un mot Grec signifiant estre engourdy, stupide & sans sentiment." In *The Mirror of Medusa*, Siebers considers the etymology – "to grow stiff or numb from palsy, fright, or cold" (p. 59).

57 "Two Versions of the Imaginary," in *The Gaze of Orpheus*, p. 79.

58 ibid., p. 85.

59 ibid., p. 89.

60 "The Essential Solitude," in *The Gaze of Orpheus*, p. 77.

61 Julia Kristeva, *Powers of Horror: An Essay on Abjection*, trans. Leon S. Roudiez (New York: Columbia University Press, 1982). Kristeva explores in abjection an other before the other, the other to whom one was attached before there was one; she is, in other words, trying to penetrate primary narcissism, attempting to locate the prelinguistic origin of a self-loathing that has to do with this attachment. Thus, the "original" "self" would be neither, already attached to an other that lacks the differentiation of otherness and who thus robs the self even as it supports it. Kristeva argues that this other is the mother, that the history of religious thought and ritual is fixed on the mother's body as an image of pollution and disgust because of attempts to abject the original dyad (primary narcissism), and that literature in particular aims at the representation of abjection. Kristeva's texts seem to coincide with Milton's strong needs for exclusion, his fears of defilement (marriage must not be called a defilement, he insists in the *Apology*), and the various purification rituals that produce the blank page that is the Miltonic necessity for writing. The "spot" removed in the sonnet appeared earlier in *Comus*, lines 214-15 and 1008, and is Adam's word for Eve's dream (*PL* 5:119).

62 To this horrific scene might be added Satan's confrontation with Sin, offspring, blocking agent, and smoother of his way; see *PL* 2:648ff.

63 See Sigmund Freud, "Medusa's Head," in *The Standard Edition of the Complete Psychological Works*, ed. James Strachey (London: The Hogarth Press, 1955), 18:273-74.

64 Jacques Lacan, *Le Séminaire, Livre XX: Encore* (Paris: Seuil, 1975), "il faut renverser, et au lieu d'*un* signifiant qu'on interroge, interroger le signifiant *Un*" (p. 23). To interrogate the notion of unity is to explore the delusion of the oneness of the imaginary; it is also to open up the lack that woman "signifies." Lacan's *Encore* is lucidly introduced by Jacqueline Rose in *Feminine Sexuality: Jacques Lacan and the Ecole Freudienne*, ed. Juliet Mitchell and Jacqueline Rose (New York: W. W. Norton, 1982), pp. 46-48.

65 Kerrigan, in *The Sacred Complex*, reads Milton's blindness as castration-before-the-crime, castration for the crime of Adam, and as Milton's license finally to write *Paradise Lost*. On anonymity and the name in the *Apology*, see Guillory,

Poetic Authority, pp. 94-103.

66 I cite the anonymous contemporary life of Milton printed in Merritt Hughes, ed., *John Milton: Complete Poems and Major Prose* (New York: Odyssey Press, 1957), p. 1044.

67 Erik Erikson, *Young Man Luther* (New York: W. W. Norton, 1958); see, for example, p. 72 and cf. "'You must preach,' he said, 'as a mother suckles her child'" (p. 198).

In the story of Milton's life, it is perhaps worth pausing over a moment of sequential confusion in Edward Phillips' life of Milton (see Hughes, p. 1031); had Milton's father already come to live with him before Mary Powell Milton returned, or only after? Phillips, who so clearly has his story from Milton, tells this part twice, and waffles on this sequence. Perhaps this reconstitution of his childhood family (his wife in place of his mother) caused Milton some anxiety? The clearest signs of his childhood remain, however, in his behavior as a father, the notorious treatment of his daughters; I would suggest, following the lead of Alice Miller in *The Drama of the Gifted Child: How Narcissistic Parents Deform the Emotional Lives of their Talented Children*, trans. Ruth Ward (New York: Basic Books, 1981), that Milton's behavior with his daughters was not simply directed at his dead wife, but at his mother and father, and that he had exacted on his daughters a version of what had been done to him. Did Sarah Milton's neighborhood charity extend to home?

68 Athanasius Kircher, *Musurgia Universalis*: "Echo is a joke of playful Nature. The Poets call her *imago vocis* . . .; the Philosophers call her reflected, repercussive, or reciprocal voice; the Hebrews call her the *bat kol*, or Daughter of the Voice." Cited in Loewenstein, *Responsive Readings,* p. 59; cf. pp. 143-48.

Index